Churchill's Horses and the Myths of American Corporations

Churchill's Horses and the Myths of American Corporations

Power, Stakeholders, and Governance

Mord Bogie

QUORUM BOOKS
Westport, Connecticut • London

Library of Congress Cataloging-in-Publication Data

Bogie, Mord, 1932–
    Churchill's horses and the myths of American corporations : power,
stakeholders, and governance / Mord Bogie.
        p.   cm.
    Includes bibliographical references (p.   ) and index.
    ISBN 1–56720–073–7 (alk. paper)
    1. Corporations—United States. I. Title.
HD2785.B63   1998
338.7'0973—dc21   97–21855

British Library Cataloguing in Publication Data is available.

Library of Congress Catalog Card Number: 97–21855
ISBN: 1–56720–073–7

First published in 1998

Quorum Books, 88 Post Road West, Westport, CT 06881
An imprint of Greenwood Publishing Group, Inc.

Printed in the United States of America

The paper used in this book complies with the
Permanent Paper Standard issued by the National
Information Standards Organization (Z39.48–1984).

10 9 8 7 6 5 4 3 2 1

To Mord M. Bogie

1903–1952

One of the old breed of investment bankers

Contents: Table of Myths

PART VI. WORKERS

How workers are motivated by public corporations,
although downsizing and layoffs are required by global
competition and the business cycle; how they benefit from
increased productivity.

PART VII. CAPITALISTS

How the financiers of public corporations serve their
corporate clients, their clients' shareholders, and the
investing public; how they exert a beneficial influence
on Churchill's Horses.

Acknowledgments

Good friends helped me with this book. Cherrill Heaton edited the first draft, leaving no page unturned, and it's a tribute to his great good sense that I accepted, as I recall, almost every one of his many suggestions. Tom Hopkins, Larry Schilling, Patrick Pleven, and Lynden Gillis offered counsel and contacts and the vital sap of encouragement. Herbert Park got me started. Eric Valentine, my editor at Quorum Books, somehow got me finished. And my wife, Sharon Nickles, saw me through the whole project. No need to add, though I will nevertheless, that the views expressed in this book are mine alone.

Introduction:
Our Underachieving Corporations

Some see private enterprise as a predatory target to be shot, others as a cow to be milked, but few are those who see it as a sturdy horse pulling the wagon.

—Prime Minister Winston Churchill[1]

The great enemy of the truth is very often not the lie—deliberate, contrived and dishonest—but the myth—persistent, persuasive and unrealistic.

—President John F. Kennedy[2]

When you think of a truly great team, what comes to mind? A strong coach or manager commanding the undivided loyalty of the team members, committing them to a specific goal, instilling in them the motivation, the emotion, the desire to attain it. For example, Vince Lombardi leading the Green Bay Packers to the National Football League title in 1966 and victory in the first Super Bowl. Then starting over the next season, winning the title again and Super Bowl II.

The goal itself, winning a game or a championship, is immediate, extending no further than the current season. Every so often a Branch Rickey comes along to build the first farm system for the St. Louis Cardinals, then move to Brooklyn and do the same thing for the Dodgers, then integrate the game, changing professional baseball (and American sports) forever. Those were long-range goals involving vision, planning, investment, risk, and careful execution. But for every Rickey taking the long view, we have a hundred Lombardis who believe that winning isn't everything, it's the only thing.

Now, change one of the rules: The season is continuous. Winners and losers don't start over each year. Last year's winners are still on top. That makes the game *real*—a business. The scoring may be against last year's performance rather than the competition, but the goal is still something immediate like higher profits this month, this quarter, this year. The percentage of American corporations run by Branch Rickeys isn't much higher than in the Major Leagues.

Few of us have played for a professional ball club, but three out of four working Americans work for business corporations.

When I started working for ITT Corporation in 1968, it was in the midst of an unbroken string of profit increases that was eventually to rival Joe Di-Maggio's hitting streak of 56 straight games, except that ITT kept its streak going for well over a dozen years, quarter by quarter, four quarters a year. During its streak ITT was widely regarded as one of the truly great corporations in the country, if not the world. The reason was its coach, manager, and chief executive officer, Harold S. Geneen. "Geneen trained many of the men who run other companies today," wrote *Forbes* magazine in 1977, Geneen's last year as CEO; "his systems and controls are as widely imitated as [our greatest industrialist] Alfred P. Sloan Jr.'s once were; his own company's record for growth and profitability are superb. But his public image is something else again"[3]—because he prized winning even more than Lombardi did.

If winning required quietly twisting the arm of the attorney general or even the president of the United States, well, ITT paid a lot of taxes.[4] It represented hundreds of thousands of shareholders and employees. Its right to speak freely and petition the government, like the right of any American, was protected by the Constitution.

If winning required secretly influencing a presidential election in Chile, ITT paid taxes in that country, too—and it owned the Chilean Telephone Company.

According to one economist, corporations produce 98% of what the private sector produces in the United States, and public corporations account for 90%.[5] And since ours is predominantly a private-enterprise system where the means of production are owned by individuals, not the government, and economic decisions are made by the market, not politicians, the private sector dominates the economy. Thus, to paraphrase Winston Churchill (quoted at the beginning of this chapter), publicly held corporations like ITT—private enterprises owned by members of the public—are the sturdy horses pulling the economy.

Churchill's Horses are very powerful. Dutchess County, where I live, is the home of two of IBM's three largest plants and across the Hudson River from the third. One out of every five jobs and 7 out of 10 manufacturing jobs used to be IBM jobs.[6] Then IBM faltered and cut its worldwide workforce in half. County tax revenues dropped, public health cases doubled, and real estate prices settled into a long slump as unemployment rose from the lowest in New York State (3%) to the highest (11%). Businesses like IBM, as one writer said, "provide the nation with its wherewithal. They starve, we starve, they prosper, we prosper. Everyone has a stake in their well-being, which is why, in the end, there is no such thing as private enterprise. It's all public."[7]

In recent decades Churchill's Horses haven't been pulling as hard as they used to. Major industries have been largely abandoned by them or moved to other countries—consumer electronics, machine tools, steelmaking, shipbuilding, textiles, shoes, subway cars.[8] In other industries like automobiles, they've failed to defend their share of the market from foreign competition. As a consequence, American factories and offices no longer satisfy the needs of American consumers. Each year we buy billions of dollars more from foreign sources than foreign consumers buy from American sources, which is why we have a large trade deficit. Not being able to satisfy the needs of American consumers from American production means that we no longer have enough good jobs paying good money to satisfy the needs of American workers.

Too many of our corporations have become underachievers. Why?

Should we blame the coaches and managers and chief executive officers? Are they having trouble keeping their eye on the ball? Have they lost the will to compete? Are they paid so much that they no longer care about winning? What about the owners—aren't they in control? Maybe they're too shortsighted, too self-involved, too greedy. Or perhaps the players—the people we used to count on to make those second efforts, outrun the other teams, win the ball games—are just interested in their own paychecks. Are they ripping off the system? And the customers, the home-team fans—are they as loyal as they used to be? They do seem to be supporting a lot of foreign teams these days.

To find out why Churchill's Horses have become underachievers, we need to look at

- how they became so powerful,
- how they relate to their stakeholders—people like those we just mentioned who depend on them (and on whom they depend),
- how they are governed, and
- whose interests they really serve.

The problem is, everything we need to look at is shrouded in myth. Ancient myths, like Apollo in his chariot pulling the sun across the sky, embody great truths, but modern myths—"notions based more on tradition or convenience than on fact,"[9] as the dictionary defines them—are, in the words of John F. Kennedy (also quoted above), *the great enemy of the truth.* Public corporations use these myths to mask their great power and disguise the interests that power serves.

Only after these myths have been exposed will we, the members of the public—shareholders who are owners, consumers who are customers, workers who are employees, just plain citizens who have a stake in their well-being—be able to understand why public corporations underachieve and what might be done about it.

So myth busting is our task. But while *they pretend to tell the truth and we pretend to believe them* may be the Journalist's Credo, that's not the credo we will follow. We can't expose myths that are *persistent, persuasive, and unrealistic* (JFK again) if we accept at face value the statements of those who live by the myths. Rather, we will be guided by the wisdom of Yogi Berra, one of the great team managers: ''You can observe a lot by just watching.''[10]

Part I

Control

How Churchill's Horses—our great public corporations—became so powerful; who owns them, who controls them, and in whose interests are they governed.

Chapter 1

Corporations Are Nothing More or Less Than Their People

Corporation, *n.* An ingenious device for obtaining individual profit without individual responsibility.
                                        —Ambrose Bierce, *The Devil's Dictionary*[1]

The ideal that a great corporation is endowed with the rights and prerogatives of a free individual is as essential to the acceptance of corporate rule in temporal affairs as was the ideal of the divine right of kings in an earlier day.
                                  —Thurman Arnold, *The Folklore of Capitalism*[2]

We said in the Introduction that publicly held corporations—private enterprises owned by members of the public—are the sturdy horses pulling the American economy. But what exactly are they?

According to John Marshall, chief justice of the United States, speaking for the Supreme Court in 1819, "A corporation is an artificial being, invisible, intangible, and existing only in contemplation of law."[3] In other words, a corporation isn't real, like a person. It can't hire anyone or produce anything. Everything it does is done by the people who own it, direct its affairs, manage its operations, produce whatever is produced in its name, and sell whatever that is. Corporations are nothing more or less than their people. What else could they be?

The law contemplating a particular corporation is usually the corporation law of some state. Delaware is the state du jour for corporations throughout the United States, being generally regarded as probusiness—and having a financial interest in the corporate fees and taxes it collects in remaining so—but corporation laws don't differ that much from state to state. After a state has issued a certificate (or "articles") of incorporation, a for-profit corporation joins the business world when its founders, acting in its behalf, issue shares of its capital stock that define who owns it. (Not-for-profit corporations don't have shares to issue or owners.) Buyers of these shares—people or artificial beings like the issuing corporation—collectively exercise their right of ownership by electing (real) people to the corporation's board of directors to manage its operations. Although the law holds directors responsible for management, the board customarily delegates this responsibility to corporate officers whom it selects, appoints, and meets periodically to supervise—or replace.

When the officers, acting on behalf of the shareholders under the supervision of the board of directors, cause the corporation to take some action such as paying employees or filing tax returns, we gloss over the realities and say that the corporation takes that action.

Three-quarters of the national income of the United States consists of employee compensation, and corporations pay most of it. Indeed, what corporations pay employees represents almost 50% of our total national income, 70% of the compensation of *all* employees (corporate and noncorporate including government), and 90% of the compensation of all *private sector* (nongovernment) employees.

Almost 4 million corporations file federal tax returns, compared to a million and a half partnerships and 15 million people doing business individually as sole proprietorships. But sole proprietorships collectively report business receipts (revenue) of $700 billion and change and partnerships not quite $550 billion. Corporate receipts add up to almost $11 *trillion*.[4]

In terms of the national economy, corporations are where the action is. And big corporations are where the big action is. (Although we have been told that small companies have replaced large ones as the source of new jobs, a study published in 1994 found that the proportion of people working for small businesses had hardly changed in three decades.)[5]

Only 1% of corporations employ more than 500 people. And only *half* of 1% report business receipts of more than $50 million. But this 0.5% accounts for almost $7.5 trillion of such receipts, twice as much as all the other 99.5%.

Most of these very large corporations are public corporations. Although there are some 12,000 public corporations overall, just 785 ranked by *Forbes* magazine in 1994 among the top 500 U.S. public corporations in terms of sales, profits, assets, or stock-market value accounted for $4 trillion in revenue (business receipts)—one-third of that produced by *all* corporations, partnerships, and sole proprietorships. The 785 corporations employed one of every six Americans working for a salary or wage.[6]

These public corporations are truly the draft horses—Churchill's Horses—of our economy. How did they get so big?

They got big by using other people's money—their shareholders' investment.

Shareholders own a corporation, but they're not like the partners who own a partnership or the individuals who own sole proprietorships. Partners and proprietors have to be actively involved in their business because if it fails, they are responsible for its unpaid debts and unfulfilled obligations. Having active investors limits the size of these organizations. A partnership with thousands of partners couldn't function any more than the U.S. House of Representatives could function if it had thousands of representatives.

Corporations, on the other hand, are endowed by corporation law with a special advantage known as *limited liability*. If the corporation fails, its owners have no responsibility for its unpaid debts and unfulfilled obligations. That's one reason for converting an unincorporated business (sole proprietorship or partnership) into what American journalist Ambrose Bierce, quoted at the beginning of this chapter, called an *ingenious device* for seeking profit without responsibility—to limit the owners' out-of-pocket loss, if the business fails, to no more that what they have already paid to buy their shares of stock.

Still, if you're an entrepreneur, that probably isn't your primary reason for incorporating your enterprise. You intend to succeed, not fail, and you plan to stay actively involved in running the business to make sure you do succeed, at least until you're able to recover your investment. But the quickest way to recover your investment is to sell shares you own to members of the public. And limited liability *is* important to public shareholders. Unlike entrepreneurs, they're passive investors. They invest not to run the business, which they likely don't know much about and couldn't run if they wanted to, but solely to earn a profit on their investment.

Now, a corporation may be artificial, invisible, and intangible, but Chief Justice Marshall also said that it was endowed by law with "immortality, and, if the expression may be allowed, individuality" so that it acts "as a single individual."[7] When the public pays millions of dollars to buy shares of a corporation's stock, all that money comes under the control of one artificial and immortal individual and makes it *very* powerful. "Size alone," wrote Supreme Court Justice Louis Brandeis in 1933,

gives to giant corporations a social significance not attached ordinarily to smaller units of private enterprise. Through size, corporations, once merely an efficient tool employed by individuals in the conduct of private business, have become an institution—an institution which has brought such concentration of economic power that so-called private corporations are sometimes able to dominate the State.[8]

In *Company Man*, Anthony Sampson observed that to its employees IBM used to be "more like a nationality than a job." William Steinhaus, chief executive of New York's Dutchess County—IBM country—grew up in an IBM family. "When we had health or family problems," he told Sampson, "my dad always said, 'IBM will take care of it.' I can't tell you how many social situations I've been in when the only thing an IBM-er could talk about was IBM.

Their family, kids, travels, were all bound up with the corporation.'' But to Father James Heron, half of whose congregation was dependent on IBM, ''the IBM community was always a myth: they provided services but no real community or personality.'' When massive layoffs came in the early 1990s, Heron said that it was as if dad had run off and abandoned his children: ''I've never experienced mass grief like this.'' George Zornetsy of JobNet, a networking group, found ex-IBM employees the hardest to reemploy. ''They're used to a gilded cage. They've never had to write a resume or to interview. They've had narrow and specialized skills, defined by their job.'' Once IBM citizens, now they were stateless. Said Walter Goldstein, a professor who once worked for the corporation, ''IBM people have been locked into such innumerable benefits that they couldn't be ready for anything else. It's like being demobilized from the Red Army.''[9]

Corporations can spend the vast amounts of money invested in them to do almost anything in business real mortals can do—buy and sell property, hire and fire employees, make and break agreements, sue. B.A.T. Industries of England bought Brown & Williamson Tobacco Corporation, which hired Jeffrey Wigand as its chief of research and had him sign a confidentiality agreement. Some years later it fired him. Two years after that Wigand was interviewed by Mike Wallace of CBS's *60 Minutes* regarding, among other things, the veracity of testimony by B&W's chief executive officer before Congress as to his belief in the nonaddictiveness of nicotine.[10] But apparently fearful of being sued by B&W for inducing Wigand to break his confidentiality agreement, CBS decided not to broadcast the interview. Thus, a U.S. media giant yielded to the threat of a lawsuit by the U.S. subsidiary of a British corporate giant.

But then the New York *Daily News*, less timid, evidently, than CBS, learned about the interview and published an article about it, whereupon B&W sued Wigand for breach of contract. It also sued to prevent him from giving testimony in a lawsuit by the state of Mississippi seeking reimbursement from tobacco companies for its costs in treating Medicaid patients for smoking-related illnesses. When Wigand went ahead with his testimony—which included an account of threats against his children—B&W sought to hold him in contempt of court. Corporations, said essayist William Hazlitt in 1824, ''are more corrupt and profligate than individuals, because they have more power to do mischief, and are less amenable to disgrace or punishment. They feel neither shame, remorse, gratitude, nor goodwill.''[11]

Still, they're not mentioned in the Constitution and, not being persons, are not protected by the Constitution from being regulated by the government. At least they weren't for 100 years. But in 1886 the Supreme Court decided that corporations *are* persons. The point was never properly decided—Chief Justice Morrison Waite told the lawyers not to bother arguing the point; the Court had already made up its mind—but it's been the law ever since.[12] A provision of the so-called Dictionary Act, which is part of the U.S. Code, includes corporations within a federal law's definition of *person*.[13]

So now corporations are persons with constitutional rights. What kind of constitutional rights do they have?

We can start and end with the First Amendment. If you believe that the pen of Thomas Jefferson (or James Madison, who wrote the amendment) is mightier than the sword, the First is the Great Amendment. According to the Supreme Court, it guarantees not only freedom of speech and religion and the press (if one is courageous enough to claim it) but also freedom to make political contributions and thereby influence how our elected officials govern us.

The Cato Institute found that the U.S. government spent $75 billion in 1995 on 125 programs conferring ''special benefits or privileges to specific firms or industries where there is no corresponding societal benefit.''[14] Indeed, the societal benefit of such corporate welfare is likely to be negative. For example, import quotas that limit foreign automobiles or steel products may be justified as protecting American jobs, but trade economist Paul Krugman says that

the jobs gained in the protected industry are lost through the indirect effects of the quota in crowding out employment throughout the rest of the economy, leaving us with nothing but higher prices and reduced competition. [Similarly,] an export subsidy normally costs the government and domestic consumers far more than it benefits producers in the industry.[15]

To corporations, societal benefits (or their lack) are immaterial. Political donations are investments in *corporate* benefits. In the first 18 months of the 1995–1996 election campaign, tobacco companies gave over $2.5 million to various Republican Party committees to stave off regulation of their business. Philip Morris alone accounted for more than $1.5 million.[16]

William Lloyd Garrison, Harriet Beecher Stowe, Julia Ward Howe, Elizabeth Cady Stanton, Susan Anthony, Carry Nation, William Randolph Hearst, Martin Luther King, Philip Morris—the First Amendment protects every person with a cause, no matter how commercial or self-interested. The person doesn't even have to be a citizen. Corporations are fortunate in that regard: Persons they may be; citizens they're not.

But when the persons are public corporations like the tobacco companies, not only are they speaking and petitioning very freely; they are also spending their shareholders' money without exactly getting their shareholders' consent. And when the corporations deduct expenditures for political activities on their tax returns as expenses of doing business, the government (that is, all of us) bears part of the burden of these activities because the deductions reduce the amount of corporate income taxes the government needs to perform its duties.

Of course, a real person can't get away with any of this. Even if you happen to come by a few hundred thousand dollars of other people's money, you can't contribute it to the party of your choice without their consent; and even if you could, you wouldn't be entitled to deduct the contribution from your taxable income.

It's a myth that corporations are nothing more or less than their people. The reality, or *anti-myth* (every myth has one), is this: **Public corporations are much more powerful than all their people put together**. Their great power derives from their ability to raise money from thousands or hundreds of thousands of shareholders, none of whom is legally responsible for what the corporation does with it, and from the Constitution, which "has served more as a shield for corporations than as a means by which their power may be contested."[17]

Of course, the Supreme Court might have decided that guaranteeing the right of free speech to an artificial being that can't pledge allegiance to the flag or write its name on a ballot or stand in a picket line, that can't be drafted to defend its country in time of war, that can't even be sent to jail if convicted of high crimes and misdemeanors, doesn't make sense. The justices might also have reasoned that a corporation doesn't even need any constitutional rights since all the people who own it, run it, and do whatever it does already have their own constitutional rights.

But they didn't. Instead, as legal philosopher Thurman Arnold wrote in *The Folklore of Capitalism*, the justices "dressed huge corporations in the clothes of simple farmers and merchants and thus made attempts to regulate them appear as attacks on liberty and the home."[18]

Fortunately, even our largest public corporations are controlled by their shareholder-owners, just as private corporations are. Corporations are corporations, after all, subject to the law that created them. Powerful as they may be, Churchill's Horses are not loose cannons.

Chapter 2

Public Corporations Are Just Private Corporations with Many Owners

I have always opposed putting Standard Oil shares on the Stock Exchange because I did not want them to become the play things of speculators. It was better that all our people concentrate their attention on developing the business rather than be distracted by the stock ticker.
— John D. Rockefeller, Sr., CEO of Standard Oil[1]

Increasingly, managers of mutual funds, and portfolio and pension fund administrators, are measuring their success in terms of relatively short-term market performance.
— William McChesney Martin, chairman of the Federal Reserve Board[2]

Of the 4 million or so corporations in the United States, only about 12,000 (less than half of 1%) are active public corporations. Powerful as they are, these corporations are controlled by the shareholders who own them, just as private corporations are. State corporation laws that determine how they're governed make no distinction between the two. So how do public and private corporations differ?

A corporation, private at the time it is incorporated, becomes public when it sells shares of stock it has registered with the Securities and Exchange Commission to the public, meaning people not involved in the founding or running of the corporation. The advantage of going public is that the corporation's stock, unlike that of a private corporation, can be freely traded by its shareholders and investors in public markets collectively referred to as the stock market. The disadvantage is that the corporation must comply with federal regulation designed to keep the trading public informed about its affairs and operations.

But aside from the burden (and cost) of this regulation, public corporations are essentially no different from private corporations. Public corporations are just private corporations with many owners. With this difference: When a corporation goes public, it acquires a mate. Forever thereafter, in sickness and in health, the corporation is married to Wall Street.

Nor do we mean just the paved thoroughfare in downtown Manhattan that runs from the graveyard of Trinity Church where Alexander Hamilton is buried to the East River that inspired John and Washington Roebling to create the Brooklyn Bridge. The stock market of choice these days isn't necessarily the New York Stock Exchange at number eleven on Manhattan's Wall Street or the American Stock Exchange behind Trinity Church. For all the stocks and bonds that are listed on a stock exchange in a fixed location, that many and more are traded by computer from offices all over the country courtesy of Nasdaq—the National Association of Securities Dealers' Automated Quotation system. Today, Wall Street exists in every city in America.

But *who* is it? When the *Wall Street Journal* grabs your attention with the lead "If you believe Wall Street's tough talk . . ." *whose* tough talk is it referring to?[3]

Let's look at the people you have to deal with once you are ready to take your corporation public and once you have completed the lawyer-intensive process of registering its stock.

1. First, there are the *underwriters* of your initial public offering, or IPO. *Underwrite* is an old word meaning "insure," but the underwriters of stocks and bonds are investment bankers, not insurance companies. They may insure your corporation against the risk that the public might not buy its stock by buying it themselves at an agreed price and reselling it to the public at a higher price. Or they may agree only to use their best efforts to sell your stock for a fee. Either way, they are handsomely compensated.

2. The underwriters may retail the stock directly to investors or wholesale it to *securities dealers* who are in the business of retailing stock and bonds. Some of these dealers may make a market in your stock by buying shares from shareholders who want to sell and selling shares to investors who want to buy. The dealers' reward is the spread between the bid price of the shares (what they pay) and the asked price (what they get).

3. Arranging buy-sell trades are *stockbrokers*, who charge each customer a commission based on the amount of that customer's purchase or sale. But since many brokerage houses are owned by investment bankers who are dealers as well as brokers (and underwriters), it's not always clear which hat these people are wearing.

4. Investment bankers employ *stock analysts* to write reports on corporations whose stock they have underwritten. A large underwriter-broker-dealer like Merrill Lynch may have a hundred analysts—and assign one to follow your corporation.

5. Publications like the *Wall Street Journal* maintain staffs of *financial journalists* who write leads like "If you believe Wall Street's tough talk" for articles they may print

about your corporation. Some of them publish stock market tables that list the price of your stock.

6. Institutional investors like mutual funds and pensions funds that invest other people's money in your corporation's stock engage *money managers* to make their investment decisions and their own stock analysts to advise them. Professionals in these categories number in the thousands.

Underwriters, dealers, stockbrokers and analysts, journalists, money managers, and their advisers—the modern Wall Street is all of these plus the investment banks, brokerage houses, financial publications, and institutional investors they work for. Getting hitched for better or for worse to this noisy crowd in order to gain access to investors among the general public changes your corporation's life as much as getting married to someone with an extended family of incurable gossips might change your own. Giving every member of the family equal treatment is a problem. Public corporations don't even treat their shareholders equally. Institutional investors, wrote economist Harvey Segal,

can not only buy newly issued securities at lower prices than small investors, but they also have much greater access to what some might regard as inside information [because corporate managers] fear that their dissatisfaction could result in a dumping of stocks and bonds, and hence, lower prices. Individual investors, unless sitting on enormous holdings, have no clout and are lucky if they get the time of day.[4]

Private corporations, by comparison, have few such problems. Unlike public corporations, they choose their shareholders. Since their stock can't be traded publicly, Wall Street ignores them. They don't have to tell anybody what they earn or anything else about their business.

Nor do private corporations have to worry about activists among their shareholders. Public corporations like Sears, Roebuck do.

For almost two years, Lens, a small investment firm founded by Robert Monks, badgered Sears to reform the way it governed itself and get rid of its financial subsidiaries so it could focus on its traditional business, retailing.[5] For almost two years, Sears stonewalled Lens. Suddenly, in September 1992, Sears announced that it would sell off part of its financial businesses to concentrate on retailing. As Sears's stock price jumped 9%, Lens claimed victory, saying it had generated more than $1 billion in shareholder value. Two years later Sears announced that it was divesting itself of its last financial business, Allstate, the car and home insurance operation it had started in 1931. Monks said that Sears had "done the whole job. Sears is home now."[6]

Lens's Nell Minow described shareholder activism as "targeting companies, preparing resolutions, meeting with executives and directors [to] improve [their] bottom lines." Unlike the days when activism focused on green issues or getting U.S. corporations out of South Africa, now "corporate performance is the central concern, and several recent studies show that, by this measure, shareholder activism can deliver.'' As an example, Minow cited the campaign that Calpers (California Public Employees Retirement System) initiated against 24 of the worst-performing stocks in its portfolio, all of which underperformed the Standard & Poor's stock index of the leading 500 public corporations. In the four years after Calpers began its campaign, according to Wilshire Associates, all 24 companies exceeded the S&P 500.

Why does shareholder activism work? ''For a simple reason,'' says Minow: ''Like subatomic particles, corporate directors and managers behave differently when they know they are being observed.''[7]

Since activist campaigns can be drawn out and expensive (the effort to reform Sears reportedly cost Lens almost $500,000), activist shareholders who have any clout tend to be institutional investors—institutions that invest other people's money. Private corporations don't (except by choice) have institutional investors among their shareholders.

In 1960, almost 90% of the shares of public corporations traded in the United States were owned by individual shareholders (mostly people) investing their own money. By 1990, individuals owned no more than 50%. The other half (or more) was owned by institutional investors, particularly pension plans like Calpers and mutual funds.[8]

Institutional investors invest in many corporations and have their own interests to serve. When AT&T was in the process of taking over NCR—a disastrous move that was to cost AT&T billions of dollars before it finally divested itself of NCR—a mutual fund manager said this to NCR's chief executive, Charles Exley:

Mr. Exley, we are against this takeover and think it would be a bad thing for both companies. However, we are told by AT&T that this takeover is inevitable. We have 18 times the investment in AT&T that we have in NCR. That being the case, we think it is in our interest to have the deal completed at the lowest possible cost to AT&T.[9]

Institutional investors are ''much more near-term oriented'' than they used to be, according to the *New York Times'* Thomas Friedman, and, it might be added, more near-term oriented than individual investors are today. Citing longtime bond expert Henry Kaufman, Friedman wrote that one of the reasons for this near-term orientation is that many institutional investors

have to mark to market each day—meaning that if they buy a bond [or stock] in the morning and it loses value in the afternoon they have to acknowledge that unrealized loss in their portfolio statements, giving them a strong incentive to quickly unload losers.[10]

Mutual funds have to mark to market each day because that's how the price at which they offer their own shares for sale the next day is determined. And mutual funds are the fastest growing institutional investors in the stock of public corporations.

To any institution that has to mark to market, the current stock price is more important than earnings or dividends. "The best indicator of having achieved benefits for clients is an increase in a portfolio company's stock price," says Robert Pozen of Fidelity Investments, the largest mutual fund company. "The next best indicator is an earnings increase, which is ultimately reflected in a higher stock price and/or higher dividend."[11] Public corporations, as a consequence, spend more and more of their time managing their stock price.

Private corporations don't have to worry about their stock price since they don't have one. They can spend all their time worrying about sales and profits— and managing their business so as to increase them.

Institutional money managers are the "great financiers of our day," wrote Tim Ferguson in the *Wall Street Journal*, "found not in banks but 'running' billions of dollars out of their own computerized crannies from [Manhattan's] Wall Street to Walla Walla. . . . Whether they're going to heaven or not, these guys represent meritocracy in a world that's too short on it. They get results or they fall."[12]

But as our modern-day Adam Smith said in *The Money Game*: "The name of the game is making money, not sitting on it."[13]

"Most portfolio managers are intelligent, careful people," says one of those people, but

in a world of instantaneous communication, when all of us hear the same news within seconds, . . . we act just like a herd of zebras who have sensed a pride of lions sneaking up on us. Wham! Off we go in an instant.[14]

To sell. Or if a stock looks like it's hot to trot, to buy. Is it any wonder that the average holding period for corporate shares dropped from *seven* years to *two* over the period that institutional ownership of those shares grew from 10% to 50%? Or that the average mutual fund turns over 75% of its investments each year—a holding period of only *one and a third years*?[15]

As the master investor (and economist) John Maynard Keynes wrote some six decades ago, professional investors and speculators "are concerned, not with what an investment is really worth to a man who buys it 'for keeps,' but with what the market will value it at, under the influence of mass psychology, three months or a year hence."[16]

Private corporations don't have to be worried about professional investors and speculators since their stock can't be traded publicly. Their shareholders necessarily invest, if not for keeps, at least for the long term.

It's a myth that public corporations are just private corporations with many shareholders as owners. **The Wall Street connection makes public corporations very different**, linking them to institutional shareholders with a common goal—maximizing the current stock price—but diverse agendas for achieving it. Some turn activist when they're dissatisfied with the stock price, others promote mergers, most just sell. Public corporations can be hard put to reconcile these often conflicting agendas and the goals of individual shareholders seeking long-term fundamental values.

But making sure that a corporation fairly represents the interests of its shareholders is one of the responsibilities of the corporation's directors, who are elected by the shareholders to control the corporation's management.

Chapter 3

The Owners of a Public Corporation Control It by Electing Its Directors

Shareowners control corporations in which they own stock by exercising their right to vote—usually for the directors, but sometimes by a direct vote on company decisions.

—New York Stock Exchange, *You and the Investment World*[1]

Contrary to legal theory, the boards of directors of most of our larger companies do not in fact control and manage their companies. . . . Instead, the management hired by the board . . . generally decides the course of operations and periodically requests the board to confirm the determinations of the management.

—Supreme Court Justice Arthur Goldberg[2]

Once a year, after auditors (independent accountants) have determined the profit or loss for the year just ended, the 12,000 or so public corporations in the United States send their shareholders an annual report. The report features, traditionally, a personal letter from the chief executive officer reciting the significant events of the year gone by, giving an upbeat prediction for the year ahead, and thanking the shareholders for their support—whether or not they gave it.

The reason for this tradition is that in all corporations, public and private, the shareholders who own the corporation have the right to elect the directors legally responsible for governing it. Thus do the owners of a corporation control it by electing its directors.

In a public corporation the directors carry out their legal responsibility by appointing officers to manage it on a day-to-day basis and supervising how they do it.

Directors come in two flavors: inside and outside. Inside directors are full-time managers of the corporation who serve additionally as directors. When analyzing how effective a board of directors is in appointing officers and controlling what they do, you have to take into account that the inside directors are managers first and directors second. You can't count on their following the best interests of the shareholders or some abstract legal duty when they're appointing and controlling *themselves*—or the officers they report to. No individual can serve two masters, or, as a former CEO put it: "Insiders can never be influential board members in their own right. They simply must vote with the CEO. They can serve other important functions, but they cannot be counted on to exert any real independence."[3]

Outside directors, on the other hand, are by definition *independent* of the management of the corporation. Many are active CEOs or executives of their own companies. Others are retired executives. Most of the rest are consultants or lawyers.

How a board is divided between inside and outside directors tends to vary with how public the corporation is.

- Private corporations, typically owned by the founders of the corporation and a limited number of other shareholders, have mostly inside directors. Corporate subsidiaries—companies owned by other companies—are usually private companies with no public shareholders and no directors from outside the parent organization.

- Semipublic corporations that have outsiders as shareholders but are still dominated by their founders or founding families generally have a contingent of outside directors but a majority of insiders.

- Truly public corporations usually have more outside directors than inside directors.

But even in truly public corporations, wrote Edward Herman, author of the Twentieth Century Fund Report *Corporate Control, Corporate Power*, it is

well understood . . . that outsiders "invited" onto a board are not the power equals of the more permanent top cadres of management. The frequent use of the word "invited" suggests a guestlike and transitory status of the outsider, and because the invitation is very often from top management, board criticism of the corporate leadership violates the law of hospitality.[4]

William Bowen, former president of Princeton University, who has served on a number of corporate as well as nonprofit boards, wrote a book about directors from the director's point of view. "Courage and the will to act are often the attributes in scarcest supply," he said, but the problem is "deeper than merely finding individuals with the requisite backbone, though that is, I suspect, the largest part of it." The deeper problem is the director's dilemma, described by a director in these terms:

Executive management must be left free to run the company uninhibited by excessive interference by the board. The issue, of course, is what is excessive interference? . . . Most conscientious directors are overly shy about being perceived as rocking the boat. . . . The catch-22 is that . . . not engaging or interfering in short-term management frequently causes directors to abdicate their responsibility for long-term direction.

There are other problems as well. One is shortage of attention, especially for directors who are actively involved in their own corporation or profession or who are also directors of other corporations. A second is lack of knowledge or experience relevant to the type of business of the corporation they direct or inability to understand that business. A third is dependence on the managers being supervised for information necessary to supervise them. Another is the phenomenon called *groupthink*: "It is surprising," Bowen wrote, "how easy it can be for a closely knit board to come to major decisions without really considering major risks and potentially adverse consequences."[5] With all these problems, one wonders why outside directors want to be directors.

It might be the challenge of the job or a desire to keep the CEO as a friend or the corporation as a client. It might even be the extra income, which is not peanuts—the fees that large corporations pay for a dozen or so days of a director's time often exceed what the average family earns in 365 days by working—although we always hear that directors are so well off that the fees don't mean anything to them. And then there's the prestige. Michael Blumenthal, onetime CEO of Burroughs and Unisys, told Bowen:

It helps your standing in the business community to be a director of, say, GE, GM, IBM, etc. That also means that, once inducted into the most prestigious "club," it inhibits asking the nasty questions. You want to *stay* a member! . . . All that is very much part of the group dynamic of "going along."[6]

As an institution charged with the governance of the draft horses of our economy—the cornerstone, indeed, of corporation law and of the entire corporate governance (spelled *shareholder empowerment*) movement—the shareholder-elected board of directors is deeply flawed. All the paradoxes involved in becoming and being and staying a director conspire to undercut the board's ability to supervise management, which is, after all, its only function. As Edward Herman concluded in *Corporate Control, Corporate Power*:

Directors in large mainstream corporations normally tend to play a passive role, as invited guests, characteristically tied to the inside hosts by some sort of personal or business relationship. Outside director power is, in consequence, typically latent at best, activated mainly in response to serious economic or political setbacks to the company, which demonstrate serious management ineptitude or malfeasance that leave management in great disarray and threaten corporate financial integrity and survival.[7]

In other words, the building has to be burning down before the owners can count on the firefighters they selected to do their job. Directors aren't much good at fire prevention. How could they be? They never even inspect the building!

Could shareholders elect better firefighters?

The election of directors of a public corporation occurs at the annual meeting of shareholders. If you're a shareholder, you've received the annual report with the CEO's letter as well as a proxy statement prepared by management that describes what the shareholders will be asked to vote on. Included with the proxy statement is a proxy that allows you to vote in advance of the annual meeting without having to attend it—the corporate equivalent of an absentee ballot. Since, as one account describes it, aside from all the people representing the corporation, the audience at an annual meeting is likely to consist largely of "retirees looking to fill an otherwise quiet afternoon," very few ballots are cast in person.[8] Issues on which shareholders vote are decided by proxy.

If you're a shareholder, that probably suits you fine. You don't have time to attend the annual meeting, which this year may be held halfway across the country, but you've invested a substantial amount of your money in the corporation and intend to exercise your right to vote. Let's say that its bread-and-butter products have come under a lot of pressure from foreign competitors, especially a major Japanese firm, and notwithstanding research and development expenditures twice what the average American company spends, it hasn't been able to develop new technology that would differentiate its products and move it into the electronic age. The stock analyst at your brokerage house has been saying for months that the corporation should cut R&D, divest all subsidiaries outside its core business, lay off a minimum of 15,000 employees, and fire the CEO if he won't take these actions immediately. But he's a stock analyst, not someone responsible for governing the corporation. You want to know what the candidates for the board of directors have to say about these issues.

This isn't a political campaign, of course; the candidates aren't holding a public debate. But the proxy statement profiles them, giving their age, years on the board, current job, past experience, and position on the key issues facing the corporation. Age and experience count, of course, but this year you're particularly interested in the R&D issue—anyone who's in favor of reducing it will have to convince you that new product development won't be hampered. You read the proxy statement, for the first time, with undivided attention. Are you enlightened?

You certainly are, but not about the issues, which aren't addressed at all. How, you ask yourself, are you supposed to decide which candidates to vote for when you don't know where they stand? Then comes the enlightenment.

The proxy statement profiles 15 candidates. The board has 15 directors. One man, one vote—just like elections in the former Soviet Union. Or Iraq, which held its first presidential election ever in October 1995. Voters were given ballots asking whether Saddam Hussein should be president for another seven years.

They could check yes or no. (Ninety-something percent checked yes.) You also can check yes or no.

Most proxy statements list only one nominee for each position on the board of directors. Occasionally, one or two outsiders may try to bootstrap themselves onto the board, but for the most part, the only nominees are management's nominees, one for each open slot. You have the choice of voting for them, voting against them (as activist shareholders sometimes do in protest), not voting at all (activist shareholders sometimes do that, too), or writing in the names of other people you'd like to see as directors. It doesn't make any difference.

The only people who are likely to be nominated (at the annual meeting) are the ones whose names are printed in the proxy statement. Votes for everyone else will be disregarded.

Of course, it is theoretically possible (if practically unheard of) for an unopposed management nominee for director to receive more *no* votes than *yes* votes. What then? Under corporate bylaws, directors usually hold their directorships until their successors are duly elected (or appointed) and take office. So one outcome is that the predecessor (who in most cases is actually the nominee running for reelection) continues to hold office. Another outcome is that management simply declares the nominee to have been elected since the election was uncontested.

"These meaningless [annual] meetings have come to resemble a play in four acts," wrote Philip Lochner of Time Warner, a public corporation, and Richard Koppes of the California Public Employees Retirement System, an activist institutional investor. This is Act Two of their play:

Directors are re-elected . . . in uncontested elections on the basis of proxies voted and mailed in by the shareholders, the vast majority of whom don't bother to attend the annual meeting. The results are known in advance and nothing that happens at the meeting can easily change the outcome.[9]

The rare *contested* election allowing you to choose among opposing slates of directors occurs when two factions vie for control of the corporation in what is referred to as a *proxy fight*. But whichever side wins, the next year you'll be given the same old Hobson's choice—one nominee for each open slot on the board of directors whom you can vote for or not; they will all be declared winners and take office as your duly elected representatives.

To elect, according to *The American Heritage Dictionary of the English Language*, is to "select by vote for an office." To *select* is to "choose from among several; make a choice." A *vote* is a "formal expression of preference for a candidate or a proposed resolution," and *preference* is the "selecting of or right to select someone or something over another or others."[10] However you slice it, a true red-white-and-blue election involves the right to make a choice among more than one alternative.

So, no, to answer our earlier question, shareholders of public corporations couldn't elect better firefighters. Normally they aren't given the opportunity to elect *any*. Directors are selected by management (or, sometimes, by the other directors) and serve at management's pleasure. Those who insist on making their own inspection of the corporation's building are likely to displease the building's management—and lose their positions. As Harvey Segal wrote in *Corporate Makeover*, ''Mavericks and inquisitors who displease CEOs and the other insiders are eliminated by the simple expedient of withdrawing their names from the management slates in shareholder elections.''[11]

It's a myth that the owners of a public corporation control it by electing its directors. **Directors aren't elected by the owners and don't control the corporation**. Public corporations are controlled by their managers.

Does that mean that shareholders are left out in the cold? Fortunately, no, because the number-one concern of all corporate management is shareholder value.

Chapter 4

The First Concern of Public Corporation Management Is Shareholder Value

Corporate executives are not capitalists seeking profit. They are men seeking careers, in a structure offering rewards of power and position rather than profit or great wealth.

—Adolf A. Berle[1]

In making administrative decisions, career managers preferred policies that favored the long-term stability and growth of their enterprises to those that maximize current profits. . . . If profits were high, they preferred to reinvest them in the enterprise rather than pay them out in dividends.

—Alfred D. Chandler, Jr., *The Visible Hand*[2]

Let's review the bidding. In corporate mythology, the shareholders control management by electing the directors who appoint and supervise the managers. This may be true enough in a private corporation or in a semipublic corporation where the founders or founding families own enough stock to control it. But in truly public corporations, the shareholders don't elect the directors, and the directors don't supervise the managers.

So who controls the vast wealth entrusted to these public corporations and the great concentration of power that wealth creates? Who contributed $1.5 million of Philip Morris shareholder equity to the Grand Old Party in 1995 and the first half of 1996? Who at CBS, in 1995, ordered Mike Wallace's interview of Jeffrey Wigand off the air? Who in the late 1980s and early 1990s selected more than 100,000 of IBM's U.S. employees and told them they had to go?

Who else but the people who manage these corporations?

What Adolf Berle and Gardner Means wrote in the early 1930s (in *The*

Modern Corporation and Private Property) is still true: The diversification of ownership of a public corporation among thousands of shareholders insulates management from shareholder control.[3] No one shareholder or group of shareholders acting in concert owns enough stock to tell management what to do. Indeed, if shareholders *weren't* insulated from management—if they were active rather than passive investors—public corporations could never have grown to the size they have. Separation of ownership and control is a *condition* of that growth as well as a result.

Although the insulation of corporate management from corporate ownership contradicts corporate mythology, it violates no law. In fact, the law tends to reinforce that insulation by denying shareholders the right to interfere with traditional management prerogatives. When, for example, shareholders seek greater control over how much management pays itself, the law usually comes down against the shareholders. The law reasons that since directors are able (and obligated) to take care of the shareholders' interests, the shareholders should mind their own business and leave the directors to mind the corporation's.

What does the law know? In today's public corporations, the board of directors is largely irrelevant. Corporations are controlled and directed and managed by their managers.

Is that bad?

The short answer is no, not at all, since the first concern of public corporation management is shareholder value. Management salaries are paid by the corporation, but it is the shareholders' money that the corporation is spending. Therefore, it is the shareholders who pay the piper and call the tune. The name of the tune (sung by the managers, of course) is "Oh, How We Maximize Shareholder Value!"

That's the theory. Is it true or is it myth?

We might ask Gordon Donaldson. In the early 1980s he researched the motivation of corporate executives at a dozen major industrial companies and set forth the results in *Managing Corporate Wealth: The Operation of a Comprehensive Financial Goals System.*[4] The goals managers pursue, he found, are personal survival, personal independence, self-sufficiency, and self-fulfillment. The complementary goal they pursue for their companies is the maximization of *corporate* value rather than shareholder value—money and other forms of wealth retained by the corporation rather than distributed to shareholders. Corporate wealth is a resource that managers can use. Managers can use it to enhance their power, prestige, and personal wealth and thereby lock in their survival goals at the same time they pursue self-fulfillment.

Personal wealth, *self*-fulfillment—what happened to *shareholder* wealth and fulfillment?

Maximization of corporate wealth is heresy to shareholder value hard-liners. They believe that management should not only maximize current earnings but also distribute every dollar of those earnings as dividends to the shareholders, retaining (or "reinvesting") none, not even the one-third to one-half of current profits that corporations typically reinvest. If the corporation needs money, they say, it should raise it by selling shares of its capital stock or borrowing it. That way is more expensive, to be sure, but it reflects the true cost of money. Spending shareholders' profits deludes managers into thinking that money is less expensive than it really is. Thinking money is less expensive than it really is leads managers to buy things they shouldn't buy, such as other corporations in unrelated businesses.

Besides, it's the shareholders' money, and the shareholders should be able to invest it someplace else if they think they can make a greater return. If they don't, they'll reinvest it in the corporation. But it'll be their decision, not the corporation's.

Okay, maybe we're overstating the hard-liners' position. In principle, at least, they might be willing to allow the corporation to reinvest *some* shareholder profits, provided the investment doesn't reduce (or *dilute*) the value of the shareholders' investment. So the hard-liners' position, or at least the *soft* hard-liners' position, comes down to this: Maximize shareholder value—don't dilute it.

Who decides whether an investment meets that condition? Well, the stock market itself, if you believe it. All-knowing, seeing all, the market computes the present value of all future profits (or cash, as some believe) that the corporation will earn forevermore from its investments—including profits from everyday operations financed by reinvested earnings—and that's the current stock price! If the corporation makes an investment that will not produce enough profits in the future, the market immediately reduces its stock price.

Smart market. All it needs is the information public corporations routinely disclose about their investments. How did it get so smart? Or as one Wall Streeter put it, "How can it be that the expected cash generation over the life of a business determines share price, given that most investors seem preoccupied with near-term accounting earnings?" His answer is that

prices in the stock market, like all other prices, are set at the margin by the smartest money in the game, leaving the majority of investors as mere price-takers. The concept of marginal pricing . . . can be illustrated by the metaphor of the *lead steers*: If you want to know where a herd of cattle is going, you need not interview every steer, only the lead steer.[5]

The market is smart because its prices are set by its lead steers, the smartest people in the market. Would the lead steers agree? Warren Buffet, who is regarded by many as *the* lead steer, gives his answer:

[When the] price of a stock can be influenced by a "herd" on Wall Street with prices set at the margin by the most emotional person, or the greediest person, or the most depressed person, it is hard to argue that the markets always price rationally. In fact, market prices are frequently nonsensical.[6]

That leaves us with two answers: The market is consistently rational because its prices are set by smart lead steers, and the market is frequently irrational because its prices are set by the emotional herd.

Was it rational or irrational on March 8, 1996, when it reduced stock market prices by 3% (a lot for one day) upon hearing of a major drop in the unemployment rate? Unemployment drops when business is good, orders are up, and corporations hire more workers to fill the increased orders. More workers then have more money to buy more things, which makes business even better. All good news, you say? Perhaps for the economy, but on Wall Street that day the steers leading the market worried that higher employment might lead to higher wages, therefore higher inflation, therefore higher interest rates because people who lend money need more interest to offset the higher inflation. Higher wages and interest rates mean higher costs and therefore lower returns from the investments that public corporations make. That's bad news.

According to cognitive psychologist Amos Tversky, human reasoning is a lot more quirky than we'd like to believe, and one of those quirks is a tendency to lend greater weight to potential risks in making decisions than to potential benefits.[7] Wall Street steers are like humans in that regard, and on this particular day (as on many others) the bad news won out over the good news. But the bad news wasn't all that bad. The unemployment rate remained well above what it was in, say, 1970, and worker compensation in real terms (net of inflation) was lower than the previous year. The steers might have waited to see whether the Federal Reserve Board, the arm of government charged with controlling inflation, thought that the threat of inflation was great enough for it to raise interest rates in order to dampen consumer spending and thus make business not so good, decrease hiring, raise unemployment, and reduce the likelihood of higher wages. Instead, the steers increased interest rates themselves by selling bonds and lowering bond prices, and then they lowered stock prices by selling stocks because interest rates had increased.

So a rosy outlook for Churchill's Horses and the economy produced a black day on Wall Street because the market has this wondrous capacity to realize its own hopes and fears as soon as it conceives them. That's why it's called *efficient*. On March 8, 1996, the fear of higher interest rates was self-fulfilled that same day and reflected in lower market values at day's end.

But, we were inquiring, were the market steers that day behaving rationally or irrationally? Heeding Tversky, we might conclude that they were behaving irrationally, letting the fear of inflation overwhelm the reality of economic progress. But we might be wrong. Rationality, no less than beauty, is in the eye of the beholder.

We learned a couple of myths ago that stock market trading is increasingly dominated by fast-turnover institutions seeking quick profits and that these institutions are concerned not so much with the long-range value of stocks as with the near-term value that other traders under the influence of mass psychology will place on them. In other words, the steers on March 8, 1996, worried not so much about inflation as about whether all the other steers would worry about inflation and how all that mass worrying about inflation would affect stock market prices.

Was their worry realistic? Not only realistic—stocks, after all, did drop 3% in the course of the day—but self-fulfilling. And not only self-fulfilling but also self-focused and biased toward the short term. The steers, that is, were not much concerned with the underlying performance of the economy or the long-term value of the businesses represented by those stocks. "Traders are hunting for returns," wrote Joel Kurtzman in *The Death of Money*. "Less and less do the fundamentals matter."[8]

From the point of view of the stock market, the world outside Wall Street is increasingly irrelevant.

Viewed from afar, the market may seem irrational much of the time, but like the corporation, the market is a paradox, something that doesn't exist apart from its people yet at the same time is much more powerful than all its people put together. As the corporation has come to be dominated by management, the stock market has come to be dominated by short-term traders and speculators and institutions holding stock in many corporations for shorter and shorter periods of time. They pay little heed to the fundamental earnings prospects of any one corporation over the long term since they won't be shareholders that long. The market, said Kurtzman, has

always contained a speculative fringe, but traditionally, long-term investors held the broad middle ground. Traditional markets were created for moving capital to companies with good ideas in return for a share of the profits. Traditional markets were supposed to be transparent, with the value of a company reflected in the price of its stock. But speculative markets treat stocks as if they were commodities where trading is the way to create profits. By definition, speculators are short-term investors. When they dominate a market, they change the market's character, and transparency goes away.[9]

In other words, today's market may not reflect the value of the corporation's stock and its shareholders' investment as it is supposed to. It may not be irrational, but then again it's not as smart or as concerned with future values as the shareholder value hard-liners or the market's own boosters, the efficient-market theorists, would have you believe. It's too focused on itself.

From the point of view of the world outside Wall Street, the stock market is increasingly irrelevant.

Why, then, should the hard-liners' tune, maximization of the current stock market value (and distribution of corporate wealth to current shareholders), be the only one that management dances to? What about shareholders interested in maximum *future* value—when they (or the people whose money they are investing) reach retirement age or their children are ready for college? And what about shareholders-to-come, buyers of the stock at some future time? Without buyers, of course, shareholder value is less because shareholders can't sell their stock and convert that value into money anytime they need it; they get money only when the corporation pays dividends.

What about the customers who buy and the workers who produce what the corporation makes? Without them, shareholder value is nothing more than the liquidation value of the corporation's assets. "The successful corporation," wrote ITT's Rand Araskog,

> has many masters in addition to the immediate, sometimes transient stockholders: the government and its agencies; the communities where its plants and factories are located; the employees who work for it; the quality of its products and the level of its services; the charities and public services to which it contributes . . . The successful corporation must be responsible to all its constituents. Shareholder values, to be sure—but not just shareholder values—must be the concern of the CEO. Too much emphasis on the immediate, the short-term, can only be deleterious to the shareholder and the business in the end. . . . To build lasting value, a corporation must be guided by long-term vision.[10]

The noisy crowd on Wall Street, of course, holds fast to the view that current shareholders are a public corporation's only proper constituents and the current value of their investment its only proper concern. But whether the only, or at least the first, concern of public corporation management *should* be shareholder value, it's a myth that it *is* shareholder value. As pointed out by Gordon Donaldson (with assists, quoted at the outset, from Berle and Chandler): **The first concern of public corporation management is its own interests**—and the corporate wealth that serves those interests.

On the other hand, since management enhances corporate wealth by maximizing current profit, which also enhances shareholder value, management serves the shareholders' interests even as it serves its own.

Part II

Shareholders

How the value of the investment of the shareholders of public corporations is maximized, measured, and distributed; why public corporations exist.

Chapter 5

Corporations Maximize Shareholder Value by Maximizing Current Profit

We presumed that the first purpose in making a capital investment is the establishment of a business that will pay satisfactory dividends and preserve and increase its capital value. The primary objective of the corporation, therefore, we declared, was to make money, not just motor cars.

—Alfred P. Sloan, Jr., CEO of General Motors[1]

The most basic reason for existence of the enterprise is to use the capital of the owners to their maximum gain.

—Pearson Hunt, Charles M. Williams, and Gordon Donaldson, *Basic Business Finance*[2]

As shareholders of public corporations, we're skating on thin ice. We've found that not only is the board of directors essentially irrelevant—the board that is supposed to govern the corporation in our interests—but also the stock market that is supposed to reflect the value of those interests. The board can't be relied on to control the corporation, and the market can't be relied on to measure shareholder value.

Churchill's Horses are running away with their owners' investment.

Only they really aren't. The saving grace, from the shareholders' point of view (and what other point of view is legitimate?), is this: Public corporations are run for profit. They have no other goal. Their managers may use this profit to enhance corporate wealth rather than shareholder wealth, as Gordon Donaldson found, and they may prefer to reinvest it in the business rather than distribute it to the shareholders, as Alfred Chandler concluded. But profit is profit. Whether you regard it as corporate wealth or shareholder wealth, it still amounts to *earn-*

ings, and it still powers the mechanism known as the *price/earnings ratio*, which (forget all the theories) is how the stock market *really* values public corporation stock and therefore shareholder equity.

Of course, the concept of earnings in the price/earnings ratio refers to *current* earnings—either the reported profit for the last four quarters or the estimated profit for the current fiscal year or the next four quarters, if Wall Street or the corporation has made such an estimate. Thus, corporations maximize shareholder value by maximizing current profit. But it doesn't make a whit of difference whether that profit is considered by business school professors, shareholder value advocates, or public corporation managers as corporate wealth or shareholder wealth. The price/earnings ratio gladly accepts *all* profit in its zeal to convert earnings per share to share price and shareholder wealth.

The market moves in mysterious ways. As shareholders, we'd best not look too closely at the smoke and mirrors and levers it manipulates to achieve its wizardry. Let us simply be grateful that in the United States, as strategy expert Michael Porter wrote,

corporate goals center on earning high returns on investment and maximizing current stock prices. Management exercises the dominant influence on corporate goals, interpreting signals about desired behavior from the external capital market, influenced by compensation based on current accounting profits or unrestricted stock options that heighten stock price sensitivity.[3]

Of course, the emphasis on current profits, high returns, and maximum current stock prices comes at the expense of long-term investment in R&D, new products, and higher productivity. Compared to both Japan and Germany, says Porter, U.S. private enterprise "is less supportive of investment overall because of its sensitivity to current returns . . . combined with corporate goals that stress current stock price over long-term corporate value."[4] And the investment that is made includes "a smaller share of long-term projects."[5]

Given the dominant position of fast-trading institutional investors among corporate shareholders and the increasing role of stock options in management compensation—devices that create "a direct link between stock market valuation and management behavior"—it's a wonder that public corporations make *any* long-term investment.

One that did is Hewlett-Packard, which built its first inkjet printer in 1984. According to the *Wall Street Journal*, Japanese companies, which made four out of five personal computer printers sold in the United States, were underwhelmed. Said the president of the U.S. division of Epson, the market leader: "Our engineers thought that if they announced such a product, they'd lose face." But HP continued to invest in its new technology. In 1988, after coming out with its plain-paper Deskjet model, it held a strategy conference. That, said one of the managers, was "when the lights went on."

Instead of marketing the inkjet as a low-cost alternative to HP's own Laserjet models, which dominated the laser printer segment of the U.S. market, the HP inkjetters decided to go head-to-head against the low-cost dot matrix models produced by the Japanese. Targeting Epson, they donned ''Beat Epson'' football jerseys, reverse-engineered Epson printers, and studied everything Epson did. Discovering that Epson got ''huge mileage'' out of developing slight variations on one basic design, HP determined to do the same. But first its engineers had to get over the mind-set that every new model required a basic new design. Product manager Judy Thorpe made them telephone their customers. The customers, it turned out, wanted the design the engineers considered a ''kludge.'' What HP learned, said Thorpe, was that ''you can tweak your not-so-latest thing and get the latest thing.'' The knowledge gave HP a jumpstart over its competition.

By the time the Japanese dot matrix companies woke up to the threat from inkjets, HP had hit its stride, achieving economies of scale and using the experience it had gained to make continuous improvements in its product line. In 1993, as NEC (Nippon Electric Corporation) introduced a monochrome inkjet into the U.S. market and Canon a color model, HP cut the price of its black-and-white printer (which cost half as much to produce as it did in 1988) by 40% and introduced a new color model. NEC withdrew its printer after four months. Said the head of Canon's inkjet printer business: ''The market is HP's garden.''

The next year, inkjet printers outsold dot matrix printers. It had taken a decade or more to achieve market dominance, but now HP had 55% of the world market in the dominant segment (inkjets) of a thriving group of growth products (desktop printers) and was one of the fastest-growing public corporations in the United States. Richard Hackborn, the manager originally in charge of the inkjet project, attributed success to ''the tremendous contribution of local innovation and accountability'' and ''central leverage''—the corporate resources HP invested in the operation.[6]

Local innovation and accountability constitute the essence of the ''HP Way,'' the management philosophy promoted by David Packard, one of HP's two founders, that ''fosters individual motivation, initiative and creativity, and a wide latitude of freedom in working toward established objectives and goals.''[7] On the other hand, according to the *Wall Street Journal*, HP senior managers ''for the most part preached high-profit, high-cost products for niche markets—which is how HP lost the calculator business.''[8] Had these same managers actually favored long-term stability and growth over maximizing current profits (to borrow Chandler's formulation from the last chapter) in order to build a low-profit, low-cost product for a mass market? Whether they were aware of it or not, that in effect is what they did when they invested in the inkjet.

It might have turned out differently had cofounder Packard not still been involved in the corporation. Wall Street's voice was not the only one it heeded.

Another of the country's fastest-growing public corporations is Motorola, and two of its most important businesses are semiconductors and cellular telephones.

But in their early days these businesses did not produce enough profits to satisfy the board of directors, the shareholders' legal representatives, and the board voted to dispose of them. In each case the board was overruled by Motorola's CEO, who was a member of the corporation's founding family.[9] Wall Street was not the dominant influence in this corporation, either.

A rival of Motorola and a younger neighbor of HP—described, indeed, as the Sparta of Silicon Valley to HP's Athens—is Intel, inventor of the microprocessor. In the 1980s, after Intel was driven out of the computer memory chip business by the Japanese, its core technology (microprocessor chips) was widely viewed as yet "another high-technology industry, pioneered by America, that was being lost to Japan" because American manufacturers were deficient in production quality and efficiency. But then, according to Craig Barrett, Intel's chief operating officer, Intel realized that "all the smart technologists in the world would not make this industry a success. We had to get down and vastly improve our manufacturing efficiency."

And they did. Design, development, and manufacturing were coordinated by requiring product designers to steer their creations through the early production process, which resulted in designs that were easier to produce. The emphasis on defect detection was redirected to defect *prevention.* Suppliers were competitively chosen and then closely monitored. Most workers now had technical degrees, not just high school diplomas with no specialized training. "Companies like Intel," said Richard Lester, director of the Massachusetts Institute of Technology's Industrial Performance Center, "have done a lot of the things that we all said American companies weren't doing—investing heavily for the long term and buckling down to really take manufacturing seriously."

In 1995 Intel opened a $2 billion plant in New Mexico that the *New York Times* said stands at the summit of "the Everest of modern manufacturing."

Intel microprocessors power four-fifths of the world's personal computers, but even as it opened its new plant, Wall Street was pricing its shares at a P/E ratio below the stock market average for all corporations. After all, the microprocessor market that Intel dominates might someday slump. What does Wall Street know?[10]

It knows—or believes—that corporations maximize shareholder value by maximizing current profit. And it's not shy about making its position known. It was "dismayed" when on January 20, 1997, Dow Jones announced plans to invest $650 million over the next three to four years to revamp its subsidiary, Telerate, which had in recent years lost some of its competitive luster. It was dismayed "in large part because [Dow Jones] executives acknowledged that the revamping would crimp profitability for at least the next two years." Since it was dismayed, that same day it lopped 10% off the value of Dow Jones' stock price.[11]

But Michael Porter believes that there is little direct connection between short-term corporate profits and long-term shareholder returns. The study he directed in the early 1990s for the Council on Competitiveness and Harvard Business

School found that although profits were higher in U.S. corporations, Japanese shareholders for two decades and German shareholders for more than a decade had earned higher returns than American shareholders, primarily through long-term capital gains from higher stock prices. Why? Porter's answer

is that by demanding high near-term profits the American system is counterproductive, sapping growth by lowering American investment to rates far below Japan and Germany. And the additional investment in Japan and Germany has paid off for everyone in the long term—shareholders, workers, companies and the economy.[12]

Would greater investment by *American* corporations pay off for everyone? Hewlett-Packard's long-term investment in inkjet printers, Motorola's in cellular telephones and Intel's in state-of-the-art microprocessors paid off for their share-holders who stayed the course. Staying the course, studies have shown, is the best way for equity investors to make money. (By contrast, studies have also shown, fewer than one out of four equity mutual funds, which by nature are traders rather than course-stayers, can be expected to beat the Standard & Poor's index of 500 leading stocks consistently.) And these investments paid off for consumers and the economy generally as well as for the corporations themselves. But can public corporations maximize long-term shareholder return without cutting back on their workforce?

Yes, said compensation guru Graef Crystal, who studied that question by correlating shareholder returns in major corporations over 10 years with the change in total number of employees—provided "long-term" is sufficiently long. Even at 7 years

there continues to be a robust relationship between shareholder return and work force growth. But [when] the time window is narrowed to five years, the relationship begins to soften. And it disappears altogether when the time window is either three years or one year.[13]

In other words, corporations may increase profitability for a few years by downsizing, but over the long run they have to grow to maximize profit and shareholder value, and growth ultimately means hiring more workers.

So, yes, everyone benefits from long-term corporate investment, not least the corporate shareholders. But U.S. corporations have become laggards when it comes to long-term investment. How can we get them to do more?

In Japan and Germany, major long-term shareholders are closely involved in the management of the corporation, and Michael Porter's solution would encourage that sort of partnership between U.S. corporations and their large investors. But under current U.S. law, mutual funds cannot own more than 10% of any one corporation, and pension funds cannot own more than 10% of their sponsors' stock. And shareholders who do own 10% of a public corporation must disclose their holdings, give up any short-term profits, and refrain from trading on the basis of inside (nonpublic) information.

These and other rules ensure that the stock market is efficient, the playing field level, and the game one that can be safely played by nonprofessional investors at minimum cost. Thus, there is a trade-off, as Amar Bhide has written, "between strict market regulation [of public corporation stock transactions] and fruitful cooperation between shareholders and executives."[14] But even changing the law to permit such fruitful cooperation would not make much difference unless institutional shareholders were first cured of their addiction to short-term trading profits.

It's a myth that corporations maximize shareholder value by maximizing current profit. The reality is: **Maximizing shareholder value requires investing in long-term profitability**. But too many institutional shareholders benefit from the myth and too few corporate executives act on the reality.

But since long-term profitability still involves profit, we now turn to an examination of profit, a more elusive construct than one might at first suppose.

Chapter 6

Corporate Profit Is the Best Measure of Real Shareholder Value

Profit: 1. The excess of revenue, proceeds, or selling price over related costs.
— Eric L. Kohler, *A Dictionary for Accountants*[1]

Accounting is largely a matter of accounting for costs. . . . Business costs are incurred for the purpose of earning income. Accordingly, in the course of time the costs are assigned to income; that is, they are deducted from the income they were instrumental in earning.
— John N. Myer, *Accounting for Non-Accountants*[2]

At the beginning of the last chapter, we quoted General Motor's legendary CEO Alfred Sloan to the effect that the primary object of the corporation was to make money, not just whatever products or services it produced. The money would be used to pay satisfactory dividends and preserve and increase its capital value, which is to say, its shareholder value. But to Sloan, the price of GM's stock was essentially irrelevant to that value.

Speculation never had any attraction for me. Other than a few professional operators, who has really got ahead by stock-market trading? Naturally, I like to see General Motors stock register a good price on the market, but that is just a matter of pride. Personally, I consider its price fluctuations inconsequential. What has counted with me is the true value of the property as a business, as an opportunity for the exercise of management talent.[3]

In corporate parlance, of course, money means profit. No one cares how much cash a public corporation has, provided it can pay its bills and doesn't accumulate so much cash that it becomes a takeover target. The profit that a public corporation reports is universally accepted as the measure of its performance in maximizing the true capital value of the corporation. Corporate profit, in short, is the best measure of real shareholder value.

How is the profit itself measured?

Again, the answer is universally accepted: Profit is measured against the corresponding quarter of the previous year (or previous years), a technique that removes seasonal fluctuations from the measure. Thus when we said (in the last chapter) that public corporations are run for profit, we really should have said that they are run for profit *increases*, quarter by quarter, relative to the corresponding quarter in the previous year.

Wal-Mart ran up 99 straight quarterly increases before the 1995 Christmas season finally did it in, setting a record for all other public corporations to try to beat. But was it running strictly on its own strength and endurance and skill?

It can help to have a supply of steroids—or some corporate equivalent. Ten years into its own string of profit increases that began when Harold Geneen became chief executive, ITT bought Hartford Fire Insurance Company, which like all casualty insurers maintained large reserves of money invested in stocks and other securities to hedge against risks like fire that it had insured its policyholders against. The accounting rules Hartford lived by required it to carry its portfolio stocks at their original purchase value, unlike, say, mutual fund companies, which have to adjust the book value of their portfolio to current market value. Thus, if ITT in its pursuit of continuous profit increases wanted to add a little to its quarterly profit, it could direct Hartford to sell undervalued stocks to realize a capital gain—and then, if necessary, buy them back at current market value. If ITT wanted to subtract a little from profit that might be hard to beat in another year, Hartford could sell overvalued stocks and take a capital loss. Geneen, wrote Floyd Norris in the *New York Times*, was "perhaps the best manager ever at understanding how sometimes-foolish accounting rules could be used to his benefit."[4]

"Whenever a company's profit projections are so completely on target," said the *Times* in a 1995 article about the old-line Singer sewing machine company, "investors should wonder how the company is pulling off the feat—especially when it is subject to wildly fluctuating currencies" (as ITT was in Geneen's day).[5] Having been taken over in 1989 by Chinese-Canadian businessman James Ting and moved offshore to the Netherlands Antilles, where accounting rules are more relaxed, Singer came to do all sorts of things besides selling sewing machines to keep profit looking good. A tenth of its profit in 1994 came from dealings with affiliated companies also controlled by Ting, and upwards of a fifth was attributable to nonoperating and nonrecurring sources like asset sales and foreign exchange gains. Booking onetime gains from affiliated companies is one of the more common financial ploys to maintain consistent profit increases.

But accountants, the professional scorekeepers of the profit game, are not so much concerned with consistency of profit as with consistency in the *measurement* of profit.

Accountants determine profit by adding up sales revenue, deducting the costs that have been incurred in generating that revenue to arrive at pretax income, and then deducting income taxes. The overriding principle is that all revenue must be matched with the costs incurred in generating it so that the profit determined from that revenue will reflect all relevant costs. "The assigning of costs," says John Myer, author of standard texts on accounting, "is the central problem of accounting."[6]

But note that a cost is *incurred* (recognized by accountants) when the obligation to pay it is created, not when the corporation actually has to pay it. The corporation might *never* have to pay it. Income taxes, for example, are calculated from pretax income. But since the rules for determining pretax income in tax returns and pretax income in financial reports are not necessarily the same, a corporation might never have to pay the income taxes stated in its financial reports. How can accountants call something that's never going to be paid a *cost?*

Accountants say that what they're trying to do is make the determination of profit more consistent from period to period. Consistency allows us to look at a corporation's profits over the past several years—or compare the latest quarter with the corresponding quarter in prior years—and figure out whether the corporation is doing better or worse or about the same. Consistency makes profit *meaningful.*

But what happens when a corporation announces a massive cutback in employees and jobs? The costs of such a restructuring—write-offs of closed facilities, moving and retraining expenses, severance payments to fired employees—don't relate to the generation of revenue in *any* period. You might think that these costs, at least, not having any revenue to be matched up against, would be accounted for as they are paid. But they're not. They are all deducted at the time the restructuring is announced, although the restructuring itself may take several months or even years to complete—or even not be completed ever. This time the principle accountants are following is *conservatism*, which John Myer defines as "an attitude that fears to overstate profits but is not so fearful of understanding them."[7] Accountants pride themselves on being conservative, but charging all the costs of a restructuring against profit in one accounting period sets consistency on its ear.

So do all the FASB rule changes.

FASB, the Financial Accounting Standards Board, is the arm of the accounting profession that determines the rules of accounting. Take health care costs. Corporations used to wait until their retired employees got sick and were treated before they accounted for the costs of the treatment that the corporations had agreed to pay. But since employees generate revenue for their corporations while they're still employed, not after they're retired, FASB decided that, beginning in 1993, all costs that will be paid by a corporation after retirement should be deducted from revenue while the employees are still employed. As a consequence, you can no longer compare current profits with pre-1993 profits without making an adjustment for the change in how health care costs are accounted for.

But observe that this change, like so many changes in accounting, doesn't have any impact on cash, the stuff we use to pay our bills. Corporations still won't have to pay their retirees' health care bills until treatment is rendered. The only impact of the FASB rule that some future health care costs have to be recognized as current costs is to shift some current profits to future years. The stock market discounts (adjusts to) all such changes as soon as it learns of them; that's why it's called efficient. So who really cares?

Three months before the rule took effect, the *New York Times* carried a news item by the Associated Press that McDonnell Douglas was canceling a nonunion retiree plan under which it provided health care at corporate expense and substituting a new plan under which the nonunion retirees would pay for the health care themselves. According to the news item, McDonnell Douglas's purpose was "to reduce the financial impact" of FASB's new rule.[8]

Who cares about the FASB rule? Well, the nonunion retirees of McDonnell Douglas might. If the news item was accurate, McDonnell Douglas used the *financial impact* of the FASB rule as a justification for canceling its contributions to their health care plans. Now they have to pay all the costs out of their own pocket. And McDonnell Douglas cares, of course—it got rid of future cash costs.

All in all, profit is an accounting contrivance that doesn't always mean what it says, isn't always consistent in the way it's calculated, and doesn't always justify the acts committed in its name. And as a measure of corporate performance, it has another drawback: It can be manipulated by the corporate managers whose performance it supposedly measures. Thus, the measurement can't be relied on as 100% objective or true or even honest.

Still, public corporations are monitored by accountants, and the accountants won't let corporations tamper too much with their contrivance without blowing the whistle. Here's how the process works.

After the end of the corporation's fiscal year, independent accountants called auditors, who are elected every year by the shareholders, certify the corporation's financial statements including how much profit the corporation made for its shareholders during the fiscal year. They do this by reviewing the corporation's accounting records and issuing a report to the shareholders describing the work they've done and expressing their professional opinion as to the propriety of the financial statements based on those records. If anything is amiss, they warn the shareholders by qualifying their report or refusing to give one. When they issue clean (unqualified) reports that the financial statements "present fairly" the financial position, operating results, and changes in financial position of the corporation, they assure us that each financial statement "conforms to overall tests of truth, justness, equity and candor."[9]

Now, if our description of auditors as independent accountants elected every year by the shareholders chanced to remind you of the myth that the owners of a public corporation control it by electing its directors, you're going to get an "A" on the exam. Managements give shareholders a choice of auditors to vote for about as often as Halley's Comet rounds the sun; the other 74 years, shareholders have only the management nominee to vote for (or against), which we know is not the same as electing. Since auditors are in reality selected by management, they can hardly be regarded as independent of management.

In addition, what management agrees to pay the auditors affects what work they do and therefore what they take responsibility for. The work is described in the audit report, but you have to understand code words like *examine* and *review*—and how they differ—to know whether the auditors performed a complete audit or something less thorough.

Let's assume that a full audit of a corporation and all its subsidiaries is conducted by one of the big accounting firms. The firm certifies the profit-and-loss statement by issuing to the shareholders its unqualified opinion that the statement presents fairly the results of the corporation's operations for the year just ended. Can we shareholders rely on the audit report? Can we assume that the profit-and-loss statement meets the tests of truth, justness, equity, and candor?

We might ask these questions of BDO Seidman, longtime auditors of the apparel maker Leslie Fay. After an eight-month investigation of false bookkeeping entries that forced it into bankruptcy, Leslie Fay restated its earnings for 1990–1992 "to reverse $81 million of pretax accounting irregularities." BDO Seidman had given its opinions that the financial statements for the first two years—1990 and 1991—were fair presentations, but later it withdrew those opinions, and now it refused to offer any opinions at all regarding the newly restated earnings.

Restating past earnings or withdrawing past opinions is the accounting equivalent of locking the barn door after all the cows have been herded to someone else's balance sheet—it does absolutely nothing for anyone who doesn't have a time machine. But perhaps we can learn something from Seidman's explanation of why it issued the now-withdrawn 1990 and 1991 opinions in the first place.

Observing that this was "a carefully concealed case of fraud involving the corporate controller and more than 20 members of his financial accounting staff," the auditors expressed confidence that nonetheless "they [the auditors] will be found to have fully complied with professional standards." By way of justification Seidman noted that "accounting irregularities due to collusive fraud may not be detected by a properly designed and executed audit."[10]

Any accountant can tell you that auditors often can't (or don't) uncover management misfeasance. And while auditing is a profession with its own professional standards, it is also a business with its own competitive pressures. Auditors don't keep clients by displeasing them. "When there's somebody down the street who will say yes," said one accountant quoted by Floyd Norris, "other

firms find themselves under enormous pressure to also say yes."[11] Norris gave
his 1992 "Mr. Magoo Award for Auditing" to another major accounting firm,

KPMG Peat Marwick, which did not notice that checks issued by the Comptronix Corporation to pay for equipment were being deposited into Comptronix's own bank account
as payment for products it had supposedly sold. In fact, none of the transactions were
real, and KPMG certified fictional profits for three years.[12]

Singer was audited by still another major accounting firm, Ernst & Young,
during the years when its profits steadily rose—1990 to 1994. But its cash flow
from operations leveled off in 1993 and went south in 1994. That's not supposed
to happen. The income statement from which profit is calculated is essentially
a distortion (intentionally made) of cash receipts and payments related to operations. When profit and cash go in different directions, says Howard Schilit
of the Center for Financial Research and Analysis, "bad things usually happen."[13]

Happen, that is, to profit, not to the real stuff, cash flow. Real profit is an
oxymoron. Profit, as we've seen, is so malleable that all that needs be done to
bring it in line with some real later-discovered disaster like the disappearance
of $81 million is to adjust the books and *restate* it. Presto! What's real is what
we use to pay our bills and buy things—cash or a promise to pay cash or a
credit card or at least an assurance that one or the other is in the mail. Profit
isn't any of those things. You can't buy anything with it or pay any bills, and
neither can a corporation.

It's a myth that corporate profit is the best measure of real shareholder value.
Corporations have prospered without it and gone bust with it. But they don't
go bust with cash or prosper for long without it. **Cash flow is a truer measure
of shareholder value and a sterner master**.

But profit, unfortunately, is soul food to Wall Street. Much as we'd like to,
we can't dismiss it that easily.

Chapter 7

Corporate Profit Is Owned by the Shareholders Who Own the Corporation

Profit: . . . 2. (economics) A payment or commitment to a person (entrepreneur) undertaking the hazards of enterprise; remuneration or reward for uncertainty-bearing.
—Eric L. Kohler, *A Dictionary for Accountants*[1]

The market does not uniformly accept the line of reasoning . . . that the more paid out in dividends, the less the value of what remained in the business. On the contrary, observation suggests that an increase in the dividend payment normally acts to raise market price rather than lower it.
—Pearson Hunt, Charles M. Williams, and Gordon Donaldson,
Basic Business Finance[2]

Cash—money—is to a business what gasoline is to your car or van or utility vehicle: It makes it go. All businesses, large and small, have to be concerned with cash. The same isn't true of profit. Profit is an accounting invention. It doesn't make anything go. Like the board of directors and the stock market, profit is essentially irrelevant to a public corporation. Or should be.

Unfortunately, what is irrelevant to Wall Street is not profit but cash, even though Wall Street finances public corporations by raising cash, not profit. But Wall Street thinks only of profit, which it relates to stock price through the price/earnings ratio. It hardly knows what to do with a price/*cash flow* ratio.

Accountants didn't even include cash flow statements with their audit reports until recently, and the ones they now include are derived from the balance sheet, which limits their utility. They show where the cash the corporation had accumulated at the end of the year came from, not how the corporation earned and spent cash in the course of its operations during the year. For that matter, even the profit-and-loss statements they prepare are singularly lacking in specifics. Balance sheets, on the other hand, are laid out in lush detail. An accountant's first love is the balance sheet, the still photo of the last day of the year, rather than the noisy movie of all 365 days. It is always the first statement referred to in the standard opinion accompanying audit reports ("present fairly the financial position"), ahead of the profit-and-loss statement ("the results of its operations"). The cash flow statement ("changes in financial position") comes last.

The Internal Revenue Service likewise prefers profit to cash flow. It's actually hostile to taxpayers who prepare their returns on a cash basis.

Reports required by government regulators like the Securities and Exchange Commission have to be based on profit. Cash flow isn't exactly on the SEC's screen.

And accumulated profit under most corporation laws is the test (or at least one test) of what a corporation may pay out in dividends. Accumulated cash or cash flow is of no consequence even though most dividends are paid in cash and a corporation can't pay them if it doesn't have any.

So, willy-nilly, we must understand profit if we're going to evaluate corporate performance from the shareholders' point of view. We know from the last chapter how an accountant defines profit. But what does it really stand for? What does profit *mean?*

Economists give several answers. Profit is reward for innovation. Profit is compensation for risk and uncertainty. Profit is the return from monopoly, the fruit of scarcity pricing. They may all come down to the same thing. An entrepreneur tries something innovative, which of course is riskier than doing what everyone else does. If successful, the innovative method or service or product is unique or at least rare—scarce—until such time as other companies develop and market a competitive method or service or product. Until they do, the successful entrepreneur has a greater or lesser monopoly and can charge a higher price than will be possible when competition puts an end to the scarcity.

To illustrate, let's indulge in a very American fantasy. You hear that the couple who own your favorite country inn by a stream near the mountain where you regularly go skiing (or did for many years before you got so busy) are retiring to the Sunbelt and offering the inn for sale to the "right person" at a very reasonable price. Although you are some years this side of your company's mandatory retirement age, everyone in your family wants you to go for it. They're all tired of corporate life and commuting, even (or especially) your kids, who just started working a few years ago. So you talk to the couple and submit a bid, and—lo and behold!—it's accepted.

Let's say that you pay for the inn in cash. Most of it is borrowed from the local bank. As the new general manager of the inn, you signed a promissory note promising to pay the loan back over 30 years with interest fixed at, say, 9% a year and a mortgage giving the bank the right to take possession of the inn and sell it if the payments aren't made. The rest of the cash—we'll make it $10,000—came out of your savings.

Also, you spent $5,000 for a barn across the road you'll need to garage your snowplows and maintenance vehicles.

Now, an economist might observe that the forecast profit-and-loss statement you had your accountant prepare for the first five years includes the interest on the mortgage and your salary as general manager but doesn't include any interest on your own investment. Since the $10,000 cash investment is riskier than the bank loan (which has the security of the mortgage), it should earn a higher return, perhaps 12% a year, meaning that an additional $1,200 (12% of $10,000) should be deducted each year from the inn's income. An additional $1,000 a year would cover rent on the barn. The profit left after these adjustments is the inn's economic profit and your return as its sole owner.

In other words, what an economist thinks of as your or the inn's profit doesn't include what you earn from either your labor or any capital (money or equipment) or land you've contributed to the enterprise. You have to deduct the *wage* you earn as a worker, the *interest* you earn as a capitalist, and the *rent* you earn as a landlord before you calculate the *profit* you earn as an entrepreneur.

We may observe in passing that it matters not to an economist whether the capital invested is in the form of equity or loan. In our example it's actually both—the bank mortgage you procured for the inn, which was invested as a loan, and the $10,000 you drew from your savings, which was invested as your equity. For that matter, land is really another form of capital and rent the equivalent of interest. The accounting and legal distinctions between these forms of capital are irrelevant to the economic sense of profit. Which may help to explain why for every economist in the United States we have eight lawyers and almost 15 accountants!

Profit in the economic sense—entrepreneurial profit—doesn't exist in the never-never land of perfect competition that economists invent sometimes to explain what they're talking about. If it existed, perfect competition would drive the price of goods and services down until it equals the cost of producing them. Since the cost of producing them includes wages, interest, and rent, you would be compensated for your labor, your capital, and your land, but there wouldn't be anything left over to reward you for what you risk and accomplish as an entrepreneur. There wouldn't be any profit in the economic sense of the word. As a consequence—one of the unintended consequences of the utopian world of perfect competition and perfectly free markets—there wouldn't be any entrepreneurs.

But, of course, this is the real world, and competition is a lot less than perfect. Your nearest competitor is a motel next to an interstate highway, not a mountain stream, with vending machines to compete with your dining room and cuisine. You are a half-hour closer to the ski lift and have a van (with a barn to keep it in) to shuttle your guests back and forth—a service you conceived of that the motel doesn't provide. Thinking competitively, you may decide to charge the same as the motel for a room and take your profit from the meals you serve. But whatever your strategy, you *do* intend to earn a profit—much more than you could justify in terms of a general manager's salary and interest or rent on your investment. The much more will reward you for the innovative management that will make your inn a unique (that is, scarce) experience for your guests. And the much more will compensate you for the uncertainties of a very hazardous enterprise, including the worst-case scenario that, given a few warm winters or rainy summers, the bank could seize your enterprise, dismiss you as general manager, ignore your $10,000 investment, and auction off the inn you mortgaged to recover the loan payments you can't make—while still holding you responsible (and perhaps seizing your barn) if it doesn't recover 100% of what's owed it.

Now, you may be entrepreneurial, but a public corporation is not. A corporation usually outgrows any entrepreneurs it had about the time it goes public. It leaves behind its youthful acceptance of high risk in the pursuit of great reward, settles down with Wall Street, puts its nose to the grindstone, and impresses its new extended family of public shareholders with its steady income. While accountants refer to that income as profit, it belongs to the shareholders, and public shareholders are capitalists, not entrepreneurs. Therefore, economists see it as return on capital invested by shareholders rather than as profit rewarding entrepreneurs for the innovations and risks of enterprise.

But whether we call it return on capital or (accounting) profit, the shareholders own it. A corporation is owned by its shareholders, and everything it earns is credited to their investment capital (equity) because it is their money. And the procedure by which that profit is distributed to the shareholders who own it couldn't be simpler: The board of directors simply declares a dividend out of not-yet-distributed profit as determined by the accountants and blessed by the auditors, and the corporation pays it.

If accounting profit isn't real, as we insisted in the last chapter, what does it mean to distribute it to the shareholders? In reality, not much. But dividends are paid in cash or (occasionally) property—at least real dividends are. (Dividends paid in additional shares of the corporation's own stock are pseudodividends.) Real dividends are real money the shareholders can spend. Real dividends are transfers of wealth that make the shareholders richer and the corporation poorer.

Since paying a dividend makes the corporation poorer, why doesn't the stock market react by lowering the stock price? Sometimes it does, if the corporation is left with less money (cash) than the market thinks it needs to prosper. Take Mesa, a natural gas producer. Its shares were trading at $160 at the beginning of the 1980s. Then, according to T. Boone Pickens, its CEO, "we just pulled all the money out of the company and gave it to the shareholders. That's not inconsistent with my philosophy."[3] But it was inconsistent with the stock market's philosophy. At the end of the 1980s, Mesa shares were trading at less than $10.

But normally dividends don't have much effect on the price of a stock. That's because Wall Street relates price to (accounting) profit through the price/earnings ratio, and dividends don't decrease profit. (Dividends do decrease equity, but equity is a balance sheet item, and few people other than accountants and the occasional book-value investor pay attention to anything on the balance sheet except working capital.) Since shareholders own all profit whether the corporation retains it or distributes it, a dividend is akin to transferring profit from a savings account to a checking account—both accounts being owned by the shareholders.

Do you believe it? Ownership is the right to possess something and use it. But as shareholders we don't have the right to possess or use any profit earned by the corporation until the board of directors formally authorizes the corporation to distribute a specific amount of that profit by declaring a dividend. That is, shareholders own the checking account but not the savings account. And even though, according to corporation law (the mother of all myths), directors are elected by and represent the shareholders, corporation law doesn't give shareholders the power to compel the directors to declare *any* dividend.

It's a myth that corporate profit is owned by the shareholders who own the corporation. **Only profit that the corporation distributes in dividends is owned by the shareholders**. Profit that's retained by the corporation (typically from one-third to one-half of total profit, though it may be more—and some corporations retain *all* the profit) is owned by the corporation.

Still, the myth that even undistributed profit belongs to the shareholders has its uses because the stock market, wending its own mysterious ways, does not distinguish between distributed and retained profit when it applies the price/earnings ratio to determine the stock price. The greater the profit—never mind who owns it or keeps it—the greater the stock price and therefore the greater the value of the shareholders' investment. And since the purpose of every public corporation is to maximize profit, it can also be said that the purpose of every public corporation is to maximize shareholder value.

Chapter 8

Corporations Exist to Maximize Shareholder Value

Profits are the carrots held out as an incentive to efficiency, and losses are the penalties paid for using inefficient methods or for devoting resources to uses not desired by spending consumers.

—Paul A. Samuelson, *Economics*[1]

There is only one boss: the customer. And he can fire everybody in the company, from the chairman on down, simply by spending his money somewhere else.

—Sam Walton, chairman and CEO of Wal-Mart[2]

Business corporations are in business to make money; that's why their founding shareholders created them in the first place. Since making money—universally measured by the artifice accountants call profit—is their reason for existence, we measure how efficient they are by how much profit they make. In other words, the purpose of corporations—why people create them—is to maximize profit.

None of this profit, we've just established, is owned by the shareholders until it is declared as a dividend. Corporations rarely declare all their profit as dividends unless they're going out of business since they need some of that money—and this time we mean cash—to invest in order to increase future profits, and investing the cash they've earned is easier and less expensive than using the cash for dividends and going out and raising new cash. Indeed, so-called growth corporations are called that not just because they are bent on faster-than-average growth but also because they reinvest all or at least a sizable portion of their current profit to attain that growth.

Maximizing growth of future profits will eventually boost the price/earnings ratio (the market's black box) and therefore the value of the shareholders' investment as measured by the stock market price. And as we learned a few myths back from Michael Porter's study, shareholders generally earn more from selling their shares at an enhanced stock price than they would earn if their corporation paid higher dividends at the expense of future profits and an enhanced stock price.

Therefore, since maximizing real shareholder value comes down to maximizing profit over the long term, both may be thought of as defining the purpose of a corporation.

How does a corporation maximize profit?

We can take a leaf out of Paul Samuelson's textbook, which has informed Economics 101 classes for upward of half a century (I still have mine), and say that corporations maximize profit (and shareholder value) by using efficient methods and devoting resources to uses desired by spending customers. The key phrase, to take a cue from Sam Walton, is *spending customers*. In the accounting world, spending customers provide the *revenue* that the corporation uses to offset expenses and, if its resources are devoted to the right business and its methods are efficient, to create profit. In the real world, spending customers provide the *cash* the corporation needs to pay its bills and stay in business.

Shareholders don't contribute revenue. (In accounting terms, they contribute equity, which doesn't offset expenses or create profit.) More important, they don't even contribute cash except on the rare occasions when the corporation itself sells shares of stock. All the cash that shareholders shell out to buy shares in the stock market goes to other shareholders—the ones selling the shares. Not a dime goes to the corporation. Not a dime goes to finance investment in product development or greater productivity or future profits.

Shareholders are like used-car dealers, writes economist John Shilling, since both trade in secondhand merchandise. The shares they buy in the stock market are simply "used certificates." Except in the case of new issues of stock,

capital gains do not result from productive investment in new capital equipment that creates new jobs. Rather they come from changes in the market's valuation of existing assets. . . . If one believes in efficient markets, all the gains from trading used stock are the result of factors unknown to the market at the time the stock is bought, which makes the trading a form of gambling.[3]

The point is worth emphasizing. Venture capitalists and other investors who buy shares of stock from the corporation (as in an initial public offering) provide money to the corporation that it may use to buy new capital equipment. If the corporation's use of their money increases the value of the corporation and therefore of its shares, then their capital gain *does* result from productive investment in new capital equipment. But shareholders who buy used shares from other shareholders are not financing new capital equipment or anything else the corporation spends money on. Therefore, any capital gain they realize (if you truly believe the market is efficient) is like hitting the jackpot in the slots at Las Vegas. No skill required. No value added.

Do these shareholders, then, serve any useful function? Indeed they do—their trading supports the stock market and the price it sets for the corporation's shares. If the corporation should decide to raise money by issuing new shares to public investors, that price will largely determine the price at which the corporation will be able to sell the new shares. If there were no stock market, of course, there wouldn't even be any public investors to sell the shares to.

But a corporation needs paying customers every day because it needs cash every day to pay its bills. It doesn't need shareholders every day. Many private corporations carry on without any significant input from their shareholders (other than in their role as managers), and not-for-profit corporations exist without any shareholders at all. But neither a private corporation nor a not-for-profit corporation engaged in a commercial activity can survive without paying customers.

Thus, of the two masters that a corporation is called on to serve, the customer has the greater claim to the corporation's attention because the customer keeps the corporation in cash to serve another day. Yet increasingly, it seems, public corporations pay more attention to their shareholders than to their customers, as when they scrimp on capital investment but spend billions to buy back their stock in order to increase its stock market price and the current value of their shareholders' investment. The balance of power is "out of whack," according to Calpers' Richard Koppes, "having swung too far toward share owners."[4]

Not favoring your shareholders over your customers (and your business) can have its risks, as Chrysler, once the poorest of Detroit's Big Three automobile companies, discovered in 1995. Backed by a loan guarantee voted by Congress in the 1970s after an intensive lobbying campaign that emphasized the thousands of jobs to be lost if Chrysler went bankrupt, Chrysler turned itself around. In due course it became Detroit's most efficient car manufacturer with the lowest costs and the highest return on investment. But in 1995, having paid back its government-guaranteed loans and stashed away $7 billion in anticipation of a cyclical downturn in its business, it and its new stash became the target of a takeover attempt by financier Kirk Kerkorian, its biggest shareholder, in league with Lee Iacocca, its former CEO. The takeover bid, Clyde Prestowitz of the Economic Strategy Institute wrote at the time, would

force Chrysler to accumulate an additional mountain of debt to finance the deal—and force the company right back into a financial hole. Its credit rating would suffer as well, greatly complicating its efforts to finance not only new domestic investments but expansion into critical emerging third-world markets and vehicle sales.[5]

All Kerkorian was interested in, it turned out, was an increase in the current stock price whether through a buyback, an increased dividend, or a takeover. "For all of his plans to redirect the company," commented the *New York Times* some months later, ''none of them focused on making cars or trucks.''[6] But he hadn't lined up the financing for his takeover bid, and Chrysler successfully defended itself by taking its case directly to its institutional investors. ''None of our institutional owners asked us to change directions,'' said Robert Eaton, Chrysler's CEO. ''Not one of them told us to compromise the future for the sake of today.''[7]

Ironically, Chrysler's case as reported in the financial press did not cite the potential loss of thousands of jobs had the raid been successful and the corporation stripped of its cash reserves. The omission tells a broad tale of the difference between Capitol Hill and Wall Street. Capitol Hill is the citizens' hill. Wall Street is the shareholders' street. Shareholders, wrote Richard Goodwin, are ''even more intent on short-term profit and growth than management. That is the nature of their interest. As shareholders they do not represent the consuming interest, much less that of the entire citizenry.''[8]

Money managers Wood, Struthers & Winthrop, who bought into Baxter International in September 1993 when they found its shares lying in the mud, are a Wall Street species commonly referred to as *bottom feeders*. Their game plan was to pressure Baxter's CEO, Vernon Loucks, to restructure the company (as Sears's CEO had done) and pressure the board to kick him out if he didn't (as Kodak's board had done to its CEO). ''This is probably Loucks's last chance to save his career,'' said Wood, Struthers's chief investment officer. ''He has a year here to turn the operations around or face a hostile board. Either model— Sears or Kodak—works to our advantage.''[9] That is, either model would cause the stock price to rise up from the bottom and allow them to realize a capital gain when they sold their shares. What happened after they cashed out wasn't their concern. Why, asks Clyde Prestowitz, should a shareholder who has just bought into the company ''have the same voting power as one who has held a share for 10 years?''[10]

Shareholders, you will say, *own* the corporation from the moment they buy their shares to the moment they sell them. That's the nature of the beast.

That's certainly the nature of the beast in a private corporation, which is owned and controlled by its founders. It's also more or less the nature of a semipublic corporation that has public shareholders but remains more or less under the control of its founders or founding families. But when a corporation goes truly public, when control passes from founders to independent managers, it can be considered *owned* by its shareholders of the moment only in a very legalistic sense of the word.

The law, as we have seen, doesn't give shareholders the right to manage the corporation, and it doesn't even insist on meaningful implementation of their right to elect the directors who *do* have the right to manage the corporation. Nor does it allow shareholders to claim any of the profit the corporation earns on their behalf with their investment except when the directors, acting (we may be sure) on the instructions of management, declare a dividend out of that profit—and the shareholders can't force the directors to declare *any* dividend.

Of course, shareholders do own their shares, and a corporation can't take some extraordinary action (such as selling off its assets) that would destroy the value of those shares without getting its shareholders' consent. But the same is true of bondholders, and no one contends that bondholders own a corporation. Owning shares of stock (or bonds) is not the same as owning the corporation.

Realistically speaking, *a public corporation has no owners.* In that respect, it's like a not-for-profit corporation that operates a (nonprofit) business but has no shareholders and therefore no owners.

If shareholders of a public corporation aren't owners, what are they? They're passive (and increasingly transient) investors, distinguished from other passive investors like lenders (bondholders) in that the return on their investment is not fixed (as interest on a loan is usually fixed) but rather depends on the dividends the corporation decides to pay. And unlike a loan, the investment itself is not repaid. Shareholders recover their investment (plus or minus any gain or loss) only by selling their shares. Although a shareholder's investment is, for these reasons, riskier than a lender's and therefore should earn more, both shareholder and lender are capitalists seeking as much return on the capital they've invested as the market will allow them. Neither one is an entrepreneur pursuing what economists call profit. Neither one controls the corporation they've invested in. Neither one owns it.

"Business," writes management philosopher Peter Drucker, "exists to supply goods and services to customers, rather than to supply jobs to workers and managers, or even dividends to shareholders."[11] Does that mean management has no responsibility for profit? Not at all.

Business management has failed if it fails to produce economic results. It has failed if it does not supply goods and services desired by the consumer at a price the consumer is willing to pay. It has failed if it does not improve, or at least maintain, the wealth-producing capacity of the economic resources entrusted to it. And this, whatever the economic or political structure or ideology of a society, means responsibility for profitability.[12]

It has failed not only its customers and investors but the country—all of us. Although what business does is

by no means the only task to be discharged in society, it is a priority task, because all other social tasks—education, health care, defense, and the advancement of knowledge—depend on the surplus of economic resources, i.e., profits and other savings, which only successful economic performance can produce. The more of these other satisfactions we want, and the more highly we value them, the more we depend on economic performance of business enterprise.[13]

But profit isn't the *purpose* of a corporation, not its function or its goal. Profit is a constraint—a condition, if you will, to its continuing to produce economic results in the future—and a measure of how well it has done so far. The true purpose of a corporation is satisfying the needs of paying customers—at a profit. Corporations that pursue profit (or the maximization of shareholder value) as a goal tend to lose their way chasing all sorts of irrelevancies such as buying a manufacturer of corporate jets, as Chrysler did under Iacocca. And—the worst business sin of all—they forget their customers.

It's a myth that public corporations exist to maximize shareholder value. **The function of a public corporation is to satisfy the needs of paying customers** by creating ever more valuable products and services with ever increasing efficiency—and selling them at a profit. The profit is a measure of its competitive success. If it earns more than it needs to meet its obligations and invest in its business, it distributes the extra amount to its shareholders. If it earns less, it goes out of business.

In the real world, that's essentially the way public corporations operate, never mind the legal niceties about ownership or the complaints about shareholder value. A public corporation can't set a course that will satisfy thousands of transient passengers with divergent itineraries. All it can do is announce its ports of call and let each investor decide when (if at all) to climb on board and when to go ashore.

But, if it's wise, it will pay closest attention to the customers who purchase its cargo—a subject we will now turn to.

Part III

Customers

How the needs of the customers of public corporations are satisfied through marketing, brand enhancement, low pricing (as required by the law of supply and demand), and innovation.

Chapter 9

Corporations Engage in Marketing to Satisfy Their Customers' Needs

Because its purpose is to create a customer, the business enterprise has two—and only these two—basic functions: marketing and innovation. Marketing and innovation produce results; all the rest are "costs."
—Peter F. Drucker, *Management: Tasks, Responsibilities, Practices*[1]

Selling is preoccupied with the seller's need to convert his product into cash, marketing with the idea of satisfying the needs of the customer by means of the product and the whole cluster of things associated with creating, delivering, and finally consuming it.
—Theodore Levitt, "Marketing Myopia"[2]

Paul Hoffman, who was involved in the economic recovery of Europe after World War II, called it an illusion "that you can industrialize a country by building factories. You don't. You industrialize it by building markets."[3] It's also an illusion that you can create a successful business by building factories. The critical task, and the hardest one, is building markets.

Building markets—converting potential customers for a corporation's products and services into actual paying customers by satisfying their needs—is what corporate marketing is all about. Corporations engage in marketing to satisfy their customers' needs. And since no business can exist without paying customers, management guru Peter Drucker lists marketing first among the two core functions a corporation has.

In terms of corporate profitability, marketing is apt to be a more critical skill than the other core function, innovation.

Take, for example, desktop computers. The first prototype, named Alto (as in

Palo Alto), was developed in the early 1970s by Xerox Corporation's Palo Alto Research Center (Xerox PARC), which also invented the first graphics user interface and graphics monitor, the first mouse, and the first laser printer. When Steve Jobs, Apple Computer's cofounder and marketing genius, was given a demonstration, he said he was so dazzled by the graphics user interface that he paid no attention to the other landmark innovations he was being shown, a network to allow the computers to communicate with one another (and their printers) and an object-oriented programming language to write application programs for the computers to run.[4]

Taking the invention he was so dazzled by, Jobs created the Macintosh computer and marketed it with great success. Some years later Bill Gates, Microsoft Corporation's founder and marketing genius, used the same invention to create Windows and marketed it with even greater success. Xerox, the inventor, did no marketing. In 1994 the *New York Times* pointed out in an article about Xerox that "when an office worker wants a few copies of a memo or letter, the person is as likely to push the 'print' button on a personal computer a couple of times as walk over to a [Xerox copying] machine and make duplicates."[5] So Xerox was spending billions of dollars trying to *recapture* the business copying market that computers—mostly Macintosh or Windows computers networked to laser printers—had taken away from it.

The mainframe computer industry has long been synonymous with IBM, but it was Sperry Rand that invented the first commercial computer (the UNIVAC), not IBM. But IBM was the superior marketer, and it got prospective buyers of computers to associate computers with it, not Sperry. Over the years, IBM made a lot more money off computers than Sperry.

Did IBM make better computers? Well, the Model 360 incorporating its own internal operating system was so innovative that it set the standard for all computers to come and triggered the growth of an entire industry, as the Model-T had done with automobiles and the DC-3 with passenger airplanes. But what defined IBM to its customers wasn't so much the computers it made as the service it delivered. With a product as complicated as the Model 360, customer service—making sure the product works the way it's supposed to—was more critical than the product itself.

Customer service is one of the cluster of things associated with creating, delivering, and consuming a product that Theodore Levitt says marketing is preoccupied with. In "Marketing Myopia," the most famous of all *Harvard Business Review* articles, Levitt drew a line in the sand to make sure that we didn't confuse marketing with sales. Selling concerns itself with the needs of the seller, wrote Levitt, and

with the tricks and techniques of getting people to exchange their cash for your product. It is not concerned [as marketing is] with the values that the exchange is all about. And it does not, as marketing invariably does, view the entire business process as consisting of a tightly integrated effort to discover, create, arouse, and satisfy customer needs.[6]

Thus, corporate marketing focuses on satisfying the needs of the buyer, not the seller (the corporation itself), because that's how the corporation creates and retains paying customers and builds markets. The focus may be as important as anything marketing people actually do. Drivers, Levitt observed, don't buy gasoline—they buy the wherewithal to drive someplace. Computer users don't buy computers. They buy the computing power that enables them to do all sorts of things they couldn't do before (or do as well) such as generate an ever-current count of their inventory or flash messages to people thousands of miles away in different time zones—or write a book.

Exxon still sells gasoline, but the oil business is less competitive and also less innovative than the computer business. IBM packages all sorts of software with its desktop computers to connect you with the Internet or help you write that book.

Given the focus on customers and their needs, what do the marketing people in public corporations actually do?

Judging by departmental budgets, the marketing function in public corporations consists largely of advertising and promotion. Advertising, which accounts for about one-third of marketing budgets, is communicating in public to potential customers. It doesn't do any good to build a better mousetrap unless the builder tells people who are bothered by mice that a new mousetrap exists and persuades them to try it. Although it often seems that advertising is full of sound and fury, signifying nothing of substance, consultant Gary Stibel concluded from a study of 15 leading advertisers in the 1980s that most of the time it ''has a quantitative positive impact''[7] on sales and market share. That is, it creates customers.

So does promotion, which accounts for the other two-thirds of corporate marketing budgets and seeks to attract customers with temporary price reductions in one form or another. (Activities like sponsoring sports events that promote the corporation's name or one of its products are really forms of advertising.) Temporary price reductions can be a risky tactic, as the automobile and airline industries found out when ever-increasing numbers of newly price-sensitized customers held off buying at sticker prices to wait for the next promotion. If enough customers act this way, the temporary price reduction can become permanent. But risky or not, the purpose of promotion is to create customers.

If corporate marketing creates customers, does it *retain* them? Do advertising and promotion contribute to the satisfaction of customer needs that keeps customers coming back to purchase more?

Advertising communicating facts about a mousetrap that better serves our needs is trying to satisfy those needs. But what about advertising telling us that GE brings good things to life? *What* things? What exactly does General Electric *do* for the consumers it broadcasts that message to? The message doesn't say. And what about advertising that's trying to persuade us to associate a particular food with family values or a particular beer with adventurous living or a particular cigarette with masculine (or feminine) independence? Wouldn't our real needs be better served if corporations saved the costs budgeted for mindless or manipulative advertising and used it, say, to reduce prices?

Wouldn't our real needs be better served if corporations applied the money budgeted for temporary price reduction devices like coupons—only 2% of which are in any event ever redeemed[8]—to everyday low prices?

You bet they would. And we consumers would respond by buying more. In economics, it's even the law: If the price of a good is cut, *more* of it will be demanded.

To Drucker, as to Levitt, marketing is entirely separate from selling. "The aim of marketing is to make selling superfluous," Drucker wrote. "The aim of marketing is to know and understand the customer so well that the product or service fits him and sells itself."[9] But no product or service is likely to sell itself if consumers feel that it is overpriced. Nevertheless, the worship of high prices and profit margins is the most pervasive of what Drucker calls the five deadly sins of American business. This sin led to "the near-collapse of Xerox in the 1970s." Xerox "invented the copier—and few products in industrial history have had greater success faster"—but then it started adding features to the product and dollars to the price. When Canon, the Japanese camera company, introduced a much less expensive copier into the American market, "Xerox barely survived."[10]

This failure of Xerox was also a marketing failure, as was the failure of the American companies that invented, developed, and first produced the fax machine (most of which are now made overseas)—ignoring the needs of customers upon whom a corporation's survival and prosperity depend. IBM's failure in the desktop computer market was of a different sort.

As soon as IBM came out with its personal computer (PC) in the early 1980s, the industry adopted its standard and took off, leaving pioneers like Commodore and Radio Shack and even Apple eating its dust. Such was the marketing power that IBM wielded as the undisputed master of mainframe computers. But desktops and mainframes were different markets because they had different customers. IBM remained the master of mainframes, but in desktops it was overthrown by Microsoft, which doesn't even make computers. What happened?

Drucker theorizes that IBM committed another deadly business sin in "slaughtering tomorrow's opportunity on the altar of yesterday." To protect its mainframe cash cow, he said, IBM refused to allow PCs to be marketed to mainframe prospects. "This did not help the mainframe business," said Drucker—"it never does."[11]

Xerox committed this same sin in ignoring the great inventions coming out of Xerox PARC. "For years," according to the *Times*, "the fear at Xerox headquarters in Stamford, Conn., had been that something would replace dry copying as thoroughly as xerography obliterated the messy, wet systems that [preceded] it."[12] That's why it never marketed the Alto or the laser printer.

If Levitt had written "Marketing Myopia" in 1990 rather than 1960, he might have used Xerox and IBM as examples of companies that defined themselves in terms of their current products rather than in terms of their customers' needs. Had IBM thought of itself as producing not mainframe computers but computing power, had Xerox thought of itself as creating not copiers but copies of documents, they might have regarded PCs as another vehicle for satisfying existing customers and creating new ones. Instead, they regarded PCs as a competitive technology threatening their product monopolies—and missed the boat to a market that (as it turned out) would flow much faster than their own.

There are no growth industries, wrote Levitt, only companies that are managed to take advantage of growth opportunities. Failure to grow is a management failure, not a technological failure, and it is caused by managers thinking of their business as producing and selling something rather than as acquiring and satisfying customers. Failure to grow is a marketing failure, not a market failure.

In most public corporations, marketing isn't really concerned with satisfying customer needs. "Just look at what the thousands of marketing people do every day," writes Al Ries. "They keep changing things. New products, new flavors, new sizes, new packaging, new pricing, new distribution." Marketers should take a lesson from airline pilots. After devoting all their energy to getting the plane off the ground and reaching cruising altitude, pilots settle back, turn on the autopilot, and relax. When a new product "reaches an optimum market share," says Ries, "a company should throttle back the marketing program and make minor corrections only."[13] But big corporations have big marketing departments and big marketing budgets to justify. So they focus on developing ever more sophisticated tricks and techniques to get us to exchange our cash for their products. That is, corporate marketers are really concerned with selling, not marketing. And like the salesmen described by Levitt, they define customer service "by looking into the mirror rather than out the window."[14]

It's a myth that public corporations engage in marketing to satisfy their customers' needs. **Corporations engage in marketing to satisfy their own needs—selling** (and justifying their own marketing activities). Still, it may be allowed that corporate marketing increases brand value, and brand value satisfies customer needs; subjects we now turn to.

Chapter 10

Corporations Invest in Brands to Increase Consumer Value

Advertising . . . not only creates and sharpens demand, but also by its impact on the competitive process, stimulates the never-ceasing quest of improvement in quality of the product.

—Governor Adlai E. Stevenson[1]

If you can convince consumers that your product tastes better than your competitor's, then you can command a premium price for it.

—George Bull, CEO of Grand Metropolitan[2]

"We live, all of us denizens of a market economy, in a buyer's paradise," wrote economist Martin Weitzman in an upbeat description of the world of marketing.

As consumers we are actively courted by the hidden persuaders of advertising; our opinions about what we like to consume are eagerly sought out and listened to; completely new products and new variations of old products are continually created to gratify our existing wants and to anticipate our future desires; sellers trip over themselves in an effort to improve in our eyes the image of their product and the quality of the services accompanying its sales and maintenance. These and other forms of non-price competition can be taken to undesirable extremes, but they do account for a substantial part of the richness, dynamism, diversity, and, yes, quality of economic life under capitalism.[3]

Most of these forms of nonprice competition are marketing activities related to brand-name products, which are products with a distinctive trademark. People buy branded products for different reasons, according to a 1992 survey by the Roper Organization, but the most important are past experience (cited by 87% of those responding), price (65%), and quality (57%). "Knowing what to expect is the most common reason for buying a particular brand. Value [price] and quality rank second and third.''[4]

Take Tide, which has dominated the laundry products market with a 30% share for half a century. Although not the cheapest brand, said its product executive at Procter & Gamble, ''Tide has endured partly because . . . the people who use it give it high marks for providing value and superior performance through innovations that better meet customer needs.'' (That covers Roper Two and Three.) Another reason (Roper One) is ''continual advertising support with a message that's consistent to this day, so consumers know exactly what Tide stands for. Even from the very first, we were selling Tide on superior performance.''[5] P&G is not only the biggest brand marketer, spending $5 billion a year on advertising, but also, arguably, the savviest.

Corporations invest in brands to increase consumer value. ''At Ford,'' the advertising slogan goes, ''quality is job one.'' (Had Ford listened to Roper, quality might have been job three and consistency job one.) And as the value of the branded product to the consumer increases, the value of the brand to the corporation increases. Indeed, P&G's chief archivist said in 1996 that the company is literally built on the Tide brand. But are the increases equal? Are the values of the brand (owned by the corporation that owns the trademark) and the brand-name product equivalent?

The way brand value—or brand *equity*, as marketing people call it—is calculated suggests that the answer to both questions is *no*.

Let's do the numbers. In September 1993 *Financial World* reported that Coke had the second-highest value of all brands and explained how it made that calculation. It first took Coca-Cola's operating profit, estimated at $2.7 billion. Then it deducted $0.3 billion representing ''what would be earned on a basic unbranded or generic version of the product.''[6] That left it with a net operating profit for just the brand (Coke) of $2.4 billion. Next it provided for income taxes (approximately 30%) and multiplied the brand's after-tax profit by another number reflecting Coke-brand (not Coca-Cola–product) strengths and weaknesses. The multiplier, which ranged from 9 to 20 for all brands and was 20 for Coke, is based on the seven components of brand strength defined by the Interbrand Group of London. The seven components are market leadership, survivability, trading environment, internationality, trend, communications effectiveness, and legal protection. None, one might observe, has much to do with quality, price, or consistency—or consumer value.

The result: Coke, the brand, was worth $33 billion to Coca-Cola, the corporation.

In a survey released in mid-1995 by Bozell, Jacobs, Kenyon & Eckhardt and *Fortune* magazine, 153 CEOs and other corporate executives considered Coke the best-managed brand in the world. Over half the respondents indicated that the principal brands of their own corporation were worth billions of dollars— the median was $5.3 billion—because they provided ''an umbrella for products and services'' and contributed to ''corporate identity.''[7] Brands, it appears, are about producers and their identity and their products, not about customers and their satisfaction and their needs. But what, precisely, is a brand?

"A brand is how a consumer feels about a product," says Charlotte Beers, CEO of the Ogilvy & Mather advertising agency. "Within every brand, there's a product, but not every product is a brand." With a product like Coca-Cola, she says, "the emotional texture and the fabric around a brand . . . are much more significant" than the product itself.[8] Indeed, 8 times more significant, judging by the profit *Financial World* attributes to the brand ($2.4 billion) versus the profit it attributes to the branded product ($0.3 billion). Or *160* times more significant if we factor in the multiplier of 20 that augments the value of the brand but not the value of the branded product.

Since a brand lies in the hearts and minds of consumers, we're not going to get a precise answer to our question of what a brand is. *A brand is how a consumer feels about a product* will have to do. Nevertheless, we would still like to know how brands like Coke become so much, much more valuable than their underlying products.

The answer seems to have a lot to do with the $100 billion spent each year in national advertising and the $70 billion spent in local advertising. While future improvements in customer service and product quality were the top brand-enhancement strategies cited by the executives in the Bozell, Jacobs/*Fortune* survey, the brand-enhancement activity that in fact had the greatest impact on their corporations' sales in the prior year was media advertising. More specifically, the answer seems to involve Weitzman's hidden persuaders of advertising. They enter the mind of the consumer and create what marketing professionals call *perceived value*. Perceived value may have no more relationship to real value than brand value has to product value, but it is what leads consumers to prefer a particular brand of that product. And brand preference or brand *loyalty* is the keystone of brand value.

Free market economists like to assume that markets are not only free (competitive) but also informed and rational. (Economists virtually own the word *rational*. If people didn't always act rationally in matters involving money, quite a few economic theories would go out the window.) We've had occasion to question these assumptions in the case of the stock market, which is, after all, only people buying and selling stocks for themselves, for other people, or for the institutions they represent. And people bring bias and emotion and the herd instinct to the trading floor and even, sometimes, inside (nonpublic) information or fraudulent intent. The stock market will never be as free or as smart or as rational as it's supposed to be.

Neither will the consumer market. And one special reason is branding. For the very function of brands is to substitute loyalty for rationality in consumer buying habits—loyalty, be it observed, to an abstract concept like Coke or an inanimate object like GE—and substitute a perception of brand value for the reality of product value. To understand this, we must not confuse the brand Coke with a bottle of Coca-Cola. When we spend, say, $.45 to drink what's in a bottle of Coca-Cola, we're paying $.05 for the reality we swallow and $.40 for the emotions and perceptions the Coca-Cola Company has buried in our head. If the Coca-Cola Company has failed to get through to us, if we haven't bought into those emotions and perceptions, we're clearly overpaying.

When a corporate consumer such as an information system manager I once did business with asserts that the corporation is "all blue" (IBM's color), the corporation is likely paying not only for the computing power of its IBM equipment but also for the perception of the information systems managers, the executives running the corporation, and even the directors on the board that they are buying the very best.

What the Bozell-*Fortune* survey found, according to Leslie Gaines-Ross, communications and marketing director for *Fortune* in New York, was that CEOs are paying attention to brand management rather than leaving it to product or brand managers. But what she found "absolutely fascinating" was that "so few CEO's [17% of those surveyed] saw brands as making it easier to price products at a premium, which has always been the value of brands."[9] And still is the reason, notwithstanding the reluctance of corporate managers to say so out loud.

Between 1983 and 1991, the price of cold breakfast cereal rose twice as fast as overall food prices. Wall Street analyst John McMillin blamed the price increases on the lack of "many substitutes for cold cereal," adding that "compared to other food categories, the consumer is definitely at a disadvantage."[10]

Disadvantage? What about *hot* cereal—isn't that a substitute? Or generic brands of cold cereal that cost less? Or bagels? The problem with these alternatives seems to be . . . our children. Weitzman's gremlins, hidden in TV sets and cereal packages, have persuaded them that the only food they can get down in the morning—the only brand, we parents might interpret, in which they *perceive value*—is (say) Kellogg's Frosted Flakes. We indulge our kids, disregard private-label or generic equivalents, and tolerate frequent price increases, which Kellogg is only too happy to impose.

In September 1993 *Financial World* reported that Kellogg's cereals brand had a value of almost $10 billion, the highest in the entire food category and 8.5% higher than the previous year. Did the value of Kellogg's cereal products also grow that year by 8.5%? This we may doubt. Kellogg's Rice Krispies and numerous other brand-name cereals have been on autopilot at cruising altitude for half a century; why would a master marketer like Kellogg tinker with them? Only the month before, McMillin reported that while marketing costs—discount coupons (which figure in almost half of all cereal purchases) and other expenditures on promotion and advertising—eat up fully $.30 out of every sales dollar, operating profits in the cereal industry are "extraordinarily high."[11] High marketing expenditures and high profits suggest that Kellogg spends little on adding value to its cereal products.

But it can charge high prices because it has invested millions in its brands—and in instilling loyalty to those brands in our kids.

It's a myth that corporations spend money on brands in order to increase the value of the branded products to consumers. **Corporations invest in brands to increase the value of the brand to themselves**. That's a surer way to increase prices, current profits, and corporate value than investing in consumer value. For once they have instilled loyalty in consumers, corporations have less to fear from their competition when they raise prices and less to fear from their own customers.

In 1993, *Financial World*'s top brand was Marlboro cigarettes with an equity of $40 billion—$7 billion more than Coke.[12] Philip Morris spends billions of dollars a year in advertising so that you'll feel good about yourself when you inhale a Marlboro riding to work, like one of the guys when you bottom-up a Miller Lite on the way home, or warm and fuzzy while you watch your kids eating Jello-O with their fingers like you used to do when you were their age. Philip Morris spends billions to buy your loyalty.

If it succeeds—if you feel good about yourself or like one of the guys or warm and fuzzy when you're consuming their product—just don't complain if Philip Morris doesn't spend as much money as you think it should on the *food* beneath Jell-O's shimmering surface or the *beer* below Miller's frosty foam or the *risk* to your kids' health should they start smoking before they're old enough to know better. Or if its prices are higher than you think they should be.

As to prices, at least, we have a law that protects us from their becoming *too* high. It's called supply and demand.

Chapter 11

Corporations Are Required by Supply and Demand to Charge Their Lowest Prices

> Supply and demand . . . may be thought of as the forces guiding economic
> life in an economy based on private property.
> —*The Columbia Encyclopedia*[1]

> Supply equals demand only in the rare case of perfect competition.
> —Martin L. Weitzman, *The Share Economy*[2]

The law of supply and demand is as sacred to all of us who live in a free market economy as the First Amendment or the Golden Rule—perhaps, given our faith in private enterprise and free markets, even more sacred. Since it's a law, every person including, of course, every corporation has to obey it.

But what exactly does it say? What do we have to do to obey it?

Suppose a corporation you founded has developed and successfully marketed a digital monkey wrench. At first you were selling all the wrenches you could make at $489 apiece and making ends meet, as shown by the following numbers:

Selling Price	$489
Variable Cost	300
Marginal Profit	189
Fixed-Cost Allocation	50
Net Profit (28%)	$139

But then a couple of guys working out of their garage started making a wrench like yours and—having no overhead to account for—priced it at $399, spoiling your market and cutting your profit to \$49 and your margin to 12% (\$49 ÷ \$399). When you sued them for patent infringement, the court ruled against you on some legal technicality and decided that your patent was invalid.

Within months of the decision a dozen or so other outfits started producing digital monkey wrenches. Since their entire R&D effort consisted of reading your patent application, which is public information, they could undersell even the guys in the garage, who at least had developed their own product even if it did infringe your patent. Today, the number of digital monkey wrenches sold each year is many times what it used to be when there was just you and the garage guys, but the price has dropped down to around \$325—and even lower when rebates are offered—where no one can make a profit anymore. Whatever control you had over the price of your product—the one you invented—is long gone. Prices are now determined by the market. You and all the other manufacturers are price *takers*, not price *makers*.

When we say that prices are determined by the market we mean that they are governed by the law of supply and demand. What the law says is this: You must lower the price of your monkey wrench until you no longer make a profit. Sounds crazy, doesn't it? Well, it's even crazier than that. If you read the fine print, what it really says is that you must lower your price until you actually *lose* money!

Now, the law was written by free market economists, not legislators or judges, so you won't go to jail if you break it. You'll simply go broke. Indeed, the fine print guarantees that you'll go broke even if you *don't* break the law.

It's a great law—for consumers. And it even makes some sense for producers like yourself. After all, as we've already discussed, you're in business to maximize profits, which you do by maximizing customer satisfaction. The way you do both simultaneously is to lower your price to increase demand (remember that other law: *If the price of a good is cut, more of it will be demanded*) until the price equals the cost of producing the next wrench—what economists call the *marginal cost*. Marginal cost is the same as variable cost in our numbers— the materials, wages, and other expenses that go into making that next wrench. (Fixed costs like interest and rent, which don't vary in amount and have to be paid whether you make a thousand wrenches or none, are not included in marginal cost.) Since your variable (marginal) cost is \$300, every wrench you can sell for more than \$300—even a buck more—adds to your total profit.

The kicker is, you can't fool all your customers all the time and you can't sell some wrenches for \$489 or \$399 or \$325 and others for \$301, not for long. In a free market, which we know that economists believe is populated with rational and knowledgeable buyers, you'll end up selling *all* your wrenches at \$301. That'll cover your marginal costs but not your fixed costs. Sooner or later, you'll go out of business.

But as we said before, your competitors have the description of your invention and therefore don't have any of your fixed costs (principally interest on money you had to borrow) that you incurred in developing it. They can undersell you.

They can price their wrenches at $325 for 11 months of the year and (unlike you) cover all their variable *and* fixed costs, then offer a $24 Christmas rebate, which covers their marginal costs (which we're assuming are $300, same as yours) while squeezing the last drop of profit out of the year's sales.

If you fail to do the same, you will be adjudged either irrational (since maximizing profit in the eyes of the law is the only rational objective of business) or incompetent or both. Worse still, you won't be able to sell any more wrenches because your competitors, acting rationally and competently, will have lowered their prices, and consumers would hardly be so irrational or incompetent as to buy from you when your competitors are selling the same product at a lower price.

So this is how the ultimate free market economy works. Competition in the pursuit of maximum profit drives the price of goods down until it equals the marginal cost of producing them—$300 in our case. At that price (economists call it the *equilibrium price*) and only at that price, supply equals demand. You and the manufacturers can sell as many wrenches as you are able (at that cost) to produce, and consumers can have as many wrenches as they want (at that price) to buy. At any lower price, which would be below marginal cost, supply would drop off because manufacturers would lose money and stop manufacturing (or go out of business); demand would then exceed supply, and consumers would bid the price back up to the equilibrium level. At any higher price, fewer people could afford or would want to buy the wrenches; supply would then exceed demand, and competition would drive the price back down until supply and demand were once again in equilibrium.

It really isn't a wonderful law, even for consumers. At prices that just cover their marginal costs, producers don't care whether they produce more, and sellers don't care whether they sell more, since they're not going to make a profit. (Anyway, they're eventually all going out of business since they can't cover their fixed costs.) Given their attitude, you can imagine what happens to quality and customer service. Worse yet, entrepreneurs stop dreaming up ways to make things better because what economists define as profit the law defines as unlawful—and economic profit, you will recall, is every entrepreneur's incentive and every successful entrepreneur's reward.

Fortunately for our buyer's paradise, no one obeys the law.

No one obeys it because it's the law only in an economist's never-never land of perfect competition. In this never-never land, prices are determined solely by the free market because no supplier is large enough or powerful enough to influence the price of what it sells. But in our land *somebody* has the power to wield *some* influence over the price of virtually *every*thing we buy.

Economists refer to the ability to influence price as *monopoly power*. Except in regulated industries like electrical utilities, monopoly power is rarely held by just one supplier and rarely amounts to total control over price. But any monopoly power is better than none. To illustrate what you can do with it, let's go back to when your corporation started selling digital monkey wrenches but this time add some real-world conditions.

Let's say your patent was ultimately upheld—your attorneys appealed the decision invalidating it and won. Your now-valid patent will keep every Tom, Dick, and Harry from jumping into the market and spoiling it. But as you expand your market, you run into competition from several manufacturers of *analog* monkey wrenches, which serve the same function as your wrench but are based on older technology and aren't quite as efficient. Since analog wrenches go for between $335 and $360, not too many people are willing to pay $489 for your wrench, even though it represents the state of the art of the industry. But at least you're not subject to a law requiring you to lower your price until you can't make a profit just so more people can afford your wrenches.

Like most suppliers, you've got both limited competition and limited monopoly power. Being, therefore, a price maker under competitive restraints, how do you go about making your price?

You need to consider two factors: what the marginal cost is of the next wrench you produce, which we've stipulated is $300, and how sensitive your customers are to any change in your price. The second question is always hard to answer, but a survey of your customers plus some trial-and-error pricing leads you to believe that if you lower your current price (which we'll say is $425) by 10%, your customers will buy 40% more wrenches. Conversely, if you *raise* your price by 10%, you will sell 40% *fewer* wrenches.

Armed with these facts, you set the price of your digital wrenches at $400. That's your optimal price, the one that maximizes your profit. Any lower price will increase the number of wrenches you can sell but reduce your total profit, whereas any higher price will reduce the number of wrenches you can sell *and* your total profit.

The formula for calculating the optimal price[3] is the marginal cost ($300) multiplied by the price-sensitive ratio (40% more wrenches sold because of a 10% reduction in price = 40% ÷ 10% = 4) divided by the price-sensitive ratio minus one (4 − 1 = 3), or

$$\$300 \times (4 \div 3) = \$400.$$

In free markets with perfect competition, consumers are infinitely price sensitive, which is another way of saying that producers have zero influence over the price at which they sell what they produce, or zero monopoly power. In that situation our formula multiplies $300 (your marginal wrench cost) by infinity divided by infinity (infinity minus one still being infinity), which calculates to 1, and produces an optimal price of $300, which in conformity with the law of supply and demand equals marginal cost—and ruin. But real-world customers are not infinitely price sensitive. The real world lets you charge a price ($400) that covers all your costs ($350), fixed as well as marginal, and make a profit of $50. And survive.

Assuming that your fixed-cost allocation of $50 per wrench covers your salary plus interest on any capital you advanced to your corporation and, if the corporation is using land you own, an appropriate charge for rent, then the $50 profit is entrepreneurial profit, not just accounting profit, as well as your reward for inventing the digital monkey wrench and successfully marketing it.

The real world will reward you even more if you can increase your monopoly power by making your customers less price sensitive. Assuming, for example, that your customers would buy only 30% fewer wrenches (rather than 40%) if you raised your price by 10%, your optimal price would be $450 instead of $400, doubling your profit (price less fixed and variable costs of $350) from $50 to $100. How might you go about doing that?

The classic way is to invest in a brand name for your product and develop it through advertising. If you succeed in instilling brand loyalty in your customers, they will be less inclined to switch off or over to a competitor if you raise your prices. As noted in the last chapter, a brand makes it easier to charge a premium price for the underlying product. That's what brands are all about.

So now you're selling your trade-marked SmartMonkey Wrenches for $450 each. You can produce more than you can sell at that price (your factory is running at less than 60% capacity), but you know that if you reduce your price to sell more, you'll also reduce total profit—not just the profit on your extra sales. Is there anything you can do short of reducing (or *spoiling*) your price to increase sales?

The trick is to lower the price of a SmartMonkey selectively without admitting that's what you're doing. If you can add new customers at $400 or $350 or even $301, you'll add to total profits *provided you can still sell as many wrenches at $450 as you used to*. And that's where consumer promotion, advertising's sibling in the corporate marketing playpen, comes into its own. For promotional activities—sweepstakes, holiday specials, clearance sales, coupons, the whole nine yards—are temporary price reductions in disguise designed to attract *new* customers.

What would a recession do to your optimal price? A recession means that demand has fallen off and people are buying less. If the recession has reduced your variable costs or increased the sensitivity of your customers to your price, the optimal-price formula will calculate a lower price. But if your costs are the same and your customers are no more (or less) price sensitive than before— they may be buying fewer wrenches, but a 10% increase in price produces the same percentage decrease (40% or, if they're brand loyal, 30%) in their purchases—you won't change your old price *even if you're selling less* because that price still brings in more total profit than any lower (or higher) price. Of course, if you are selling less (at the optimal price), you will reduce production and lay off workers to compensate for the reduction in demand.

What happens if a competitor comes out with a new state-of-the-art *virtual wrench* that threatens your digital wrench with obsolescence? The answer is the same as in a recession—it all depends on whether your customers are more (or less) price sensitive and whether your variable costs have changed.

What happens if inflation (or scarcity—or supply and demand) increases your costs? The price-setting formula raises your optimal price because your marginal cost has increased, but if nothing changes the price sensitivity of your customers, you won't shave the new higher price increase to stimulate demand. If your higher price reduces the demand for your wrenches, you will reduce production and lay off workers just as you would in the event of recession or competitive obsolescence.

Is all this *microeconomics* written in stone? Not in a communist country like the former Soviet Union where, in contrast to our own economy, the production of consumer goods is constrained, the price of consumer goods controlled, and the supply of consumer goods never as great as demand. In the United States the ability to sell is highly valued and the ability to buy taken for granted. In the Soviet Union, the opposite was true—the *buyer* highly valued, the seller needing little skill. Writing in the early 1980s, Martin Weitzman said that

the buyer can consider himself fortunate if the "car salesman" . . . condescends even to see him without special favors. So it is not difficult to understand the leisurely pace of technological progress in the Soviet automobile industry, the rather restrained concern about quality, and the reason why service is nonexistent.[4]

If that description is reminiscent of our description of the never-never land of pure competition, the reason is the same: The producer or seller cannot profit by improving quality and service to its customers and therefore has little incentive to do so.

In capitalist economies, producers have that incentive because they have some power to influence their prices—monopoly power—and therefore their profits. Exploiting their monopoly power, says Weitzman, "producers *set* prices, in systematic relation to costs, so that supply exceeds demand in 95 percent of the product markets of advanced capitalist countries" and then seek to sell everything they can produce at those prices, which always represent a markup over costs.[5] And producers, especially the large public corporations that dominate our economy, are always seeking to increase their monopoly power. While a free market economist may view competition as the way to decrease monopoly power, from a free market competitor's point of view competition is the never-ending struggle to *increase* monopoly power.

It's a myth that corporations are required by the law of supply and demand to charge low prices. The law is fiction. Rather than lowering their prices to stimulate demand as the law requires, **corporations mark up their prices and limit demand to maximize profit**. In the real world of capitalism, supply exceeds demand and prices exceed costs.

Were it otherwise, entrepreneurs would disappear, and corporations would never innovate to satisfy their customers' needs.

Chapter 12

Corporations Innovate to Satisfy Their Customers' Needs

The second function of a business is . . . *innovation*—the provision of different economic satisfactions. . . . It is not necessary for a business to grow bigger; but it is necessary that it constantly grow better.
  —Peter F. Drucker, *Management: Tasks, Responsibilities, Practices*[1]

With the benefit of hindsight, we now know that the Good Years really ended in 1973, and that their end was essentially due to one factor and one factor only: the slowdown in productivity growth.
  —Paul Krugman, *Peddling Prosperity*[2]

Theodore Levitt said that we celebrate Henry Ford of Model-T fame for the wrong reason.

His real genius was marketing. We think he was able to cut his selling price and therefore sell millions of $500 cars because his invention of the assembly line had reduced the costs. Actually, he invented the assembly line because he had concluded that at $500 he could sell millions of cars. Mass production was the *result* not the cause of his low prices.[3]

What Ford did is what Peter Drucker terms *price-driven costing*, which Drucker contrasts to the usual practice of cost-driven pricing—setting prices by adding up existing costs and tacking on a profit. Cost-driven pricing, he says, is "irrelevant. . . . The only sound way to price is to start out with what the market is willing to pay . . . and design to that price specification."[4]

As Ford himself noted, what good is it to know the cost of something if it exceeds the price at which you can sell it? Besides, he said, calculating a cost tells you what a cost is, not what it should be. Ford's technique for finding out what a cost should be was to stipulate "a price so low as to force everybody in the [corporation] to the highest point of efficiency. The low price makes everybody dig for profits. We make more discoveries concerning manufacturing and selling under this forced method than by any method of leisurely investigation."[5]

The concept of a car priced for the mass market, the invention of the moving assembly line to manufacture it at a cost lower than that price, and last but not at all least, the discipline that regards cost as a function of price and price as a function of the market (rather than the other way around) are three great innovations that were rolled into one great product, the Model-T. Like all great innovations, they were customer focused. Corporations innovate to satisfy their customers' needs.

When corporations stop innovating, their products obsolesce, their services deteriorate, and their customers migrate to their competitors. The consequences can be devastating, as the Great Innovator, Henry Ford himself, was to discover.

The Model-T came in one design and one color, black, with no ashtray. Since Ford believed that everyone would enter the automotive age by buying his Model-T, he saw no reason to offer any variety. But the market was changing as more cars were produced and more people bought them. Over at General Motors, Alfred Sloan realized that the used car, not a new one, had become the typical car buyer's first purchase. Brand-new cars had become a subsequent and more emotional purchase.[6] New-car shoppers were looking for something different from their last car, something that made *them* look different. To meet their need for variety, GM's Chevrolet Division produced different models each year in different colors—with ashtrays.

By the time Henry Ford realized the need for a new model, GM had overtaken Ford and become the largest automobile company in the world. Having lost so many customers to GM, Ford Motor Company also lost profitability and didn't regain it until years later when Henry Ford was ousted in the corporate equivalent of a coup d'état by his grandson. A lesser corporation would not have survived so long.

Not all innovations cost money. One thinks of the elimination of two-way tolls. We customers of the road now pay twice as much in one direction and none in the other. The productivity of each toll collector (and toll booth) is doubled, the inconvenience (negative productivity) to each motorist cut in half. The innovation costs nothing except the expense of dismantling half the booths and (perhaps) some loss in revenue—assuming, of course, that half the collectors can be productively employed in other tasks and don't have to be paid severance.

But most innovations require investment, lots of it, and the investment is not, of course, risk free. Kodak spent billions on R&D at twice the rate of U.S. industry in general but came up with little to show for it. The failure may have cost its CEO, Kay Whitmore, his job. RCA spent more money developing the videodisc to compete with the made-in-Japan videocassette recorder (VCR) than it had on any other product in its history but was unsuccessful in marketing it. The failure may have cost RCA its independence (it was bought by GE), but 15 years later, the Japanese VCR was still going strong.

Corporate investment in researching, developing, and marketing technological innovation is the primary means by which the economy becomes more productive, and becoming more productive is the primary means by which the economy grows. As economist Paul Krugman put it, "[T]echnology in the broad sense— not just new kinds of hardware, but also 'soft' innovations like just-in-time inventory management—is crucial to productivity growth" and long-run economic growth, which "would grind to a halt without continuous technological progress."[7]

Increased productivity means the ability to produce more output with the same resources or (same thing) to produce the same output with fewer resources. When a corporation markets a more fuel-efficient motor, it increases its customers' productivity. When it learns how to produce the new motor with fewer man-hours, it increases its own productivity. Who profits from these innovations and in what proportion depend on how much the customer pays for the motor and how much it charges *its* customers. But regardless of how the financial profits are divvied up, all productivity gains benefit the economy. The economy produces more (grows) and thereby becomes wealthier. Collectively—ignoring how the wealth is distributed—we all become wealthier.

Since 1973 we have (collectively) all become wealthier at a slower rate than we used to.

For the four or five decades before World War II, productivity increased so as to double living standards in America every 40 years. For the three decades after World War II, productivity increased so as to double living standards every 25 years. In the two decades beginning in 1973, productivity increased so as to double living standards only every 80 years. What happened?

Corporate investment has a lot to do with it.

In a day when 85% of all U.S. goods contained steel, 40% of the country's jobs were dependent one way or another on the production of steel. But U.S. steelmakers came to be plagued, in the words of the *New York Times*, by "a full plate of inefficiencies: overstaffing, outmoded production processes and poor quality control."[8] Japanese and European companies moved in to supply the market the U.S. companies used to dominate. Blaming cheap foreign labor and unfair competition rather than their own inefficiency, the industry and the steel unions got Congress to enact higher tariffs on imported steel. Still the industry languished. U.S. Steel, largest of the integrated steel corporations, bought Marathon Oil rather than investing in its own business.

Eventually, after many years, the industry "got serious about survival," as the *Times* reported, "slashed payrolls, shuttered the most antiquated of their hulking mills and spent billions on new technology and equipment."[9] Productivity increased dramatically. In 1975 it took 12.5 man-hours for the big mills to produce a metric ton of cold-rolled sheet steel. In 1995 it took less than 4.5 man-hours, less even than Japanese and European manufacturers.

But the effort was too little and too late. From 1970 to 1981, net imports (imports minus exports) of iron and steelmill products grew 10-fold—from $.75 billion to $7.5 billion—even though total U.S. consumption declined as U.S. goods used more plastic and aluminum and less steel. The dramatic gains in productivity extended only to a shrunken industry that was no longer large enough to satisfy even a shrunken domestic market. Despite $1.6 billion of new investment by Bethlehem Steel in its plant at Sparrows Point, Maryland, in 1995, the plant had the capacity to produce only one-third as much steel as it used to.

The foreign camel that had stuck its nose under the steel tent without getting whacked didn't upset the tent. It moved in and set up an import business.

Faced with more innovative models from Chevrolet, Henry Ford finally re-placed the Model-T with the Model-A, but his great invention, the moving assembly line, became the production model not only of the American car in-dustry but of mass-production industries throughout the world. American car companies, however, avoided the small, inexpensive, fuel-efficient cars that Volkswagen and other European manufacturers produced after World War II because they believed that they couldn't make enough profit from them. The Japanese showed them how.

The lead camel this time was Toyota, which had pioneered a revolutionary new manufacturing technique called *lean production*. In contrast to the assembly line technique, now referred to as *Fordism*, lean production emphasizes ease of assembly, flexibility on the part of its workers, and the ability of its suppliers to provide the materials it needed *just in time*.[10] It also is said to use half the R&D effort and half the time to develop a new product with many fewer defects and half the man-hours, half the tools, and half the factory space to manufacture it.

Suddenly the Japanese car companies had the world's highest productivity, lowest cost, and fastest reaction to changes in customer preference and market demand.

As their compact cars proved a success and the Honda Accord became Amer-ica's best-selling car, the Japanese, thinking strategically, reinvested their profits to develop larger models for more lucrative markets. Within a few years, they accumulated the products, know-how, and financial resources to compete suc-cessfully against not only GM, Ford, and Chrysler but also Germany's BMW and Mercedes-Benz.

U.S. automobile companies, like the steel companies, turned to the govern-ment for help and got it to negotiate an agreement with the Japanese limiting their exports to the United States. Otherwise, Detroit's reaction to the Japanese threat was remarkably laid back. Whereas the Japanese spent billions to study the U.S. market and (when forced by their export quotas) to build plants in the United States to satisfy that market, the U.S. companies spent almost nothing on the Japanese market and got almost nothing in return. ''The biggest strategic mistake that we made over the last 30 years,'' said the president of North American operations at GM in 1995, ''was not aggressively attacking the Japanese market.''[11]

But then in late 1985, after five years and $3 billion of development, Ford Motor Company, nearly bankrupt but very serious about survival, introduced two new midsize models, the Ford Taurus and its Mercury Division twin, the Sable. ''Their design, a futuristic 'jelly bean' shape, was a radical departure from any American car on the road at the time,'' said the *New York Times*. ''Critics questioned whether Ford had gone too far, but the public embraced the styling, and other manufacturers rushed to produce their own jelly beans.''[12]

In an industry ''saturated by ordinary quite-good cars of all sizes and prices,'' wrote Edward Luttwak of the Center for Strategic and International Studies, ''design leadership that produces radical innovation at moderate cost is all-important . . . because true qualitative distinction allows sellers some exemption from head-to-head price competition.''[13]

A year after its introduction, the Taurus/Sable made Ford more profitable than GM (despite lower sales revenue) for the first time since the Model-T. By the early 1990s the Taurus had caught up with the Honda Accord as the country's top-selling car. Ford's share of the U.S. car market shot up from 14% to 38%.

So, did Ford follow the successful Japanese strategy and reinvest the exceptional profits generated by the Taurus/Sable to maintain its leadership through continued innovation? Not at all, said Luttwak. Ford invested in the financial services and defense industries, where it had little experience, and eventually lost billions of dollars. This strategic diversification came at the cost of investment in its own cars, which Luttwak asserted was much less than what the Japanese were investing.

Thus Ford neglected to grow better by innovation, violating the Drucker mandate, and it ignored the needs of its longtime customers, violating the Levitt precept. Furthermore, it gave its rivals the catch-up time they needed to design cars that were fully competitive with the Taurus/Sable. The consequences, Luttwak wrote in 1993, were predictable. Taurus/Sable clones could be found in the showrooms of domestic and foreign car dealers all over the country.

Luttwak believes that what Ford did is representative of the larger story of American R&D expenditures, which in 1991 were 27% less per person than Japanese expenditures. ''Why is this happening in America?'' asks Luttwak. His answer is that

the Calvinist virtues that have long offset our extreme individualism and greed—self-restraint, and the urge to save and invest—have waned. Quick fixes and fast money are in; patient research, development and investment are out.[14]

Should we care? Having jelly beans in every showroom gives consumers more choice. But when American corporations underinvest in their own corporate growth, and imports are required to make up the deficit in what they produce compared to what the country consumes, they are underinvesting in American jobs. For the 10 years from 1985 to 1994 that annual trade deficit (as measured by the balance on current account) averaged $110 billion a year.[15] That's more than $100 billion of goods and services that might be produced each year by American workers but aren't. The trade deficit is less than 2% of total U.S. production, to be sure, but it used to be the other way around. Exporting more than it imported, America used to be the world's largest creditor nation. Now it's the world's largest debtor.

The single biggest item in the trade deficit represents imports of Japanese cars. Even at Ford, engineers working on the most innovative and successful American passenger car produced in years consider the Toyota Camry to be their benchmark. And the *Times* said in 1995 that the Camry "still beat[s] the Taurus in terms of pep, ride comfort and drivetrain smoothness."[16]

When American corporations underinvest in their own productivity growth, they are underinvesting in American prosperity. If this trend goes on long enough, we'll have a lot of jelly beans to choose from but not so many pennies to spend on them.

Why is this happening in America? It's a myth that corporations innovate to satisfy their customers' needs. Heeding their shareholders more than their customers, concerned with the current value of their shares of stock more than the ongoing value of their products and services, **public corporations *under*invest in innovation** necessary for productivity increase and corporate growth even as they *over*invest in acquisitions of existing assets, often in unrelated industries with unfamiliar technologies, markets, and customers—and unpredictable outcomes.

We must look to management for the reason why.

Part IV

Managers

How the managers of public corporations are entrepreneurial, strategic, and capable of running any business; how their competence is enhanced through team management.

Chapter 13

Corporate Management Is Entrepreneurial

Few great men could pass Personnel.
　　　　　　　　　　　—Paul Goodman, *Growing Up Absurd*[1]

Company policy absolutely prohibits acceptance or evaluation of *any* unsolicited ideas.
　　　　　　　　　　　—Legal advice by corporate counsel[2]

The fight of the century for the corporate heavyweight crown of the world was fought in the 1920s. In one corner stood Henry Ford, champion entrepreneur, pioneer of the automobile age, inventor of the moving assembly line. In the other stood Alfred P. Sloan, Jr., professional manager, master of the decentralized corporation, developer of the techniques of modern management.

Ford threw in the towel in 1927 when he closed his plant at River Rouge where the Model-T was produced to retool for a new model, the Model-A. When the plant reopened, Sloan's General Motors had replaced Ford Motor Company as the largest manufacturing enterprise in the world.

The professional manager had beaten America's champion entrepreneur.

Yet we Americans exalt our entrepreneurs, not our professional managers.

Entrepreneur is defined by *The American Heritage Dictionary of the English Language* as "a person who organizes, operates, and assumes the risk for business ventures."[3] That's what all young business managers want to be. Few, however, actually organize their own ventures. Most join corporations like Ford Motor Company that someone else started as a venture, perhaps many years before. But even in a large public corporation, they can still be organizers, operators, risk takers. They can be innovators. They can be *entrepreneurial.*

And that's what we believe: Corporate management is entrepreneurial.

But why is it that few managers become entrepreneurs, organizing and operating their own ventures?

According to venture capitalist A. David Silver, entrepreneurs are typically dissatisfied graduates of middle-class value systems, deprived childhoods, absent fathers, disappointed mothers, failed marriages—though rarely of Ivy League colleges; they would have dropped out to pursue their great innovation and then felt guilty about it. ("It is difficult," he says, "to name . . . three successful entrepreneurs who received their degrees from Princeton University.")[4] Not that they're unique. Many artists have similar backgrounds, "and the result is a beautiful articulation of the world's problems flowing from their pens, a representation of the world's problems that decorate their canvasses, and a cacophonous description of the world's problems through melodies and related sounds."[5] Artists, however, lack the energy to solve the problems they identify even though they may have developed a solution on paper. Others (Silver specifically mentions consultants) may be both dissatisfied and energetic enough to do something about it but lack the insight to see a business problem from all angles and the creativity to develop an appropriate solution.

Entrepreneurs, according to Silver, combine dissatisfaction, energy, insight, and creativity plus a few other key qualities like selling and communication skills and not being able to conceive of failure—and they're happy to boot. Does that sound like many managerial people in public corporations?

Experience teaches us, however, that real entrepreneurs, talented as they are, rarely have the ability to make a large public corporation out of a small private enterprise. "To believe that entrepreneurs are capable of taking their companies from zero sales to $1 billion . . . without standing down as their chief executive officer, is to believe in Santa Claus," wrote Silver in 1985.

Name 10 entrepreneurs who have achieved this kind of success in post–World War II America, and you have all [nine] of them: Charles McCowen (MCI Communications), Robert E. Noyce (Intel), Kenneth E. Olsen (Digital Equipment), David Packard (Hewlett-Packard), H. Ross Perot (EDS), Dr. Henry E. Singleton (Teledyne), Saul Steinberg (Reliance), Charles Tandy (Tandy), and Dr. Ansu Wang (Wang Laboratories).[6]

Plus Bill Gates (Microsoft) and perhaps a couple of others. That's still a small fraction of the number of entrepreneurs *starting* new ventures.

In the great majority of cases, if the successful entrepreneurial venture is to prosper as a large corporation with public shareholders, professional management is needed. But the entrepreneur who organized, operated, and assumed the risk of the original enterprise is rarely comfortable in a professionally managed corporation. Thus, when a successful enterprise grows beyond the limitations of one-person control, it usually parts ways with its founding entrepreneur.

About the time of the parting, it also changes its stripes.

I joined ITT in its heyday, 1968, from a big U.S. government agency that everyone, I'm sure, would consider bureaucratic. In those days ITT was widely regarded as one of the best-managed of the multiindustry corporations called conglomerates. On my first day a seasoned executive heading up a new foreign venture that ITT had started with another company told me with awe in his voice that it was impossible for this venture *not* to make a profit and *not* to generate more cash than it needed. Having just spent several years financing foreign ventures of U.S. companies that never seemed to make a profit and always seemed in need of cash, I decided that ITT was a place I was going to enjoy.

And I did, much of the time, especially after I left the corporate treasury a few years later to join that same foreign venture as part of a new team of managers. During the intervening years the venture never made a profit and always needed cash, and the seasoned executive and his team were eventually benched. We moved our headquarters to Europe, where most of the problems were, and managed to turn the venture around. In time it became one of ITT's most profitable businesses.

But while I was still in the treasury department, I'd reached the conclusion, startling to me even today, that there were more similarities between ITT and the bureaucratic government agency I had left than dissimilarities. Maybe it hit me the day I wrote a memorandum to the chief financial officer saying, "I recommend that you approve" such-and-such action, and my immediate superior (a person I greatly respected then and thereafter) suggested rephrasing it to read, "It is recommended that" such-and-such action "be approved." Personal responsibility on the part of both originator and recipient of the memorandum was to be diffused.

Diffusion of personal responsibility is the hallmark of bureaucracy.

But taking personal responsibility is part and parcel of being entrepreneurial. You can't be a risk taker if the risk is someone else's responsibility, not yours, and you can't be innovative without taking risks. You can't be entrepreneurial and bureaucratic at the same time.

After leaving ITT, I became a consultant and saw how a lot of different organizations functioned. Then I came to believe that *any* institution, be it corporation, nonprofit, labor union, or government agency, inevitably takes on the characteristics of a bureaucracy once it reaches a certain size. For a public corporation, the threshold seems to be reached about the time it goes public and hires a professional personnel manager—and certainly by the time that personnel manager requires every position to have a job description. How do you write a job description for an entrepreneur?

A common characteristic of the bureaucratic organization is arrogance, as in the NIH syndrome—if it was *not invented here*, it's not worth considering. That's a customer-unfriendly attitude, discouraging innovation, but when it's held by the human resources department, it's *people*-unfriendly, discouraging *any* initiative. Yet in corporation after corporation, it seems that HR people are as arrogant as any. At ITT we used to say that personnel people hated personnel.

When a full-time lawyer joins the personnel manager on corporate staff, you may assume that any entrepreneurial flame has been extinguished for good.

In the countries of the world that keep such statistics, there are approximately 5 lawyers for every 10,000 persons. In the United States there are 6 times as many—30 lawyers for every 10,000 persons. Lawyers advise clients and write contracts, of course, but more and more what they do is engage in litigation, particularly the litigation of tort claims, since that's where the money is. In 1994 the U.S. tort system cost the economy more than $150 billion, 2% of the gross domestic product—and more than twice the average tort-to-GDP ratio of all the industrial countries in the world.

For as long as anyone's been counting, tort costs in the United States have been growing *much* faster than the economy as a whole.

The people who claim to have been injured by the torts get about $70 billion of the $150 billion total cost to the economy—less than 50%. The rest is absorbed by lawyers and courts and the expenses of defending against the claims. And only about half of the $70 billion awarded to the claimants represents compensation for economic loss. The rest is paid to them for other reasons, including punishing the defendant.[7]

When a plaintiff sues General Motors for injury or damage caused by one of its trucks and the legal system allows the jury to award the plaintiff $1 million for damages and $100 million to punish GM, we may well question the sanity of the legal system. If the $1 million was based on proof of loss, what was the $100 million based on? In criminal trials, punitive fines are imposed by judges under statutory guidelines. What competence do civil jurors have to impose fines (called *punitive damages*) without *any* guidelines? Fines in criminal cases are paid to the state. Why should punitive damages in civil cases be paid to the plaintiff—and, of course, to the plaintiff's lawyers?

Punitive damages is the number-one target of tort reform, but tort reform of any kind is the number-one target of the large numbers of attorneys who make their living prosecuting tort claims.

Paying out no more than one-quarter of its economic costs to compensate victims for actual losses they have suffered, the tort system can hardly be considered a model of efficiency, but it *is* effective in reducing risk taking by large public corporations, which as the defendants of choice (they have the money) pay most of the costs. The corporations, of course, pass these costs on to their customers in the form of higher prices, so the public ultimately bears the burden. But heeding the tort-avoiding advice of their own lawyers, the corporations also become increasingly risk averse, concerned more about avoiding liability and protecting the bottom line than about improving the product line and building sales. Inevitably they become less innovative.

Since innovation is the wellspring of increased productivity and increased productivity is the font of higher living standards, the public loses again.

Corporate lawyers, a conservative lot, would die happy if their clients never took *any* risks, never mind that a corporation following their advice would probably go belly up before they did. And they spend a lot of time trying to achieve that goal—their time, their clients' time, and the time of the corporations their clients do business with. Practicing corporate law at a firm in New York for a few years (my first job) persuaded me that if all business transactions were funneled through lawyers, the national economy would shrink to roughly one-quarter its present size. The one-quarter was pure guess, of course, but the reaction I usually got was that it was too high!

The negative attitude toward risk, the NIH syndrome, and the avoidance of personal responsibility characteristic of public corporations (and large organizations in general) go far to explain why public corporations tend to be underachievers. How could anyone with an entrepreneurial spirit be happy in such an environment? They would have to change their stripes to match the corporation's dull colors—or leave.

If they leave, where might they go? Perhaps to "an industry that is chock-full of risk and keen competition. Customers are fickle. Markets are volatile." New products aren't protected—or even kept secret. "Welcome to Wall Street," writes financial adviser Susan Webber, where

- making money takes precedence over all else,
- egos and politics don't stand in the way of business,
- even the most senior executives . . . work regularly with clients,
- very often, even for higher-ups, pay depends not on seniority or title but on performance,

and where "insecurity and opportunity—also known as fear and greed"—are the basic motivators.[8]

Webber's Wall Street is the antipodes of corporate country. It's myth that corporate management is entrepreneurial. **Public corporations are too bureaucratic for management to be entrepreneurial**.

But at least corporate management is strategic. Strategy doesn't require entrepreneurs.

Chapter 14

Corporate Management Is Strategic

Business is like war in one respect. If its grand strategy is correct, any number of tactical errors can be made and yet the enterprise proves suceesful.
—General Robert E. Wood, CEO of Sears, Roebuck[1]

Plans are nothing; planning is everything.
—General Dwight D. Eisenhower[2]

Strategy is a military concept derived from the ancient Greek word for *general*. More indirectly, through Latin and medieval French, the word *stratagem* comes from the same root. But don't let the slyness of stratagem, a trick or ruse, cloud the forthright meaning of strategy, which is generalship in its broadest sense. And don't confuse strategy with tactics. According to *The Random House Dictionary of the English Language*, tactics "deals with the use and deployment of troops in actual combat," whereas strategy "is the utilization, during both peace and war, of all of a nation's forces, through large-scale, long-range planning and development, to ensure security or victory."[3]

Substituting a few words, we could define business strategy as *the utilization, in a more or less hostile competitive environment, of all of a corporation's resources, through large-scale, long-range planning and development, to ensure profitability or market dominance.*

The management function in a corporation can be thought of as having two faces, like Janus, the gatekeeper of Roman mythology. The face looking backward is either putting out yesterday's fires or implementing current (that is, yesterday's) strategy. This is how most managers earn their keep. The face looking forward is engaged in large-scale, long-term planning and development of corporate resources so that those resources produce the greatest benefit in future years. This is how corporate generals earn their keep. At the top, corporate management is strategic.

How large is *large-scale* and how long is *long-range?*

In 1970, when Canon, the Japanese camera company, decided to enter the photocopier business, that business was dominated by what Gary Hamel and C. K. Prahalad called "the $4 billion Xerox powerhouse." But Canon and other Japanese corporations that sought to become world-class companies "created an obsession with winning at all levels of the organization and then sustained that obsession over the 10-to 20-year quest for global leadership. We term this obsession 'strategic intent.' "[4]

Fifteen years later Canon had caught up with Xerox in the number of photocopiers sold throughout the world. To Canon, *long-range* meant a decade and a half, and *large-scale* was measured by the size of the global copier market.

In their 1989 article, "Strategic Intent," Hamel and Prahalad describe how Canon did it.

Canon first studied Xerox's patents, then licensed technology from other sources to give it experience in making its own photocopier, then—taking a leaf from Henry Ford's book on price-based costing—gave its engineers the task of designing a copier that could sell for several thousand dollars less than Xerox's. After its engineers developed a disposable cartridge to replace the complex image-transfer mechanism that Xerox used, Canon introduced its product in Europe and licensed its new technology to other manufacturers in order to accumulate marketing experience and resources before confronting Xerox on Xerox's home turf.

When it finally entered the U.S. market, Canon did so on its own terms. It priced its copiers at a thousand dollars and pitched them to the office people who would actually use them rather than to purchasing managers who had been buying the more expensive Xerox machines. It sold its copiers through independent office-product stores; Xerox employed (and paid for) a large direct-sales force. It used standardized parts in all its copiers so that the office-product stores would be able to repair them; Xerox had (and paid for) its own national service network.

In *Competitive Strategy*, a book widely read by managers and management consultants specializing in strategic planning, Michael Porter defined the five forces driving competition in any industry, whether local, national, or global: rivalry among existing firms; potential new entrants; potential substitute products or services; bargaining power among suppliers; and bargaining power among buyers or customers. "The goal of competitive strategy for a business unit in an industry," he wrote, "is to find a position in the industry where the company can best defend itself against these competitive forces or can influence them in its favor" and thereby maximize its profit and return on investment.[5]

Competitive strategy usually seeks to achieve either low-cost leadership in the industry; differentiation of products or services so that they are perceived as unique (as through branding); or domination with respect to a particular group of customers, a product line segment, or a geographic market niche.

The position Canon, the new entrant, staked out in Xerox's garden was untended (and undefended) space at the low-price end that Xerox considered unfruitful. But Canon's low-cost leadership made that segment profitable. While IBM and Kodak were competing head-on against Xerox, Canon took over the low-price end, boxed Xerox and Kodak in at the high-price end, and drove IBM out of the market altogether. Xerox dismissed the threat from Canon, Paul Allaire admitted after becoming CEO, until it realized that Americans were buying Canon copiers at a price that was less than what it cost Xerox to *make* its copiers.

According to Hamel and Prahalad, the competitive strategy of Far Eastern companies engaged in global competition focuses on building and leveraging resources (such as Canon's knowledge of imaging) to attain long-term goals beyond their present means. Western companies, by contrast, seek goals *within* their present means. One suspects that if the positions of Xerox and Canon had been reversed in 1970, Xerox management would have stuck to cameras and never thought to challenge Canon in copiers.

The approach to competitive risk also differs. Japanese companies counter risk by developing a broad range of corporate-wide advantages. Large multiindustry American corporations typically adopt a portfolio approach, "harvesting" the cash from "Cash Cow" businesses to finance high-growth "Wildcats" (or "Question Marks") and convert them to high-market-share "Stars" (which turn into Cash Cows when growth slows down), meanwhile stripping the remaining cash from low-growth, low-market-share "Dogs" before dispatching them to the pound. The only corporate-wide advantage they pursue is money.

According to Michael Porter, techniques for portfolio analysis like the Boston Consulting Group's star-cat-cow-dog matrix depicting market share and growth potential (or GE's three-by-three matrix depicting industry attractiveness and competitive position) "provide simple frameworks for charting or categorizing the different businesses in a firm's portfolio and determining the implications for resource allocation."

[These techniques] have their greatest applicability in developing [portfolio] strategy at the corporate level and in aiding corporate review of business units, rather than in developing competitive strategy in individual industries. Nevertheless, if their limitations are understood, these techniques can play a part in answering some of the questions in competitor analysis, . . . particularly if a firm is competing with a diversified rival who uses them in its strategic planning.[6]

That is, portfolio techniques aren't much use in formulating *competitive* strategies to ensure profitability or market dominance, but they can be useful in developing *portfolio* strategies for allocating money among various businesses or in analyzing the strategy of a competitor that uses portfolio analysis in its planning. As to the latter: "We're glad to find a competitor managing by the portfolio concept," one global company executive told Hamel and Prahalad, because "we can almost predict how much share we'll have to take away to put the business on the CEO's 'sell list.' "[7]

Focusing on portfolios of individual businesses rather than on development of core competencies for the corporation as a whole, many U.S. multiindustry corporations in the 1970s and 1980s were quick to place business under competitive attack on their sell list. Ford, GE, GTE, Motorola, Rockwell, Teledyne, and Westinghouse all quit making television sets during this period. Consumer electronics had become a mature (low-growth) industry, and the entry of foreign competitors with low labor costs turned it into a dog.

The piano business is also mature—isn't it? Yamaha's response, quoted by Hamel and Prahalad, sounds like its executives had been reading Theodore Levitt: "Only if we can't take any market share from anybody anywhere in the world and still make money. And anyway, we're not in the 'piano' business; we're in the 'keyboard' business."[8]

Still, lower labor costs in many foreign countries give manufacturers in those countries a cost advantage that U.S. companies cannot compete against. As the World Economic Forum in Switzerland confirmed as late as 1995, low-cost producers in the newly industrialized countries of the world are flooding the industrialized world with cheap goods. Aren't they? Trade specialist Paul Krugman's response is no, they're not: "[T]he vision of a Western economy battered by low-wage competition . . . is a fantasy with hardly any basis in reality."[9] Industrialized countries do most of their trading with other industrialized countries having roughly comparable wage scales. A study by Robert Lawrence of the Kennedy School at Harvard found that in 1990 only 2.7% of U.S. imports came from countries with wage rates 50% or less of U.S. wage rates, not much more than in 1960 (2%). Considering all trade, the countries that the United States trades with have a weighted average wage rate equal to 90% of the U.S. wage rate.[10]

Rather than blaming mature markets or cheap labor costs when U.S. corporations fail to ensure profitability or market dominance in global competition, we might look to the mind-set of their generals. Is their deployment (or disposal) of corporate resources based on large-scale, long-range planning?

At ITT, we spent a lot of time during the summer months preparing and reviewing business plans covering the next five years. Our strategic planning staff (such as it was) created the planning forms but didn't do any planning; planning was (as it should be) a line management function. In its business plan, each unit set forth its forecast P&L for the current year, the plan P&L for the next two years (Plan Years 1 and 2), and key numbers for the fifth year. That was pretty much it. A lot of numbers. Little planning. No strategy.

And when the plans were presented to senior management for approval—a process involving a shifting cast of literally scores of executives over many weeks—the later years were largely ignored. The several hours' discussion of each unit's presentation was typically divided about evenly between the forecast for the current year—or rather the remaining few months of the current year—and Plan Year 1. Plan Year 2 might or might not merit a brief discussion. I don't recall hearing Plan Year 5 ever mentioned.

A 300-company survey in the early 1990s by the Council on Competitiveness and Harvard Business School found that almost half (47%) of the development projects undertaken by Japanese companies and three-fifths (61%) of those undertaken by European companies counted as long-term projects, defined by the survey to mean *no profit expected for five years*. In the case of U.S. companies, only one out of five (21%) projects met that definition.[11]

In most public corporations, *long-term* and *long-range* mean no more than two or three or (at a stretch) four years from now. Five years is over the horizon. They may call their plans *strategic*, but they're not. "Aiming to be number one in a business is the essence of strategic intent," said Hamel and Prahalad, "but imposing a three-to four-year horizon on the effort simply invites disaster."[12]

What ever happened to the vision of Alfred Sloan and Henry Ford? Are our modern corporate generals too set in their ways to realize they need new glasses? Looking forward to wealthy retirement, have they lost the will to compete? Or should we round up different suspects for questioning?

In discussing the myth that public corporations are just private corporations with many owners, we noted that from the 1960s to the 1990s, while institutional ownership of corporate shares was increasing from 10% to 50% or more, the average holding period for those shares dropped from seven years to two. If the average corporate shareholder won't be a shareholder two years from now—and if it's an institutional investor, perhaps not even one year from now—how interested will that shareholder be in an investment project from which no profit is expected for five years?

If the average shareholder isn't likely to be supportive of long-term investments and long-range strategies—which are riskier, of course, everything else being equal, than short-term investments and strategies—why should corporate managers stick their necks out? Especially managers who profess to live by the myth (as most public corporation managers do) that their first concern is shareholder value?

It's a myth that corporate management is strategic. For the most part, **public corporation planning is too short term for strategic management**—and too simplistic. And in many cases the corporation is involved in too many different industries for management to develop a competitive strategy at the corporate level that goes beyond the allocation of money among its business units.

Does the lack of strategy matter to the rest of us? We have indicated in earlier myths that corporate investment, particularly long-term investment, benefits shareholders, customers, workers, and the economy as a whole—but that Churchill's Horses don't do enough of it. One of the reasons, certainly, is their managers' lack of strategic focus. But when a whole industry like consumer electronics moves abroad, isn't that just the play of a global free market rewarding low-cost producers to the benefit of consumers everywhere? If Americans develop the first, or best, next-generation TV technology, won't the free market bring the industry back home?

Possibly, but, as Paul Krugman says, "in the world of QWERTY one cannot trust markets to get it right" because "the outcome of market competition often depends crucially on historical accident."[13] QWERTY, of course, refers to the layout of the standard typewriter keyboard developed a century ago. Numerous other keyboards have been designed, all touted as more efficient, but the added efficiency is not worth the effort of developing new digital reflexes, not to you, not to me, and not to the millions of other people who use more than two digits to type. The movie industry is concentrated in Hollywood because that's where most people in the industry work because that's where the resources are concentrated because (in Hollywood's case) that's where the industry started— never mind whether the best movies are made there.

No one in the United States makes TV sets anymore. Zenith, the last U.S. TV manufacturer, sold out to a Korean company in 1995.

If the next-generation TV is developed here, it may still have to be manufactured by the people with manufacturing resources and experience where those people and resources and experience are concentrated—overseas. In other words, once an industry is let go, there's no guarantee it—or the jobs associated with it—will ever come back.

So the strategic myopia and risk aversion of our corporate generals do have ongoing consequences for the rest of us—and the economy. But if our generals aren't strategic, at least they're versatile. They have to be to manage so many different businesses.

Chapter 15

Professional Managers Can Run Any Corporate Business

Geneen, along with other conglomerateurs of the 1960s and 1970s, had an overriding business philosophy that strong managers could manage anything, no matter how separate or incongruent.
—Rand V. Araskog, *The ITT Wars*[1]

Happily, governments and quasi-governmental authorities . . . haven't instituted the formal licensing of corporate managers, and they may never. But much the same effect is achieved by limiting executive-track jobs to graduates of prestigious business schools.
—Harvey H. Segal, *Corporate Makeover*[2]

In the late 1980s, Korn/Ferry, an executive recruiting (headhunting) firm, surveyed 1,500 chief executives about the qualities they expected their successors to need. Japanese CEOs stressed technical and R&D experience. U.S. CEOs emphasized marketing and finance.[3]

American CEOs emphasize marketing and finance because that, in many cases, is where they came from. (According to the president of the research arm of the Bell operating companies, only 18% of American CEOs have technical training compared to 36% in Japan.) Having mastered these two subjects, professional managers can run any business or a conglomeration of many businesses because the basic principles of marketing and finance are the same in all businesses. The providing of financial services may have nothing in common with, say, the manufacturing of cigarettes, food products, or computers—and tobacco and food manufacturing may be rather different from computer manufacturing—but all these industries share common marketing principles, and a dollar of profit is a dollar of profit, no matter where it comes from.

Living proof that well-trained professional managers can run any corporate business is provided by Louis Gerstner. He has been

- principal of McKinsey & Company, a prestigious management consulting firm,
- high executive at American Express, a global financial services corporation,
- head of RJR Nabisco, a tobacco and food marketing conglomerate, and
- CEO of IBM, the world's leading computer company, having been appointed to that position at the age of 51.

Many professional managers learn marketing and finance in a two-year graduate business school they attend after college. Since two years isn't enough time to teach students every business or even *any* business, a business school zeros in on these generic subjects because they apply to every business and qualify their graduates as managers in any type of corporation. (Both marketing and finance are heavily numbers oriented—marketing in demographics and market share, finance in accounting and profit and loss—so it isn't that difficult to become conversant in both disciplines.) But is the Master of Business Administration degree that business school graduates earn worth two years' loss of income and on-the-job experience plus the pricey tuition that business schools charge?

While Louis Gerstner (who received his M.B.A. from Harvard Business School) might say "yes," J. Sterling Livingston, who taught at that school, might disagree. In "Myth of the Well-Educated Manager," Livingston wrote that "formal management education programs in both universities and industry [have been unable] to develop explicitly the traits, knowledge, and skills that are essential to career success and leadership in any business organization."[4] The reason, he said, is that business schools and corporate management programs

typically emphasize the development of problem-solving and decision-making skills, for instance, but give little attention to the development of skills required to find the problems that need to be solved, to plan for the attainment of desired results, or to carry out operating plans once they are made. Success in real life depends on how well a person is able to find and exploit the opportunities that are available . . . and, at the same time, discover and deal with potential serious problems before they become critical.[5]

These skills can be learned *only* on the job. "A manager cannot learn how to find opportunities or problems without doing it," said Livingston. "The doing is essential to the learning."[6] Having been not only a professor of business administration but also a corporate president and a manager of hundreds of M.B.A. graduates, Livingston might just know what he is talking about.

So perhaps an M.B.A. doesn't really qualify a manager to manage anything. Perhaps the only place to learn marketing and finance is in a corporation that is an expert in these disciplines.

John Sculley was regarded as a marketing whiz at Pepsi-Cola and its parent,

PepsiCo, the world's leading snack food company, when he was recruited to run Apple Computer. Michael Jordan had been PepsiCo's chief financial officer when Westinghouse's board tapped him to become CEO. Gordon Tucker was in charge of strategic development for PepsiCo's KFC (Kentucky Fried Chicken) business unit when he was made head of Micrografx, a computer software company.

But can either an M.B.A. or on-the-job experience in generic subjects really qualify managers to run a business they aren't familiar with? Gary Hamel and C. K. Prahalad don't think so. Business schools, they say, have wrongly "perpetuated the notion that a manager with net present value calculations in one hand and portfolio planning in the other can manage any business anywhere."[7] Net present value calculations reduce (discount) future values to what they're worth today, taking into account the cost of money and risk, just as the efficient stock market is supposed to do. (The devil, of course, is in the assumptions— what the future will hold and how much it should be discounted.) Portfolio planning, as we learned in the previous chapter, is what passes in many conglomerate corporations for competitive strategy formulation.

Large corporations, say Hamel and Prahalad, compound the problem of lack of experience by moving their managers around

so many times as part of their "career development" that they often do not understand the nuances of the business they are managing. . . . Regardless of ability and effort, fast-track managers are unlikely to develop the deep business knowledge they need to discuss technology options, competitors' strategies, and global opportunities substantively. Invariably, therefore, discussions gravitate to "the numbers," while the value added of managers is limited to the financial and planning savvy they carry from job to job. Knowledge of the company's internal planning and accounting systems substitutes for substantive knowledge of the business, making competitive innovation unlikely.[8]

Although M.B.A.s were scarce when I was at ITT, managing by the numbers was what its CEO, Harold Geneen, a trained accountant, was best known for. "He apotheosized the rational and analytic," wrote his (unauthorized) biographer, but the flip side of the coin was—and is today in many public corporations—

a ruinous tendency to overprize management-by-the-numbers. The analysts, the accountants, the dealmakers, the lawyers, the controllers—all the number crunchers—they took over and no one was left to do any honest work. Production and the product were no longer glamorous. It was reason run amok, effacing the purpose of the enterprise.[9]

Even under Geneen, managing by the numbers had its limitations, like any generic management technique, when not enlightened by the deep business knowledge that comes from long experience in the particular business. For example, it took a number of years to make the international Yellow Pages venture I was associated with profitable, but at least we had one of the leading U.S.

companies in the business as a partner. All we had to do was learn when to listen to it—and when not to.

It took much longer to make the Sheraton Hotels acquisition profitable. Private hotel corporations (as Sheraton was when it was acquired by ITT) are often run as real estate operations, minimizing current profits and income taxes through maximum interest and depreciation deductions while staking future profits on the rising value of the hotel properties. But public corporations like ITT pursue quarter-by-quarter and year-to-year increases in current profits. ITT-Sheraton had to be reoriented. That didn't happen overnight. An astute and farsighted manager with net present value calculations in his hand could well have concluded (the devil, remember, is in the assumptions) that the value of ITT's investment in Sheraton to ITT and its shareholders was *negative from day one and would never turn positive*—even after Sheraton eventually became profitable!

Through the green eyeshade of management by the numbers, hotels don't appear all that different from telephones (ITT's original business) or computers from junk food—and telephones and computers appear to be virtual twins. Futurists may have been wearing the same eyeshade when, as the 1980s unfolded, they predicted that before the decade was out AT&T, the world's largest telephone company, and IBM, the world's largest computer company, would duke it out in the marketplace formed by the convergence of computer and communication technology. AT&T's managers took the prediction seriously even if IBM's didn't. In preparation for the fight, AT&T shed its Bell operating company subsidiaries and the fat gained as a government-regulated monopoly and began training to become a market-oriented computer champion.

The fight, as we now know, never took place. The promoters were wrong—computer and communication technology didn't converge. According to marketing maven Al Ries, technologies rarely do.[10] The paperless office of the future is still in the future. Advent never made the home entertainment center happen. American Express never became the global financial supermarket. Following the law of entropy, technologies usually divide, as when the department store of yore split into the likes of Foot Locker, The Limited, Toys 'R' Us, Office Depot, and Blockbuster Video. With technologies as with their markets, the name of the game is *segmentation*, not convergence.

And AT&T, despite its training, still didn't look much like a computer champion. The corporation that had developed the landmark transistor, UNIX operating system, and C and C++ programming languages—developed but never really marketed them—couldn't crack the personal computer market. To get help, it entered into a *strategic partnership* (a phrase embracing almost any type of collaboration) with Olivetti, the Italian computer maker. When that association failed, in 1991, it executed a $7.5 billion hostile acquisition of NCR, the former National Cash Register, leader in point-of-sale computers, real-time inventory management, and automated teller machines and arguably the most successful of the original bunch of mainframe companies competing against IBM. AT&T told NCR to do what AT&T had failed at—market desktop computers.

Mergers and acquisitions (the same thing, really) are a favorite tactic of corporate managers with generic skills (and of many without), especially after they have squeezed all the profit they can out of cost cutting and downsizing and must now address the more difficult task of increasing revenue. If they can't increase revenue through advertising or promotion, and customers or competitors won't let them raise prices, they grow the revenue line (as they would say) by acquiring another corporation. That's quicker than developing new products and services, and surer. Or so it may appear.

But the dirty little secret is: *Acquisitions generally fail.* McKinsey & Company (Gerstner's old firm) concluded from a study in 1988 that most acquiring corporations would have made more money by depositing their money in a bank than they did from the acquisition.[11] Since money costs more than what banks pay their depositors—banks, after all, have to make a profit like everyone else—the McKinsey findings suggest that the net present value of most investments in an acquired corporation is negative.

The won't-go-away problem with acquisitions is the clash of cultures. Each corporation has its own. "Once the personality of an organization is fixed," wrote Thurman Arnold in *The Folklore of Capitalism*, "it is as difficult to change as the habits of an individual. The same type of people succeed each other, moved by the same attitudes as their predecessors."[12] AT&T managers found competing in a market-regulated environment was tough sledding indeed—even with the corporation they had cut their teeth on. How did they think they could manage a new (and unfamiliar) corporation with a distinct (and unfamiliar) personality in a different business that neither corporation was experienced in—especially when the new corporation had been acquired against the will of its managers? (Even in a friendly acquisition, most senior managers of the acquired corporation leave within a short time, such is the shock of trying to blend two different cultures.) *Hubris*, the ancient Greeks would have called it.

And just as they did in Homer's Greece, the gods got even. In 1995, after billions of dollars of losses, AT&T announced that it was getting rid of NCR by spinning it off—that is, handing it and all its problems—to its shareholders. AT&T also spun off its manufacturing arm (the old Western Electric Corporation), took $6 billion in write-offs, and got rid of 40,000 managers and employees.

Initially, NCR shares traded at a value that indicated that NCR was worth about $3.5 billion. Although that was less than half of what AT&T had paid for it, some analysts thought the value was too high. "Their products are pretty good," said one, "but from a marketing perspective their presence is zero. The difference between when AT&T bought them and now is that a lot of other people have caught up. Their lack of direction for many years has really hurt them."[13]

How many acquisitions succeed? The answer, of course, depends on the definition of success. But according to one Wall Street pessimist, if success is defined as achieving "all their synergistic goals," corporate acquisitions succeed "about ten percent of the time."[14]

It's a myth that professional management can run any corporate business. If anything, the opposite is true. At the very least, **professional management requires on-the-job experience and in-depth knowledge** gained from years of experience in the business they're managing.

Not that the people whose business it is to fit managers into management slots seem to notice. Gerald Roche, chairman of Heidrick & Struggles, one of the leading headhunting firms, placed John Sculley, the PepsiCo marketing whiz, as CEO of Apple Computer. It was, he allowed, the search he was most proud of. (His "dream search" is to headhunt the president of the United States.) But Sculley and Apple parted company on less than the best of terms. Part of the problem, it appears, was that Sculley didn't really understand Apple's technology and never felt at ease with its engineers.[15] He aggressively promoted the palm-sized computer Apple was developing, as he later said, to inspire the team that was designing it and build support for the product—and nearly destroyed the project. Team members quit; one had a breakdown; another killed himself. And when the product was finally released, over a year behind schedule, the Newton, as it was called, was far less than the twenty-first-century device Sculley had touted.

Headhunting, Roche concedes, is "a very inexact science."[16]

If other public corporations haven't all fared as badly as Apple, one reason may be that their management acts as a team. Team management compensates for the shortcomings of individual managers—including the CEO.

Chapter 16

Corporate Management Is Strong Because It's Team Management

It takes a team, and the team ought to get credit for the wins and the losses.
—Philip Caldwell, CEO of Ford Motor Company[1]

Or as Yogi Berra, a great player, manager and malapropist, said when asked what makes a good manager: "A good ball club."
—*Economist* magazine[2]

After I left ITT for smaller pastures, I joined a modest-size semipublic corporation with some interesting assets. One was a digital phototypesetter (a real product, unlike the digital monkey wrench of our own mythology) that was state-of-the-art.

Among our competitors was Rockwell International, a corporation many times greater in resources, experience, and sophistication. But phototypesetters were small potatoes to Rockwell, and one day it announced that it was getting out of that business. Suddenly every Rockwell customer became a prime prospect for our sales force. The opportunity was all the more golden for being free. There was nothing we had to buy or invest in.

Free, that is, until our CEO, who together with his brother had founded the company and still controlled a majority of its stock, decided to make Rockwell an offer to *buy* the business it was closing down. Nothing we said would dissuade him. The offer we made didn't specify a sum of money—our CEO, after all, didn't want to risk insulting Rockwell management before negotiations even began—so when Rockwell management recovered from its astonishment, it formed a team to sit down with ours and work out the price.

Our objectives were quite clear, even if they confounded Rockwell. One, of course, was to obtain the lowest price we could. But to everyone but our CEO, that was a fallback objective. The primary one was to introduce conditions like an appraisal of Rockwell's business that Rockwell would not agree to—hardly a difficult task considering that Rockwell had previously decided simply to shut the business down. After a couple of days of negotiations going nowhere, we succeeded. Rockwell packed its bags and went home. Our CEO, however, pleaded with Rockwell to return. And this time he told us why. He could just see the press release: "XYZ Corporation, the world's leading manufacturer of digital phototypesetters, announced today that it would acquire the phototype-setting business of Rockwell International, a major U.S. aerospace company and defense contractor. Terms were not disclosed. . . ."

Well, in the end we still won, and so did our corporation, which presumably gained a lot of new customers without buying anything, although I departed to become a consultant before the results were in. It was, really, a management *team* victory. Our CEO never got his David-acquires-club-from-Goliath press release, but even he, I suspect, came to see that it wasn't worth the money he would have been paying for something he could have for free.

This account may strike you as a left-handed example (if you're right-handed) of management teamwork in action, but it wasn't so different from the triage practiced by ITT managers when Harold Geneen was CEO. In meetings, Geneen was a human Gatling-gun firing suggestions, commands, instructions, and ideas in all directions at friend and foe alike. After he left the field, his staff would emerge from their foxholes to separate the targets that had received direct hits and had to be operated on from those that had been riddled by off-the-wall ricochets and could be buried quietly. Burials usually outnumbered op-erations.

Although with rare exceptions only the CEO of a public corporation reports to the board of directors while all the other officers report (directly or through another officer) to the CEO, the CEO shares authority, responsibility, and power with a team of managers because the job of running the corporation is too big for one person. Top management, says Peter Drucker, "is a team job. . . . What-ever the titles on the organization chart, the top-management job in a healthy company is almost always actually done by a team."[3] Corporate management is strong because it's team management.

Who are the players on team management?

Judging from a 1992 survey of some 1,400 senior managers by Cornell Uni-versity and the headhunting firm Paul Ray Berndtson, they are mostly white (94%), male (93%), and middle-aged (average 46 years). Seven out of 10 agree with the statement, "In most ways, my life is close to ideal." Still, they are "satisfied" with their job only 30 out of the 56 hours a week they spend at it, "dissatisfied" 15 hours, and "neutral" the remaining 11 hours. And the typical respondent in this survey—two rungs below the CEO in a corporation averag-ing $1.5 billion in sales and 5,000 employees—was on the lookout for a new job, as were three out of four CEOs. But the survey found that lack of job security is not the leading cause of stress on the job. The leading cause of stress is the "degree to which politics, not performance, affects organizational decisions."[4]

The *politics* that causes stress on the job is the "use of intrigue or strategy in obtaining any position of power or control, as in a business," to quote *The Random House Dictionary of the English Language*.[5] But the "power game is a part of management, and it is played best by those who enjoy it most," wrote J. Sterling Livingston in "Myth of the Well-Educated Manager." It is a part of management because the drive for power is one of the three characteristics of people who learn to manage effectively. (The other two characteristics are the will to manage and the capacity for empathy.) Individuals who lack the drive for power and scorn company politics are not likely to advance very far up the managerial ladder.

What does this drive for power tell us about the managers who reach the top of the ladder, the once, present and future CEOs? For one thing, said Livingston, they are not likely to tolerate any system of participatory management:

The power drive that carries men to the top also accounts for their tendency to use authoritative rather than consultative or participative methods of management. . . . Few men who strive hard to gain and hold positions of power can be expected to be permissive, particularly if their authority is challenged.

For another thing, they are not likely to share their power with other managers:

Since their satisfaction comes from the exercise of authority, they are not likely to share much of it with lower-level managers who eventually will replace them, even though most higher-level executives try diligently to avoid the appearance of being authoritarian.[6]

Once in a blue moon you run into a power-sharing arrangement, as when two people form a corporation and one becomes chairperson and the other president. But in three out of four corporations, the CEO holds both offices (in Britain it's only one out of four), and in almost all of the others the chairperson *or* the president—whoever is designated CEO—is clearly in charge. The latest trend, exemplified by GE and IBM, is to eliminate the office of president altogether[7]

Call it team management if you will—but more and more it looks like a one-person (white, male, middle-aged) team. And the group of would-be team players, the managers reporting to the CEO, has gotten a lot smaller.

Since the latter 1980s, corporate America has been downsizing its management. Spencer Stuart (another headhunting firm) estimated that in 1994 more than 500,000 people lost jobs in corporations resulting in the "wholesale evaporation" of management positions with P&L responsibility.[8] From 1990 to 1995, large consumer-goods corporations that it surveyed including Coca-Cola and Procter & Gamble reduced general management jobs with profit responsibility by one-third. "In large organizations," wrote James Champy, author of *Reengineering Management*, "middle managers serve the purpose of relaying information up and down—orders down, numbers up." But modern technology and corporate reengineering have made their functions obsolete. Thus, large organizations have reason "to shed 'information relayers' and make those who remain do more 'value-added work,' that is, something customers will actually pay for."[9]

Is that good, having managers do more value–added work and less management work? Are there any downside consequences?

Work in a corporation involves routines—the "forms, rules, procedures, conventions, strategies and technology" by which it operates as well as "the structures of beliefs and cultural codes that reinforce, elaborate, and sometimes contradict the formally prescribed routines." These routines substitute for a real person's memory. "Routinization of activity in an organization," wrote Robert Cole in the premier issue of *Quality Management Journal*, "constitutes the most important form of storage of the organization's specific operational knowledge"—the accumulated know-how that defines it. The other way operational knowledge is stored is in written rules and records.

Routines, of course, are performed by the corporation's people—that's how the corporation *remembers*—and when many people who know those routines leave the corporation, the routines get disrupted and misinterpreted and mutated. The first casualties are apt to be quality and the customer satisfaction that goes with it. Corporations with high turnover typically try to compensate for the loss of experienced personnel by relying on written rules and records. The problem, says Cole,

is that the more demanding the job, the more likely it is that the written rules and records won't provide sufficient nuances; they are hard to keep updated and/or are often difficult to access in a timely fashion. . . . At the management level, it is particularly important to know how to get things done, and this requires an intimate knowledge of the politics of the organization. This is not the "stuff" of documentation.[10]

So management downsizing tends to reduce quality (which requires not only organization experience but also teamwork) and decrease customer satisfaction. That's one downside consequence. Another is the loss of managers with the general management (P&L) experience that qualifies them to become tomorrow's officers and top executives. "Functional responsibility doesn't qualify you," says a former Kraft and Borden executive, "and you rely on a person at the top to run everything. Most of the time is spent trying to figure out who messed up what, instead of focusing on objectives. Nobody is purely responsible for anything."[11]

Finally, management downsizing inevitably increases the CEO's power and frequently turns him or (7% of the time) her into a celebrity synonymous with the corporation. *Sculley turns Apple around . . . Iacocca saves Chrysler.* Only in recent years, observed Paul Krugman, have business leaders "received the kind of treatment once reserved for victorious generals." Our taste for business heroes, he adds, is dubious. "Almost without exception the celebrity businessmen whose biographies climb the best-seller lists have been promoters rather than producers, experts in making deals rather than in making high-quality products."[12]

In the Roman Republic of Cicero's day, when a national emergency occurred, the elected consuls could appoint one person with supreme authority to run the government. The Latin word for this person was *dictator*, and from 500 B.C. to 44 B.C. Rome appointed one every five years, on average—about as often as we elect a new president. Although each dictatorship was limited to six months, during that period the dictator had essentially unrestrained authority except in matters financial.

Dictator carries ugly connotations for us today, but in the Roman Republic, it was an honorable title.

The last dictator was Julius Caesar, who was appointed, unlawfully, for life. (The ancient Athenians would have called him a *tyrant*, someone exercising absolute authority illegally.) Caesar's assassination in 44 B.C. marked the end of Roman dictatorships *and* the Roman Republic.

Now, think of a public corporation as the Roman Republic in a never-ending competitive crisis, its directors as the consuls, and its CEO as the wise and honorable citizen they appoint to be its dictator. (If it's a myth, as we have observed, that directors appoint the CEO, it's also a myth that consuls made Julius Caesar a dictator-for-life.) Although the appointment is nominally for one year, because it's renewable and because the corporate dictator has essentially unrestrained authority (with financial matters *not* excepted), the appointment is really for an indefinite period. If the dictatorship is benevolent, meaning one that satisfies the aristocrats (shareholders) and their consuls—never mind what consumers and the people who work there, the ordinary Roman citizens, think— well enough and good. If it's not, all the consuls can do is stick a knife in Caesar's back.

Yet according to a study by a trio of finance professors at New York University and the University of Georgia, CEOs rarely suffer Caesar's fate. When their companies start losing money, CEOs use their CEO power to sell assets and divisions and lay off employees (typically 5% of the workforce in the first year), all the while blaming economic conditions, foreign competition, accounting changes—anything but management. CEOs "never, never blame themselves," said Larry Lang, one of the professors, and unless the corporation is actually close to bankruptcy, "CEOs don't suffer."[13]

It's a myth that public corporate management is team management. **Corporate management is CEO management, and corporate power is CEO power,** even when the CEO chooses to delegate management authority or share management responsibility.

Were it not for an occasional Brutus among the outside directors, CEO power would be virtually absolute.

Part V

CEOs

How the chief executives of public corporations are controlled by outside directors; how they are fairly compensated; how their compensation is linked to performance; how they perform.

Chapter 17

In Public Corporations the CEO Is Controlled by Independent Directors

When you look at it, anybody who runs a company, it's kind of like their own fiefdom. The other management people serve at the pleasure of the chairman, and the board of directors pretty well serves at the pleasure of the chairman. So who really watches the chairman?
— T. Boone Pickens, chairman and CEO of Mesa[1]

A board of directors may remove any officer at any time with or without cause.
— American Bar Association, *Model Business Corporation Act*[2]

The CEO, we've established, controls management, and management controls the corporation. So who really controls the CEO?

The answer, at law and in fact, is the board of directors. Although the board of a public corporation is not able to govern it (as we found in exploring the myth about the owners of a corporation electing its directors), it *is* able to control the CEO. It controls the CEO by removing the CEO from office. But not all members of the board can be counted on to participate in this function. Inside directors, as we know, report to the CEO and therefore can themselves be removed by the CEO. They can't be counted on because they're dependent on the CEO for their position and paycheck. But outside directors, who in most truly public corporations represent a majority of the board, are by definition *independent*. Thus we may say that in public corporations the CEO is controlled by independent directors.

Independence is usually defined as not working for the corporation (except in the capacity of outside director) and sometimes also, to cover retirees, as *never* having worked for the corporation. Ultimately, however, it's not what the directors don't do or didn't do that determines independence but how they think. Independence is a frame of mind, like loyalty or allegiance. Let's take a closer look.

Suppose you're selecting outside directors from scratch. We'll say that you're the new CEO of a private corporation controlled by your family. The business was started by your father, and there are five directors including your father, your mother, and yourself. But now your parents are ready to pass the torch to a new generation and retire from active management, and you (the oldest in that generation) want to grow the business by acquiring other corporations after raising the money (and registering the stock) for these acquisitions by going public.

To make sure your public investors will be satisfied that the corporation is well managed, you recommend that the board modify the bylaws so as to increase the number of directors to 15 and appoint three members of your new management team to sit on it. Counting yourself and your parents, that makes 6 inside directors. That done, your next task is to invite nine outsiders to serve on the board. Whom will you invite?

You'd do well to invite wisely since those nine directors could band together someday and fire you! Even if you and the corporation enter into a contract approved by the board appointing you as CEO until death do you part, the board can still fire you. Breach of contract it may be—in which case the corporation, not the directors, will be liable to you for damages—but since the directors are legally responsible for directing the corporation, the law gives them the power to change officers anytime they think that's necessary.

With this possibility (however remote) in mind, very carefully you invite

1. The owner of the company that supplies you with your principal raw material. He has your best interests at heart, since they're close to his own best interests. He wants your corporation to grow and prosper, and he has quoted you the lowest prices in the market ever since you picked his company to replace your father's supplier.

2. The president of the insurance firm that sold you your corporation's group health policy. He now wants to set up and manage a 401(k) pension plan for you, but you told him that you had to get this public offering out of the way first.

3. A fellow director on the board of another company run by somebody you went to school with. This woman is a very successful executive search consultant who holds her own with dignity and grace, as the only female director of that company.

4. Your classmate, the CEO of that company, who took it public a year or so before he invited you to join his board. Profited very handsomely, too—could probably give you a few pointers.

5. A member of the admissions committee of your country club. Since you became the committee chairman, you've gotten to know him quite well. He recently sold his investment advisory business and is now retired. Well known in the community and always soft-spoken and cordial.

6. A vice president of the largest bank in the state. Not your corporation's bank, but you never know, and besides, a little financial expertise never hurts. He didn't leap at the idea when you mentioned it the last time you teed off together, but he didn't turn you down, either.

7. The dean of the business school at the university you attended. He serves on a half-dozen or so boards and would be a good source of information about the business community and the economy in general.

8. An executive of the local power company whom your father added to the board a number of years ago.

9. Either the former chief operating officer of the corporation under your father, who became a director while he was COO and stayed on after he retired, or the local chapter head of United Way, if he has time, or the independent investor who helped your father start the business and is still a substantial stockholder. You're leaning toward the former COO, since he's already a director and a very loyal person.

If these people join your board, they will pretty much match the profile of outside directors of the major industrial corporations in the United States.[3] How many of them will have a truly independent frame of mind?

Ask the question a different way: Who's likely to give you trouble if things don't go as well as you expect? The people who do business with your company? Not if they don't want to risk losing that business. The director you've sat with on another board? She never made any waves there. Your old friend, the CEO of that company? He values director loyalty as much as anyone. Personal friends and golfing partners? You don't think that's very likely. Professional directors like the business school dean? That isn't how he got on all those boards. The two directors appointed by your father? Not while your father's around, and besides, they've always been in your camp.

The selection of outside directors, said Edward Herman in the Twentieth Century Fund study *Corporate Control, Corporate Power*, reflects "the interest of the power core of the corporations in establishing and consolidating their control—which calls for outside directors who are *not* very independent of the company, its dominant personalities, and its lines of influence."[4]

But most CEOs of public corporations don't start from scratch when they take office. They've got a board, one that was already constituted before they were appointed. One, indeed, that legally appointed them CEO. There's the rub.

On Sunday, November 1, 1992, an article by Susan Antilla in the *New York Times* observed that the stock of General Motors had rallied on rumors that Robert Stempel was on his way out.[5] GM had lost billions in the two years since Stempel had become CEO, and Wall Street was clearly out for blood. The weeklong rally, which added almost 18% to the price of the stock, peaked when the board that had appointed Stempel belatedly decided that what GM needed was a surgeon, not a general practitioner, and fired the GP. The rally then faltered as Wall Street took stock of GM's prospects regardless of who was CEO and lost some of its cockiness. Still, at the end of the second week (when the article was published), the stock was almost 6% ahead of where it had been at the start of the rally.

The lead role of Brutus in this performance of *Julius Caesar* was played by outside director John Smale, retired CEO of Procter & Gamble.[6] Most outside directors of public corporations are active executives of other corporations. Corporate Caesar should beware of *retired* executives and particularly *retired CEOs* with a hefty pension and no day job to worry about—and nothing to lose but their reputation.

(You just changed your mind and decided to invite the United Way chapter head to join your board instead of your father's now-retired COO.)

But even retired CEOs don't act on their own. As the stock rally indicated, Wall Street was behind the move, especially money managers of institutional investors like index funds that would rather fight than switch investments. The winter of 1992–1993 they were fighting mad and talking tough.

Antilla's article, after disposing of Stempel, named five other blue-chip investments that money managers said would benefit from a 5% to 20% rally if the CEO departed: American Express, IBM, ITT, Kodak, and Westinghouse.

In January 1993, less than three months later, John Akers was forced out at IBM, Paul Lego at Westinghouse, and James Robinson III at American Express. Lead roles were performed, respectively, by outside directors James Burke, retired CEO of Johnson & Johnson, Rene McPherson, retired CEO of Dana Corporation, and Rawleigh Warner, retired CEO of Mobil.

Some months later Kodak's board, led by outside directors John Phelan, Jr., former CEO of the New York Stock Exchange, and Roberto Goizueta, current CEO of Coca-Cola, dismissed Kay Whitmore.

In all four cases the market staged a *CEO rally* as predicted. (Similar rallies have been staged in recent years to celebrate the departure of CEOs from companies such as Bausch & Lomb, Allied Signal, Tenneco, and Goodyear.)[7] Wall Street was happy. The only disappointment was ITT. Rand Araskog retained control of his outside directors and his job as CEO.

Retaining control of the outside directors is key, but new CEOs have to have the political skill and will to *gain* control before they can retain it. The first step is to get their own directors on the board. Given a little time, most CEOs manage to do just that. Although many boards of public corporations have their own nominating committees for selecting new directors, Korn/Ferry concluded from its 1992 board survey that 9 out of 10 corporations still find board members through the recommendation of their chairperson. The chairperson, of course, is almost always the CEO.

When the CEO chairs the board of directors, said a former CEO and chairman quoted in William Bowen's book on directors, what you've got is "a dictatorship. It may be benign and it may even be enlightened, but it is nonetheless a dictatorship."[8]

Which brings us back to where we ended the last chapter and began this one: Public corporations are run by their CEO as a dictatorship, and when the dictatorship is neither benign nor enlightened, the remedy is the corporate equivalent of assassination—firing the CEO. But the remedy is administered only rarely because it's so extreme, particularly in the eyes of those who must apply it, active CEOs and executives of other corporations (for the most part) who have been invited onto the board as guests, often by the very CEO whose head is being demanded. (The spate of corporate executions in late 1992 and early 1993 may be collectively thought of as that oxymoron, the exception that proves the rule, the rule being that CEOs are fired—but only in exceptional circumstances.) Is firing the only remedy available to directors?

Well, most boards also have a compensation committee, which determines what the CEO is paid. Does the power of the purse offset the power of the dictator?

Not according to Graef Crystal, former compensation consultant, publisher of a newsletter on executive compensation and author of *In Search of Excess: The Overcompensation of American Executives*. Directors on the compensation committee tend not to be very knowledgeable about compensation matters and rarely invest the time and effort to become knowledgeable. Why? According to Crystal, serving on this committee is

considered to be "the pits" by many outside directors. In most companies, there is a sort of hierarchy of committee service, and at the top is the executive committee, followed by the audit committee. At or close to the bottom is the compensation committee.[9]

Not having developed their own expertise in compensation matters, directors on the committee have little option but to react to the compensation plan proposed by the CEO, which is typically prepared and presented by an outside consultant of the CEO's own selection. Under these circumstances, it is pretty much a foregone conclusion that the board will accept the CEO's (consultant's) recommendations. In the boardrooms of U.S. corporations, says Crystal,

it is considered well-nigh traitorous to buck the CEO. If things get bad enough, you can fire the CEO. But until you do, you'd better support him. Indeed, about the only time I have seen a board attack a CEO on his pay has been when it has already decided to get rid of him.[10]

The power of the purse, in other words, is invoked only after the assassination plan has been approved, when it is superfluous. It's a myth that CEOs of public corporations are controlled by (outside) independent directors. The CEO is essentially a dictator, and **directors are rarely independent and rarely invoke their only control—dismissal**. At best, outside directors serve (in Herman's words) as "the focal point of constraints on management."[11] The *sources* of those constraints are the corporation's institutional investors.

CEOs don't have to worry about a Brutus among the outside directors once they have won over their institutional investors. How do they do that? For years

Campbell Soup, which the *New York Times* called a "once-dozing giant," suffered from disappointing sales and taking its preeminence in the soup business
for granted. Then, in September 1996, David Johnson, Campbell's CEO, assem-
bled 90 stock analysts at a meeting in Manhattan and announced a $160 million
restructuring plan, a 30% increase in advertising expenditures, a $210 million
acquisition of a German soup company, and a $2.5 billion stock repurchase
plan. The stock price immediately rose 6.5% to a record high. The restructuring
plan included downsizing of Campbell's headquarters staff by over 10%. Wall
Street likes the taste of downsizings with their soupçon of lower costs in the
future, but the icing on the cake may well have been the stock repurchase plan.
Stock repurchasing exerts an immediate, direct, upward pressure on the stock
price.

"The company has historically been conservative," said one of the analysts,
"and the repurchase plan represents a change in mentality. It's large, since most
food companies normally buy back 3 to 5% of their shares outstanding." Campbell's $2.5 billion represented 15% of shares outstanding. "Unlike mortals,"
Johnson told the analysts, "this company can live forever."[12]

Johnson and CEOs like him are worth a lot of money to the corporation and
its shareholders. If they are paid a lot of money, they're paid only what they're
worth.

Chapter 18

CEOs Are Paid What They're Worth

We're overpaying him, but he's worth it.

—Samuel Goldwyn[1]

The only way to keep score in business is to add up how much money you make.

—Harry B. Helmsley[2]

We have observed that while boards of directors generally accept what CEOs propose to pay themselves without engaging in any meaningful negotiations over that pay, CEOs are worth a lot of money. We just can't claim, in the absence of meaningful negotiations (or a public auction of CEOs), that their worth is objectively determined by the give and take of supply and demand, the Scylla and Charybdis of any free market. We have to take it on faith that CEOs are paid what they're worth.

Still, the proposition might warrant a closer look. Perhaps we can establish a baseline.

Under the military pay scale revised by Congress as of January 1, 1992, the chairman of the Joint Chiefs of Staff, grade O-10, earned $8,733 a month, part of which reflects the many years of hard work and loyal service it takes to achieve that position. Privates and seamen, grade E-2 (E-1s are recruits in boot camp), earned $873 a month.[3] In other words, ignoring perks like a private mess, personal aides, and government airplanes, the top military honcho in the United States gets paid exactly 10 times as much as the lowest-paid full-time workers.

In the early 1990s, that honcho was Colin Powell.

Ordered by his commander-in-chief to plan and execute Desert Shield and then Desert Storm to counter Iraq's invasion of Kuwait, General Powell, most Americans would agree, did a very creditable job. That is, General Powell together with all his workers, noncommissioned officers, and officers from E-2s right on up to General Norman Schwarzkopf did a very creditable job.

Better, it seems, than IBM was doing in those years. From the late 1980s to 1993, sales of mainframe computers, the product line that made IBM the richest corporation in the world in terms of market capitalization (the aggregate price of all its shares of stock), dropped by nearly 50%. The price of its shares—and its market cap—fell by 75%. In 1993 IBM slashed its dividend and announced the first involuntary layoffs in its 90-year history, reversing a lifetime employment policy. In January of that year, also for the first time, it fired its CEO, John Akers.[4]

The previous year (1992) IBM paid Akers $1.3 million in salary and bonus, or $108,333 a month.[5] That's 12 times what the U.S. government paid General Powell. Of course, one is in business and the other in the military, and few taxpayers believe that the pay scales should be equal. But if you're inclined to assume that the justification for the inequality is the greater job security in the military, you might recall that after the armed forces became all-volunteer in the 1970s, they instituted a standard of "perform or get out"—a standard IBM did not adopt for another two decades.

Now, do you think that IBM's lowest-paid full-time workers (not trainees) made one-tenth of what their CEO did, ignoring perks like a private dining room, personal assistants, and company airplanes—like E-2s in the armed forces? That IBM paid every worker at least $10,833 a month? How about one-*one-hundredth*—$1,083 a month—approximately one and a half times the minimum wage?

Longtime compensation expert Graef Crystal compares CEO compensation to average wages rather than to what the lowest-paid worker makes. He also includes noncash compensation such as stock options that most CEOs (but not many workers) get. Crystal wrote in 1991 that "a typical CEO today earns pay that is around 120 times that of an average manufacturing worker and about 150 times that of the average worker in both manufacturing and service industries."[6]

By comparison, British CEOs received about 35 times what their average workers made. In Japan the ratio was less than 20.

The Japanese, as we know, are those people we're having trade problems with. We buy too much of what they make because we like it and the price is right, and they buy too little of what we make. But we pay our CEOs a lot more than they pay their CEOs relative to what our workers and their workers are paid.

And Colin Powell? The chairman of the Joint Chiefs of Staff made just a little over *six* times the average pay of the enlisted men and women (excluding recruits) on active duty in the U.S. armed forces.

Do these comparisons tell us anything about our concepts of personal worth? How can we get a handle on the value of a CEO to a corporation?

Let's make you a diligent new outside director of an up-and-coming computer company that the financial press is calling the next IBM who has agreed to serve on the compensation committee. The CEO, who appointed you on the recommendation of one of your very best clients, made it clear to you that everyone in the company is paid what she or he is worth, no more, no less, no exceptions. Compensation not being one of your areas of expertise, you decide to do some homework, especially since the CEO's compensation for the upcoming fiscal year is the first item on the agenda of your first committee meeting.

For background you look at *Business Week*'s annual surveys of CEO compensation in major public corporations. In 1990, the CEOs of these corporations received compensation averaging almost $2 million, which *Business Week* noted was 40 times what an engineer in these corporations made (a little less than $50,000) and 85 times what the average worker was paid ($23,000).[7] The comparisons for 1960, 1970, 1980, and 1990 are shown below.

CEO Pay as a Multiple of the Pay

in . . .	1960	1970	1980	1990
of . . .				
Engineers	19	37	22	40
Workers	41	79	42	85

CEO compensation and the ratios to engineer and worker compensation jumped up after 1990, but the 1990 ratios were pretty close to what they were in 1970; so you figure 1990 is a sound base to work with.

On the basis of information you've dug up you estimate that approximately 60% of the average 1990 CEO compensation of $2 million, or $1.2 million, represents cash payments—salary and bonus—with the balance represented by stock rights and options. You further estimate that about two-thirds of the cash payments, or $800,000, is regular salary, and the remaining $400,000 is a year-end performance bonus. In terms of just salary, then, CEOs of major public corporations earn roughly 35 times what an average employee makes ($800,000 divided by $23,000)—or at any rate did in 1990, the year you're using as a reference. Does the 35:1 ratio make sense for an up-and-coming corporation like the one you're now a director of?

The average employee in the corporation must be doing something right, or the corporation wouldn't be considered up-and-coming. So, you ask yourself, what does it mean to be 35 times more valuable—or at least valued—than an average worker doing a competent job? Not 5 times as much. Not 10 or even 20 times as much—*35 times*.

In large corporations a CEO typically makes at least twice as much as the next-highest-paid executive. (In smaller corporations it's less, but smaller companies may have to be more cost conscious than the IBMs of the world to survive.) This salary difference suggests that when a CEO retires and is replaced by the number-two executive, the latter becomes twice as valuable to the corporation and its shareholders the instant he or she is promoted to CEO. Does *that* make sense?

It may be that CEOs of certain other companies will talk to the chief executive officer but not to the chief operating officer or anyone else. So in opening doors and other ways, the CEO *is* more valuable because the power and prestige and authority of that position make the occupant—any occupant—more valuable. Whether or not the *person* just promoted to that position is smarter or more skillful than the day before, the opportunities and responsibilities are greater. This, perhaps, is the justification for doubling the CEO's pay, although one may be excused for suspecting that the doubling is also a reward for having won the grueling marathon (course length: 26+ years) to the top.

But is the average CEO of a public company worth 35 times more than the average worker?

In fact, with bonuses and stock options and the like included, the ratio in 1990 was 85 times more than the average worker, not 35 times. Paul Krugman wrote in 1994 that the widening gap in income distribution is "one of the two central facts about the U.S. economy over the past twenty years."[8] (The other is the slowdown in productivity growth.) In 1995, according to the *New York Times*—five years after the *Business Week* survey we were using—CEOs of the 500 largest U.S. corporations averaged *$4 million* in total compensation, almost *200 times* as much as the average worker.[9] Are CEOs getting better? (Are their workers getting worse?) Are they in short supply and great demand? (Consider all the managers who have been let go in the 1990s as corporations downsized.) Have their salaries been ratcheted up by global competition when global salaries haven't?

How, you wonder, do the directors of other corporations rationalize their CEO's compensation?

According to your calculations, CEO salaries average $800,000 in salary before bonus, but what if your CEO is earning only $600,000? Since no corporation you've ever dealt with has a policy of paying *below* average, you'd certainly be willing to go along with a $200,000 raise.

But now suppose that your CEO earns not $600,000 but $1 million. Are you going to suggest a $200,000 *reduction*? You never heard of that being done either, although it might make sense to reduce the *increases* your CEO receives in the future. But you could also rationalize a recommendation of no reduction of any kind on the grounds that the company is a top performer and should pay top salaries—at least to top management. You've read that one corporation out of three has a policy of aiming for the 75th percentile, meaning it sets executive salaries to exceed those of 75% of the corporations it compares itself to. That seems like a sound policy for the next IBM.

Thus, says Graef Crystal, is CEO compensation determined. Surveys calculate average CEO compensation, with some corporations necessarily below the average and some above. The corporations below the average bring their compensation up to average, but the ones above the average don't reduce their compensation. So the next year the average increases.

Crystal's term for the perennial increase is *survey ratcheting*.[10] CEO compensation has a lot to do with survey ratcheting—and keeping score—but not much to do with worth.

It's a myth that CEOs are paid what they're worth. Unconstrained by supply and demand, **CEO pay has little or nothing to do with worth**. "No one has been able to measure the value of a chief executive," says management expert Nancy Rose.[11]

The Internal Revenue Code of the United States has long allowed a deduction from business income for "all the ordinary and necessary expenses paid or incurred during the taxable year in carrying on any trade or business, including . . . a reasonable allowance for salaries or other compensation for personal services actually rendered."[12] But as regards what a public corporation pays its CEO and deducts from taxable income, it's as if none of the statutory conditions existed. No matter how lofty, CEO compensation is accepted by tax people as ordinary, necessary, and reasonable.

But then in 1993 Congress enacted a specific limit on the amount of executive compensation that will be allowed as a tax deduction. Compensation in excess of $1 million a year—approximately 40 times what the average worker made when the law was passed—is no longer deductible unless

- it is paid solely for attaining performance goals established by a committee of two or more outside directors,
- those directors certify that the goals have been met, and
- both the compensation and the goals have been approved by the shareholders.

What is meant by *performance goals*? As far as the law is concerned, they are whatever the corporation's committee of outside directors establishes as performance goals and gets the shareholders to approve—presumably by voting yes or no, since it's unlikely the shareholders will be given any alternatives to choose from.

With "loopholes as big as the Grand Canyon," as one consultant put it, the law affects *how* a CEO is paid, not *how much*.[13] It makes it "a little harder to be a fat cat," said another consultant. "You have to jump through some hurdles. But if you're able to jump, you could still do pretty well."[14]

Stock options, which tie CEO pay to the corporation's stock, have become a greater part of CEO compensation since the law was passed. But few stock options are indexed to general stock prices. Thus, in a bull market such as the one that began in the early 1980s and was still going strong in the mid-1990s, stock options increase in value as the price of the corporation's stock increases even though its stock price rises no faster than—and perhaps not as fast as— the stock market generally. "There are so many factors that go into a big corporation's performance, other than what the CEO does," says Rose. "But if you tie [the CEO's] pay to the stock and stock prices go up, then [the CEO] gets the credit."[15]

Not that you're likely to hear institutional investors or anyone else on Wall Street object. As they see it, a higher stock price *is* corporate performance. Stock options tie CEO compensation to their definition of performance.

Chapter 19

CEO Compensation Is Linked to Corporate Performance

Stock option plans reward the executive for doing the wrong thing. . . . It is encouragement to loot the corporation.

—Peter F. Drucker[1]

As salaries [and stock options] climb into [the millions of dollars], there is simply too much at stake for any executive turtle to stick his neck out of the shell. Very, very few in aerospace or any other industry are concerned about the future beyond the next quarterly stockholders' report.

—Ben R. Rich, head of Lockheed's Skunk Works[2]

Outside directors, those Horatios at the bridge keeping CEOs from absolute power and uncounted wealth, aren't terribly good at their job. Witness this description of the chairman of a corporate compensation committee by one of his fellow directors: "His ability to defend sizable increases for the top officers was totally unconnected with how well or how badly the company was doing at any given time."[3]

But times are said to be changing. Up until the early 1980s, according to Richard Koppes of Calpers (California Public Employees Retirement System), management held most of the power that rightfully belonged to the shareholders and their legal representatives, the directors. But "as corporate governance activism grew, share owners, from the short-term Wall Street traders to the long-term investors like Calpers, became increasingly influential, and managers began to heed their share owners' bidding."[4]

The best way to get managers and particularly CEOs to heed their share owners' bidding is to make them share owners themselves so that they will think like share owners while they're managing the corporation and manage it in the share owners' interests, which is now the same as their own interests. To this end the board of directors awards them stock and stock rights and sometimes even requires them to purchase stock. And the board grants them options to purchase stock at a stipulated price sometime in the future.

Although the stock option is the most flexible and most favored device for transforming managers into shareholders, all of these devices in one way or another link CEO compensation to corporate performance. How effective are they?

If you were to examine the annual *Business Week* surveys of what major corporations pay their CEO, you would have to conclude that the link is tenuous at best. Take the 1992 survey.[5] It compares the shareholders' return on investment (ROI) in terms of dividends and increased market price of their shares from 1990 through 1992 to what the CEO received in salary, bonus, and long-term compensation (stock options and rights) over the same three years. The results are very uneven.

At one extreme are the shareholders of Berkshire Hathaway, who earned a return of 35%, while CEO Warren Buffet was paid $300,000. At the other extreme are the shareholders of H. J. Heinz, who also earned a return of 35%, while CEO Anthony O'Reilly was paid $115,269,000—almost 400 times what Warren Buffett got. Virtually all the difference is attributable to stock options— which Buffett, who is also the major shareholder of Berkshire Hathaway (and, some believe, primus inter pares among steers leading the stock market), reportedly doesn't believe in.

The *Business Week* surveys also compare the corporation's ROI—corporate net income divided by shareholder equity—to CEO compensation. In the 1992 survey, one of the five executives whose corporation did the best relative to his pay was Martin Emmett, CEO of Tambrands. His total compensation from 1990 to 1992 totalled $7,331,000 of which more than $5,000,000 was earned through the exercise of stock options. Over the same three years, Tambrands' ROI averaged nearly 50% a year. According to *Business Week*'s algorithm for relating corporate ROI to CEO pay, Tambrands came out fifth highest among the 365 major corporations surveyed.

Business Week published the survey in its April 26, 1993, issue. Five weeks later the board of directors of Tambrands fired Martin Emmett. What did the directors know that the *Business Week* surveyors and editors didn't?

An article in the *Wall Street Journal* on August 23, 1993, provides some insights. The story begins in 1988 when outside director Robert Williams, a venture capitalist and the grandson of one of Tambrands' founders as well as a major shareholder of the company, grew "restless with Tambrands' sluggish stock, which languished in the $29 range." Enter Martin Emmett, former president of Standard Brands and senior executive vice president of Nabisco, who was being promoted by a consulting firm named Personal Corp. of America. In

April 1989, largely at director Williams's behest, Tambrands' board named Emmett CEO.

Emmett went right to work. He sold off some peripheral businesses that Williams didn't like, cut the workforce by 31%, and bought up Tambrands shares in the market to increase the price of the stock. In March 1991, two years after he became CEO, he told stock analysts that Tambrands' profits would increase 15% a year for the next five years.

The news pleased Wall Street. By 1992, the stock had doubled and was selling above $60 a share.

Emmett didn't stop there. Seeking to capitalize on the brand loyalty of Tambrands' customers, he raised the price of the company's main product by more than half. Customers fled to other brands, sales fell, and Tambrands' share of the market dropped below 50% for the first time in years. In March 1993, when Emmett told analysts that he now had reservations about achieving the previously announced 15% annual profit increase, the stock price dropped from $63 to $56.

When Tambrands' earnings report for the first quarter of 1993 revealed that Emmett had cut marketing expenditures in that quarter by almost 20%, the stock price ducked below $40.

In the second quarter, sales fell 12% and earnings 41%. But by then Emmett was gone, dismissed by the same directors who had delivered the corporation into his hands four years earlier. He left a wealthy man, however, largely because of the stock options he exercised in 1992 before the stock market woke up to the damage he had inflicted on the corporation. Who goofed?

Not Personnel Corp. of America, the consultants who had backed Emmett to become CEO in the first place. These people "were very capable and energetic advocates" on Emmett's behalf, according to the consultant hired by Tambrands' compensation committee. A former Tambrands director said that Emmett's consultants "did everything in their power to get Martin the most lucrative compensation scheme they could." But the Tambrands directors weren't exactly innocent bystanders. In 1990, a year into Emmett's reign, Personnel Corp. recommended that the directors of Tambrands approve a 54% increase in their annual retainers and grant themselves annual stock options. (A well-compensated and politically savvy CEO always leaves something on the table for the directors.) The recommendations were duly adopted.[6]

If the directors let themselves be seduced by Emmett, the stock analysts were hardly more virtuous. But the real villain may have been Wall Street's chosen instrument for linking CEO compensation to corporate performance: the stock option itself.

Assuming for the nonce that a corporation's performance is synonymous with the performance of its stock price, the *short-term* link between Emmett's earnings and Tambrands' performance was positive. Emmett and any shareholders who followed his example by selling their stock during the early run-up in its price profited very well. But the corporation and the shareholders who held on to their stock profited very little relative to the market as a whole. The *long-term* link between Emmett's earnings and corporate performance was minimal.

That's one problem with stock options. Because executives "usually exercise the option and sell the shares immediately, for a tidy profit," according to Louis Rorimer, a lawyer who specializes in executive compensation, there is little incentive to create a long-term increase even in the share price.[7] CEOs don't stay shareholders that long. Steve Huddart and Mark Lang made a study of stock option plans and found that "90% of the stock acquired by exercising [stock options] was sold immediately."[8] Some CEOs sell even before exercising by shorting the stock ahead of exercise time and then, after exercising, using the optioned stock to cover the short sale. "It is a terribly wrong thing to do," commented another lawyer. "It is like taking your favorite football team and betting against it."[9] Other CEOs short but then don't bother to cover—thus saving themselves the capital gains tax that would be due if they did cover.[10]

CEOs have a number of resources to manage the stock price in the short term. Look what Emmett did when he became CEO. He sold off noncore businesses, laid off almost a third of the workforce, and repurchased Tambrands' shares in the market—all moves that the stock market applauds. And then he told the stock analysts that he would increase profits by 15% a year? Did he increase profits by 15% a year? The all-knowing stock market didn't bother to wait and see. Being efficient, it discounted the future as it heard it from Emmett's lips and proceeded to double the stock price.

That's another problem with stock options. They're linked to stock price performance, not real-world performance for paying customers as measured by profits and earnings per share. Although profits, being profits and not cash flow, can also be managed, especially in the short term, stock prices are more readily influenced than profits by what a CEO does—and says.

One reason may be that Main Street customers aren't as easy to fool as Wall Street analysts. Tambrands' customers weren't. When Emmett raised their prices, they walked, sending Tambrands' market share over the cliff. But the analysts appear not to have figured out what was going on until Emmett told them—after he'd exercised his stock options.

Calpers' Richard Koppes, upset at how some managements have used layoffs to raise stock prices in the near term, asserts that "the balance of power is out of whack, this time having swung too far toward share owners."[11] Who's to blame? Apparently not Calpers or other advocates of shareholder empowerment. The real culprits, he says, are the directors.

That's one interpretation of what happened when CEOs began to heed their share owners' bidding. Another is that CEOs learned that by playing the stock option game they could not only heed their share owners' (and now Congress's) bidding but also become enormously wealthy in a very short time. In this second scenario the directors aren't culprits. They're just no more effectual than they ever were.

Let it be said that you don't have to be a particle physicist to design a stock option that serves long-term as well as short-term goals—or to satisfy the interests of long-term investors like Calpers as well as those of short-term traders. One could, for example, create a 10-year stock option of which one-tenth was exercisable during each of the 10 years (whether or not the holder was still an employee) but not exercisable in any other year. Provided the prices at which the option could be exercised in each year were accurately calculated to reward performance and properly indexed to offset changes in overall market averages, such an option would spread its incentive more or less evenly over the 10-year period. The CEO (or other holder) would profit as much by what the corporation did in the tenth year as in any other year.

Of course, such an option would still reward market performance rather than profit performance, but in the long term, market performance (properly indexed) tends to track profit performance just as in the long run profit performance tends to track fundamental performance—satisfying one's paying customers better than the competition. Even the wiliest CEO can't fool all of Wall Street all of the time—at least not most of the time.

But incentive stock options are generally slanted to the short term. Many have an exercise price at or only slightly above the price of the stock at the time the option is issued. Few are indexed to overall stock market prices. In years when money pouring into equity mutual funds creates a demand for stocks in excess of the supply of new stocks from initial public offerings, the increase in stock prices may be called a bull market rather than inflation (Wall Street being a bear on inflation except in its own lair), but the result is the same: Holders of unindexed stock options can profit just by sitting on their hands. Not much of an incentive to executive action!

It's a myth that CEO pay is linked to corporate performance. The way most public corporations design executive stock options, **the link between CEO pay and corporate performance is tenuous at best**.

Why do corporations issue such options?

We already know the answer: CEOs in public corporations essentially control their own (as well as the other executives') compensation. Why make getting wealthy difficult when you can make it easy?

The same answer explains why public corporations were so opposed to FASB's proposal, announced in the early 1990s, to require the value of stock options to be treated as a P&L expense when they are issued.

Issuing stocks option doesn't require an outlay of cash and, unlike health care coverage for workers after they retire, never will. So why treat it as an expense? Well, stock options have value as compensation to the employees who receive them even if they don't involve any cash outlay. (Could any CEO honestly disagree?) And when the options are exercised, the gain to the holder of the option—the difference between the exercise price and the current stock price—represents a loss of cash to the corporation compared to an arm's-length sale of the same stock. So what FASB proposed that corporations should do (presumably in the interests of accounting conservatism) was charge the discounted present value of that future loss to P&L as compensation expense when the options were issued.

How would corporations go about calculating the present value of the options?

The standard method for calculating the present value of any option is the Black-Scholes model, named after the two finance professors who developed it and published it in the *Journal of Political Economy* in 1973. That was the year the Chicago Board of Options Exchange opened for business. Up until that time, trading in options was negligible. But because of the model, wrote Joel Kurtzman in 1993 in *The Death of Money*, "more money is now spent purchasing stock options than is spent purchasing stocks. The [Chicago Board of Options Exchange] . . . trades twice the dollar volume of what the . . . New York [Stock Exchange] trades each day."[12]

If options traders trading twice the dollar volume of the Big Board can calculate the current value of an option using Black-Scholes (or some variation), so presumably can corporations. Can't they? No, insists the Business Roundtable, an organization representing some 200 CEOs, because there is no known way to price options "with reasonable accuracy."[13] Nor did it stand alone. Other head-in-the-sanders predicted that FASB's proposal would cause the stock market to collapse and keep venture companies from going public. Faced with opposition that the *New York Times* said was "the strongest of any [FASB] proposal, including some that had far greater impact on profit and loss statements [such as] accounting for pensions and for post-retirement health benefits," FASB finally backed down.[14]

In the other FASB proposals, business made the same argument: There was no way to calculate the future costs of pensions and health benefits with reasonable accuracy. But FASB prevailed in those cases, and the *Times'* Floyd Norris wrote that "when corporate boards were finally forced to look at reasonable estimates of the costs, companies began to control those costs."[15]

If corporate boards were finally forced to look at reasonable estimates of the value of stock options that were being deducted from corporate profits, they might begin to control the issuance of stock options. Then CEOs might earn less. This last consequence explains why the opposition to FASB was extra strong: CEOs might earn less.

But would it make a difference in their performance? Labor economist Richard Freeman doesn't think so. "These executives are hard-working, driven guys, and if you give then $1 million instead of $10 million, they are still going to be very motivated."[16]

Chapter 20

CEOs Devote Full Time to Managing Their Corporation

It isn't immediately clear to everyone that CEOs work. Flying off in a sleek jet with an attentive aide to deliver a short talk may sound like work to you, but a cable overhauler could get used to it.

—Alan Farnham, *Fortune* magazine[1]

People who have office jobs, say, at the managerial level—these people mostly are doing what I do when I am shirking work. Eating lunch, talking on the phone, shuffling papers, drinking coffee. I walk around offices and I never see anyone working, I see them chatting.

—Fran Lebowitz, *Mirabella* magazine[2]

Some years ago a Harvard Law School professor by the name of Henry Hart used to devote one class in his course on the federal courts to analyzing how the nine Supreme Court justices spent their time. It took the entire class hour, since Professor Hart examined not just a typical workday but all 24 hours and even parts of hours, seven days a week, 52 weeks a year. At the end of the class, Hart's students understood that there aren't enough hours in the year for the Supreme Court to decide many more than 100 cases, even though the justices devote full time to their jobs.

We need a Professor Hart to tell us what the hard-working, driven, very motivated CEOs of public corporations do during the full time they devote to managing their corporations.

When Harold Geneen ran ITT, managing was the only game in our town. ITT didn't buy businesses to spruce them up and sell them. It wasn't a trader. It may have favored managing by the numbers rather than, say, managing by walking around, as David Packard had done at Hewlett-Packard, but businesses were manageable operations, not cows to milk or dogs to starve. ITT didn't dump them if they didn't become number one or two in their industry within so many years. It bought businesses to *manage* them, and managing them was a full-time job.

Geneen wasn't even a director of any outside businesses. He didn't have time, and neither did any other ITT executives—at least not without his permission.

But CEOs vary widely in personality. Not all may be as interested as Geneen was in managing the business. A wheeler-dealer CEO might be more interested in selling it—and buying another. Take, for example, Donald Kelly.

In November 1993, Kelly was recalling his participation in the $8 billion buyout of Beatrice Foods, which personally netted him $150 million, and 10 other transactions over his 50-year career that each involved a billion dollars or more. "A nostalgic hush fell over the crowded room in U.S. bankruptcy court," wrote Jeff Bailey in the *Wall Street Journal*, as Kelly testified in defense of his $2 million salary as CEO of Envirodyne Industries, a sausage-casings maker, now insolvent, that employed 4,500 people but was one of his smaller buyouts (not even a billion dollars) and, he said, his only failure. The years at Enviro-dyne, Bailey wrote, raised doubts about whether Kelly was able "to manage a stable company, rather than buy and sell assets."

Back in the early 1980s, Kelly was CEO of the old Swift meat-packing com-pany, renamed Esmark, and after selling off half its operations, he was left with nothing to do but manage the other half. "What am I going to do now?" he recalled wondering. "I got kind of bored." But then the fun began again after another corporation made a move to buy Esmark. Kelly sold the remaining half of Esmark to Beatrice, then bought Beatrice. "I guess I'm a dealer, and that's the way it is." Buying or selling—"I don't think there's any difference." But *managing* a sausage-casings business?

During the four years he was CEO, the value of Envirodyne, according to Kelly's own testimony, decreased by 25%, or $200 million. He blamed intense price competition in the casings business—certainly not management or him-self.[3]

"A lot of deals are a substitute for hard day-to-day management of a com-pany," said James O'Toole, former director of the Leadership Institute at the University of Southern California. "When you get to be a CEO, people expect you to make grand moves." So in 1990 AT&T, under Robert Allen, spent $7.5 billion to buy NCR in order to take advantage of the upcoming convergence of communications and computers. If the moves don't work out—and most don't, as we learned in discussing the myth that professional managers can run any business—CEOs who are movers and shakers undo them. After AT&T spent additional billions trying unsuccessfully to manage NCR, Allen announced that AT&T would spin off NCR and also its communications equipment business (including Bell Labs, considered by many to be a *national* resource) to its share-holders and confine itself to long-distance telephoning, eliminating 40,000 jobs in the process. AT&T's stock rose 11% on the announcement. Stock prices usually bounce up when a grand move or unmove is announced because movers and shakers are close to Wall Street's heart. A deal, said O'Toole, "buys you time, makes you look forceful, makes you look like a visionary."[4]

The look may be misleading. Warren Bennis, who writes about leadership, thinks that deals are often a *substitute* for vision. These days, he said in 1995, "no one can clearly articulate a vision, and in lieu of vision they are buying things and selling things."[5] And buying and selling things absorb a lot of money and management attention that might otherwise be invested in researching and developing the new processes and products and services that keep corporations competitive and their customers coming back. A study of over 750 industrial corporations by Michael Hitt from 1985 to 1991, demonstrated that corporations with "an aggressive acquisitions strategy spent less on R&D and produced fewer innovations" than less acquisition-minded companies.[6]

In 1995, when AT&T's grand unmove was announced, Allen received stock options that brought his compensation for the year from $6.7 million up to $16 million.[7] Does compensation have anything to do with grand moves? In a study of more than 100 large mergers from 1989 to 1992, Mathew Hayward and Donald Hambrick took CEO compensation—specifically, the ratio of a CEO's compensation to that of the corporation's second-in-command—as one measure of CEO ego and linked that ego to the price paid to acquire other companies.[8] The higher the ego, they found, the higher the premium paid over the market price of the acquired company. For example, each highly favorable article about the CEO in the national press (another measure of ego) added 5.4% to the premium. So compensation (how they keep score) does have something to do with the moves that CEOs make by fueling the egos that prompt the moves.

Perks can also play a part in corporate moves, perks like proximity of the executive suite to the executive mansion. After he became CEO of London Fog, Arnold Cohen, who lived in Westport, Connecticut, moved the corporate headquarters from Eldersburg, Maryland, to Darien, Connecticut, in order (he said) to be near the fashion industry in New York. The next year a new CEO moved it back to Eldersburg. Dana Mead, who lived in Greenwich, Connecticut, moved International Paper's headquarters from New York City to the suburbs close to Greenwich. When he became CEO of Tenneco, he moved Tenneco's headquarters from Houston to Greenwich itself (not just close to). Greenwich, said Mead, "is as close as you can get to New York and still be in Connecticut."

Albert Dunlap moved Scott Paper Company from Philadelphia to Boca Raton, Florida, a week after he bought a $2 million home in Boca Raton. His decision "was done solely on economics," Dunlap said. (Four months later he sold Scott to Kimberly-Clark in Dallas.) W. R. Grace moved from New York to Boca Raton after making what the company said was "an extensive three-year study of 100 cities on the Eastern Seaboard." The business justification for corporate moves has "always been the big joke in the real estate business," said one executive in that business. Serious realtors "find out where the chairman lives and show him a building nearby."

More and more CEOs seem to have homes in Boca Raton or nearby where you can play golf all year long and swim in the ocean. But corporate relocations cost a lot of money—money that belongs to the shareholders, according to Anne Hansen of the Council of Institutional Investors.[9]

If shareholders (as they believe) pay for a corporate relocation with their money, all the workers the corporation leaves behind pay with their jobs.

Nor is it just shareholders and workers who pay for a CEO's fancy or personal aggrandizement. Customers pay, too.

Deal-specialist Martin Wygod built Medco Containment Services from a private $20 million mail-order drug company into a public $2 billion discount-drug powerhouse that supplied drugs at reduced prices to large health plans run by the likes of GE, GM, and Calpers.[10] The key to Medco's success was its ability, as vendor to health plans covering some 30 million people, to negotiate favorable prices from the pharmaceutical companies from which it bought the drugs it sold to the health plans. Medco could demand favorable prices because the pharmaceutical companies knew that it could always drop a drug from its inventory or, if an alternative existed, seek to obtain a better price from the alternative drug's manufacturer.

And then Wygod sold Medco to Merck, the country's largest pharmaceutical company and one of Medco's suppliers, in a transaction that made him Merck's largest shareholder. (It also made him the odds-on favorite to become Merck's next CEO. When the odds makers were proved wrong and he didn't get the nod, he quit Merck—and Medco—in search of another deal.) But merging Medco into Merck ended Medco's independence and compromised its ability to negotiate favorable discounts from Merck's competitors, the other pharmaceutical companies that supplied Medco. Ultimately, the vast wealth that came to Wygod while he was the CEO (and principal mover and shaker) of Medco was paid for in some part by the health plans Medco serviced and the millions of people participating in them.

In 1985 financier Carl Icahn gained control of Howard Hughes's old airline, TWA, after a long battle with another financier, Frank Lorenzo.[11] In 1988 Icahn took TWA private in a buyout of public shareholders that enabled him to recover most of his original investment in one fell swoop while saddling TWA with the debt incurred to pay for the transaction. Then Icahn had TWA cut costs and sell some of its best transatlantic routes to pay the debt and, when these measures didn't generate enough cash, file for bankruptcy protection from its creditors. Eventually, after Icahn had taken off, TWA emerged from bankruptcy, but it had fewer employees, fewer routes, fewer customers, and fewer resources to fall back on than it had before Icahn.

The takeover of Continental Air by Lorenzo's company, Texas Air, followed somewhat the same pattern—Continental went into bankruptcy but continued flying and eventually outlasted Lorenzo. But another subsidiary of Texas Air, the venerable Eastern Airlines, for years run by World War I ace (and World War II hero) Eddie Rickenbacker, didn't. While Lorenzo was still in charge, Eastern went into bankruptcy—and was liquidated.

Although Geneen acquired other companies to manage them, his successor, Rank Araskog, quickly got rid of many of Geneen's troublesome acquisitions and finally sold the core itself, the foreign telephone manufacturing companies that ITT acquired in the 1920s when antitrust regulators forced AT&T to get rid of them. (According to one study, troublesome acquisitions are four times more likely to be dumped in the year after a new CEO takes over than at any other time.) But Araskog, like Geneen, steadfastly refused shareholder demands to split the conglomerate into separate parts so that Wall Street could properly value them, denouncing those urging such action as profiteers seeking to tear down the house that Geneen built.

Steadfastly, that is, until Araskog was well into the corporate retirement zone. When he was 63, two years from normal retirement age, he announced that ITT would split itself into three separate corporations through spinoffs. (According to another study, two-thirds of corporate spinoffs are initiated by CEOs age 58 or older.)[12] Araskog himself would remain CEO of the corporation owning Sheraton, Caesar's World, and Madison Square Garden. "I expect," said Araskog, "that I could be going on at ITT with the approval of the board as long as I wanted to and thought I could do a good job."[13]

The CEO's age may have something to do not only with spinoffs of subsidiary businesses but also with disposing of the whole corporation, particularly in banking where government regulations make takeovers almost impossible without the CEO's consent. "A company with a strong chairman approaching retirement age, without clearly visible succession, potentially can be a candidate for a merger or sale," according to John Leonard, a banking analyst. James Marx, editor of the newsletter *Bank Mergers & Acquisitions*, arrived at a similar conclusion. "A lot of deals . . . are being done," he said, "because managers wish to cash out before retiring."[14]

What do CEOs do? Basically, whatever they want. Whatever they want may include performing the task for which they are so handsomely rewarded—preserving and adding value to the corporate resources that have been entrusted to them—but it may include a lot of other things, too, like doing deals, undoing them, and moving the corporation nearer home. And it may include activities essentially unrelated to the real function of the corporation—satisfying the needs of paying customers—like serving on other boards of directors (and pocketing the fees), sponsoring United Way fund drives (perhaps even volunteering the services of corporate employees to solicit contributions from other corporate employees), or contributing corporate funds to the arts. Or traveling to a celebrity event, as 300-plus CEOs did one weekend in August 1989 (many by corporate jet) when Malcolm Forbes of *Forbes* magazine threw a birthday party for Forbes (or *Forbes*) in Tangier, which is in Africa. (Forbes' and *Forbes*'

offices being located in New York.) "Nobody knows," wrote Nicholas von
Hoffman in *Capitalist Fools*,

how much executives overpay for a host/salesman's product or service after a thorough
wining and dining. Doubtless the cost is great, but no greater than the damage done by
stealing the time, the attention and the energy executives should be applying to their
work.[15]

It's a myth that CEOs devote full time to managing their corporation. **CEOs
pursue their own interests**, which may (in well-managed companies) or may
not serve the best interests of the corporation and its stockholders but almost
always contribute to their own personal aggrandizement.

You've got a lot of options once you've made it to the top of the corporate
food chain. And a lot of responsibilities, starting with preservation of the value
of the corporation and the resources it requires to satisfy the needs of paying
customers. The most important of those resources, 9 out of 10 senior executives
told the Towers Perrin consulting firm, is the corporation's workforce—our next
subject.

Part VI

Workers

How workers are motivated by public corporations, although down-sizing and layoffs are required by global competition and the business cycle; how they benefit from increased productivity.

Chapter 21

Public Corporations Are Proficient at Motivating Their Workers

Those guys [at Lockheed's Skunk Works], from engineers to shop workers, stayed focused. They worried about being on time, getting it right, and staying on budget. You just didn't find that kind of attitude anywhere else at Lockheed or any other company in the industry.

—Roy Anderson, CEO of Lockheed[1]

Management is nothing more than motivating other people.

—Lee Iacocca, CEO of Chrysler[2]

The most important resources a corporation has, 9 out of 10 senior executives told Towers Perrin, are its workers. But in terms of the issues they identified as most critical, worker performance and investment in worker performance both ranked (with marketing) well below customer satisfaction, financial performance, competitiveness, and quality of products and services. "They almost universally said people are the most important thing," said Patricia Milligan, a managing principal, but when she asked them how their corporate planning dealt with people, "they looked at me like I was from another planet."[3]

"Employers don't want employees," said Carol Kleiman, author of *The Career Coach*. "They resent paying them."[4] If they had their druthers, they'd have machines they don't have to pay or (next best) contingent workers they don't have to give benefits to and can get rid of without any fuss. Which is why Manpower Inc., the temporary-help provider, is the largest employer in the country.

But as line managers are more apt to appreciate, satisfying customers (and fulfilling the senior executives' other priorities) ultimately depends on the corporation's workers and how they perform. Contingent workers, unless they're former employees, don't have the knowledge. How permanent workers perform, in turn, depends on such factors as training, productivity, and above all, motivation. Even corporations averse to investing in training and productivity can get a lot out of their workers by motivating them. Motivated workers, said the CEO of Harman International Industries, "can do things that will blow your mind."[5]

Having studied the problem for decades, public corporations are proficient at motivating their workers. Basically, they use carrots like salary or wages and benefits and sometimes a year-end bonus geared to results, and they use sticks like threatening to fire employees who don't perform satisfactorily. Compensation and job security can motivate people. Carrots and sticks get results.

More or less. Of nearly 900 companies surveyed by the Wyatt Company in 1992, 10% were "satisfied" with their programs for rewarding performance and 60% were "somewhat satisfied"—the other 30% were "dissatisfied." In 1989, 16% had been satisfied, 78% somewhat satisfied, and only 7% dissatisfied. The trend was moving in the wrong direction.[6]

In Frederick Herzberg's view, corporations are mixing apples and carrots. In his 1968 article "One More Time: How Do You Motivate Employees?" Herzberg said the findings from his and at least 16 other studies as well as "many other investigations" suggest that

the factors involved in producing job satisfaction (and motivation) are separate and distinct from the factors that lead to job dissatisfaction. . . . It follows that these two feelings are not opposites of each other. The opposite of job satisfaction is not job dissatisfaction but, rather, *no* job satisfaction; and, similarly, the opposite of job dissatisfaction is not job satisfaction, but *no* job dissatisfaction.[7]

Herzberg's job satisfaction and job dissatisfaction factors harken back to psychologist Abraham Maslow's hierarchy of needs: physiological, safety, love, esteem, and at the top, self-realization. "It is quite true," wrote Maslow in *Motivation and Personality*, "that man lives by bread alone—when there is no bread." But when there's plenty of bread, the need for personal safety takes precedence, and when these needs are satisfied, "new (and still higher) needs emerge, and so on."[8] Both the first need level (food, water, sex) and the second (security and survival) are essentially finite and capable of being satisfied through material and economic means. The upper-level needs for family and friends, respect and recognition, and finally, self-actualization are not finite and can be satisfied only by symbolic rewards.

Corporations satisfy physiological and safety needs with compensation and job security, but to Herzberg these are hygiene factors or job *dis*satisfiers, not the job satisfiers that motivate employees to perform better. If compensation or job security is inadequate, motivation will be negative. If they're adequate, motivation won't be negative—but it won't be positive either. Indeed, even when classified (by some respondents) as a motivator, neither factor was very significant. In the 12 investigations tabulated in Herzberg's article, salary was cited as leading to *extreme dissatisfaction* or *extreme satisfaction* by only 15% of the respondents—85% didn't mention it at all. And security was cited less than 5% of the time!

So increasing salaries or wages or benefits or job security won't improve the job performance of most workers. While it can eliminate job dissatisfaction, it doesn't motivate. Nor do symbolic rewards that address social needs—relations with supervisors, peers, and others on the job.

What it takes to motivate—and produce job satisfaction—is satisfaction of Maslow's esteem and self-realization needs through the opportunity for achievement and recognition, advancement and growth, responsibility, and the work itself. Work with responsibility seems to be the key motivator. As stated in the foreword to Herzberg's article, "The only way to motivate the employee is to give him challenging work in which he can assume responsibility."[9]

Should we be surprised? In the myth about corporations investing in brands to increase consumer value, we quoted Charlotte Beers to the effect that a brand is how a consumer feels about a product. We might just as well say that *motivation is how a worker feels about a job*—the emotional commitment to perform it well. Salary can be a powerful incentive to go to work and do what's expected of us, but it's not how we feel about work. Earning it is not an emotional experience and doesn't require an emotional commitment like achieving or taking responsibility. It's not likely to induce us to do things that blow the CEO's mind. Salary is not a true motivator.

Nor is the threat of being fired. That's an emotional experience, to be sure, but the emotion is negative, not the kind to inspire a commitment to perform a job well. How one feels about a job and how one feels about being fired from it are entirely different feelings.

Herzberg illustrates how true motivators increase performance with the case of a small staff at a large public corporation that responded to shareholder inquiries.[10] Although management regarded the job as challenging, the employees, who were carefully selected and highly trained, regarded the challenge as nonexistent. (Herzberg doesn't specifically list *challenge* as either a job motivator or a job dissatisfier, but it appears nonetheless to be closely associated with some of the principal motivators that he does list—responsibility, achievement, and the nature of the work itself.) And almost all indexes of performance and attitude were low.

The corporation then introduced a job motivation program—Herzberg's term for it is *job enrichment*—that gave selected employees more responsibility for their work and reduced supervision. For example, personal responsibility for the quality and accuracy of letters was transferred from supervisor to correspondent, and correspondents were encouraged to write in a more personal way and sign their letters rather than preparing form letters for their supervisor's signature. Job performance in terms of quality, accuracy, and speed of response was measured by the corporation for six months against a control group that was not part of the program. After an initial decline lasting three months (as, presumably, the workers got used to the new routine), job performance improved rapidly, equaling the control group at four months and exceeding it by 20% at the end of the six-month measuring period. In job *satisfaction* the test group's score grew steadily away from the control group's score from day one.

In *Principles of Management*, Robert Ford and Cherrill Heaton illustrate how the typical corporate focus on compensation and benefits as motivating factors works in the case of airline pilots. Pilots have very prestigious jobs as well as the social status that goes with that prestige, but they fly when and where they're told to fly under tightly regulated conditions, which is why Ford and Heaton refer to them as "expensive taxi drivers." The disconnect between job status and job reality creates a problem not only for the pilots but also for the airlines. In contract negotiations, "pilots typically negotiate for more decision-making power, and management typically offers more money. The pilots try to fill an unsatisfied need, and management offers further satisfaction of a need that is already satisfied." And the outcome, say the authors, is that often the

pilots wind up settling for more money and *more time off from flying.* In their leisure time, they frequently go into creative or expressive hobbies such as running a flower shop or managing a cattle ranch. Ideally, management should find a way to help the pilots satisfy these creative urges in the job itself. That does not happen, so the pilots seem to be saying, "If you're going to prevent me from having my needs satisfied on the job, then you're really going to pay for it."[11]

What if a corporation gives its workers the responsibility for an entire operation, not just for their own jobs, as LTV did when it built a new galvanizing plant in Cleveland, Ohio, to make rustproof steel for cars? This plant, one of the very few instances of participatory management sponsored by Churchill's Horses, employs "about half" as many workers per shift as a normal plant and therefore has almost double the productivity. It "is run largely by self-managing groups of workers," who perform all the hiring and sales and customer service functions "and help select suppliers." A production supervisor is the only manager on duty at the plant.

The open sesame was *no job classifications*, a major concession by the steelworkers' union. "Instead, LTV pays more to workers who cross-train and become multiskilled, able to perform any job in the plant, including maintenance." That is, anyone can change a light bulb. LTV doesn't have to call an electrician, as in many unionized plants, and then call someone else to carry the ladder.[12]

Cross-training minus job classifications increases productivity not only by enhancing job flexibility but also by motivating the people who do the work. Economist Alan Blinder wrote that when earnings soared at Corning's participatory management plant in Blacksburg, Virginia, where job classifications were reduced from 47 to 4 and "carefully selected production workers could rotate jobs and acquire new skills,'' Corning's CEO said: ''In my gut I can tell you a large part of our profit increase has come about because of our embarking on this way of life.'' And what was this way of life? To the plant manager, it was simply ''challenging people instead of forcing them to do dumb, stupid jobs.''[13] Shades of Herzberg.

If participatory management does such good things for performance and productivity and profit—at relatively little cost—why is it so rare in this country? ''For managers, this seems like the ultimate risk,'' said Harley Shaiken, a professor of labor and technology who used to be an autoworker. ''It is easy to talk about listening to employees, but quite another to give them real responsibility.''[14]

It's a myth that corporations are proficient at motivating their workers to improve performance. For the most part, **corporations rely on carrots and sticks, which are not effective motivators**, and ignore challenge and responsibility, which are.

Shaiken, who as an autoworker was presumably a member of the United Auto Workers, might also have cited the attitude of labor unions. Presided over (according to The *Wall Street Journal*) by ''35 mostly white, mostly male, largely over-60 members'' of the executive council of the AFL-CIO (American Federation of Labor and Congress of Industrial Organizations), its national federation, what the labor movement does best is take care of its own.[15] Although union members may be paid, on average, 12 to 20% more than their nonunion counterparts, economist Harvey Segal believes that ''the power of unions to push up wages is not great,'' especially now that unions represent far less of the nation's workforce than they used to and win far fewer organizing elections: ''Wage levels don't rise unless unions encounter managers who are compliant by virtue of a permissive business climate.''[16]

But unions still tend to oppose any changes like reduced job classifications that would lessen the number of their own members on the job, never mind considerations of job satisfaction, productivity, competitiveness, and the survival needs of the corporation employing them. At the same time, they seem less concerned about the future of labor or even about new members, as when they accept two-tiered wage agreements that favor present workers at the expense of new ones. ''The whole history of unionism,'' Paul Samuelson once said, ''has been a history in which unions wield their most specific influence in determining how industries in decline are accelerated toward their extinction.''[17]

But the nature of work is changing. The lean production pioneered by Toyota and being adopted by U.S. corporations—Boeing used lean production techniques in designing and manufacturing the 777 airliner—relies on teamwork and flexibility while deemphasizing the skilled labor on the shop floor that once formed the core of industrial labor union membership. Unions will have to shape up or ship out. But teamwork and flexibility also require continuity of employment and motivated employees—neither of which is promoted by the corporate propensity toward mass layoffs.

Chapter 22

Corporations Stay Competitive in a Global Economy by Downsizing

There are some good economic reasons for a current restructuring, long overdue, of the American workplace. But the human costs are enormous. Some profound betrayal of the American dynamic itself (work hard, obey the rules, succeed) runs through this process like a computer virus.

—Lance Morrow, *Time* magazine[1]

We believe that if men have the talent to invent new machines that put men out of work, they have the talent to put those men back to work.

—President John F. Kennedy[2]

In the last chapter we observed that compensation and job security are not motivators or job satisfiers but, rather, job *dis*satisfiers. That is, not feeling secure in your job tends to make you dissatisfied, demotivate you, and offset the effect of any satisfiers like having an interesting job with lots of challenge and responsibility—*if* job security is important to you.

Job security wasn't very important to Frederick Herzberg's respondents when he wrote his article in 1968. Recent studies suggest that job security is of much greater concern today.

A poll conducted by the *New York Times* in December 1996 found that fully half of the country was concerned that they or someone in their household would be laid off within the next two to three years. The number expressing concern varied from 43% of those earning more than $50,000 to 57% of those earning less than $15,000.[3]

Their concern may be warranted.

In the early 1990s the number of workers laid off during the year topped 3 million and stayed at that level. According to figures revised by the U.S. Bureau of Labor Statistics in the fall of 1996, almost 9.5 million people—8% of the total workforce—were laid off their jobs during the three-year period 1992–1995. Yet the economy was not in recession in those years. Indeed, it was generating many more jobs than it was destroying. Unemployment was going down. The number of employed workers was going up—to $125 million in mid-1996. On the other hand, most of these 9.5 million people weren't being *temporarily* laid off, as the euphemism implies—they were being *fired*. Corporations were downsizing and eliminating their jobs.

To labor economist Frank Levy, the layoff statistics "suggest a long-term upward trend as a natural cost of having a more competitive economy."[4] In other words, corporations stay competitive in the new global economy by downsizing.

General Electric, the Man o' War of Churchill's Horses, started the downsizing trend by eliminating 100,000 jobs—1 out of 4—in the 1980s. Shucking marginal operations and non-value-added jobs, GE and the overweight horses that followed its lead sought to focus on their core competencies, outsource requirements that could be filled by independent suppliers, and prune their overhead personnel, particularly first-tier and middle managers.[5] A 1,400-company survey by the American Management Association in the fall of 1996 found that two supervisors and three middle managers were being dismissed for every one hired. The reverse was true of technical and professional workers: two hired for every one dismissed.[6]

What Churchill's Horses were and are hoping to gain is more productivity—more (revenue) bang for the (expense) buck. Increasing productivity not only increases profitability (which measures the ratio of buck to bang) but also makes the corporation more competitive by lowering its costs.

To the national economy, greater productivity means that the economy can produce more with the same resources and particularly (zeroing in on the greatest cost) with the same number of workers working the same number of hours. The United States doesn't really have the option to reduce the size of its workforce. But U.S. corporations do. And greater productivity to corporations in downsize mode usually means—at least in the short term—producing the same (or less) with *fewer* workers.

What happens to all the workers that downsizing corporations leave behind?

According to the same Bureau of Labor Statistics data (as analyzed by the *Times*), one-third get another full-time job at equal or higher pay. One-quarter get a full-time job at lower pay. Another one-quarter are split between those who stop trying to find work (withdraw from the labor force) and those who keep trying but are unsuccessful (become unemployed). And the remaining one-sixth is divided between those who become self-employed (including unpaid family workers) and those who take part-time work. Among the reemployeds, a little over half find their new jobs within three and a half months (15 weeks).[7]

Studies by Henry Farber and Ann Huff Stevens indicate that the average pay cut of everyone who takes a new full-time job (including, presumably, the ones who earn the same or more) is 10%.[8] Thus, for the workforce as a whole, being downsized is like taking a 10% pay cut—*if* you're among the 60% who are able to find a new full-time job.

When you're reemployed in a full-time or part-time job that you expect to end within a finite time like a year, your job is now classified by the BLS as *contingent*—nonpermanent. The significance of contingent employment is not only that your job is transitory but also that you are less likely than noncontingent employees to receive health insurance and other benefits from your employer. In its first survey of such jobs in 1995, the BLS found that upward of 6 million workers held them—5% of the workforce. The 6 million includes 1.2 million working for temporary-help agencies like Manpower. But the count of 1.2 million temps is about half of what the Labor Department shows in its report on business establishments. "Most labor market analysts will find [the BLS] levels of contingent employment surprisingly low," said Eileen Appelbaum of the Economic Policy Institute.[9]

In mid-1996 there were almost 4.5 million people working part-time because they couldn't find full-time jobs and another half million who were too discouraged even to look for work.[10] Both groups were classified as *hidden unemployment* but not included in the official civilian unemployment rate, which stood at 5.4% of the employed and unemployed workforce. Had they been included, the unemployment rate would have risen to 8.7%—1 person out of every 12 who worked (contingently or otherwise) or wanted to work for someone else as a full-time employee.

And there are those who might think that *that* figure is too low, including Herbert Barchoff, who once served on President Truman's Council of Economic Advisors. Barchoff wrote in 1994 that "the employment picture is far worse than it appears"—among other reasons because people "holding two part-time jobs, as about seven million Americans do, are counted twice; and roughly a million hold three jobs."[11]

Downsizing is traumatic to downsized employees. And it can be demoralizing even to the survivors. "After downsizing, people began to notice that the demoralized, traumatized work force was not able to carry out their jobs in the way they were expected," said Steve Worth, executive director of an association of outplacement firms. "And if the purpose of the process is to enhance productivity, cutting the fat is one issue. Making sure that the muscle, the survivor, is able to function is equally important."[12]

The process is tricky. Said the *Economist*: "Downsizing can have a devastating impact on innovation, as skills and contacts that have been developed over the years are destroyed at a stroke."[13] Corporations have to know who their best workers are and which ones know where the dead horses are buried and how things really get done (never mind the formal routines)—and keep them. Not only keep them, but keep them motivated.

But Churchill's Horses derive as much as 30% of their revenue and profit (much more than other U.S. corporations) from the global economy,[14] which the collapse of the Soviet Union and the lowering of trade barriers have made very competitive by introducing "more than a billion cheap workers" into the labor market. To survive, they have had to become more productive and lower their costs. The way they did this was by downsizing. Michael Jensen of Harvard Business School thinks that the worst is yet to come.[15]

But considering how tricky the process can be, how good a bet is it that downsizing really cuts costs and increases productivity?

No better than fair, according to a 1992 survey of 800 corporations by the American Management Association.[16] Of those that had laid off employees since 1987, fewer than half reported greater profit.

In 1993, a study of over 500 large corporations by the Wyatt Company also found that the results were a mixed bag.[17] Of corporations that had cut jobs in the previous few years,

- only 61% had reduced costs,
- only 46% had increased profit, and
- no more than 34% had raised productivity—

but within the first year more than 50% had restored some of the positions they had just eliminated.

"Companies still think that all they need to do is cut heads," said Wyatt's John Parkington. "But that won't yield what they're looking for. Downsizing requires more planning and thought in order to be effective."[18]

Although there are many explanations for the slow growth in productivity, Louis Uchitelle wrote in the *New York Times*, "[M]ass layoffs [are] rising toward the top of the list, the explanation being that they destroy loyalty, job stability and continuity, [which are] increasingly recognized as ingredients of productivity."[19]

A 1991 study found that downsizing companies underperformed stock market averages three years after the downsizing was announced.[20]

"Most companies are just shrinking, not changing how they do work," said consultant Michael Hammer, coauthor of *Reengineering the Corporation*:

The traditional meat-cleaver approach of just cutting people is a strategy for decline. To succeed, companies have to change the way they work instead of just throwing people over the edge, and most companies are not making basic changes.[21]

It's a myth that corporations stay competitive by downsizing—unless a lot more is done. Since unplanned cuts like across-the-board reductions take their pound of flesh indiscriminately from both high-productivity and low-productivity operations, the cuts themselves, if they are to benefit the corporation, have to be carefully planned and implemented. Furthermore, the employees who remain have to be able to accomplish the work assigned to them, and that may mean reducing the amount of work (as the number of workers is reduced) or changing the way it is done. **Just cutting jobs isn't likely to make a corporation more productive or competitive**. Indeed, by undercutting motivation and know-how, downsizing may well *decrease* productivity and make the corporation *less* competitive.

Wall Street, however, may not agree.

From the *New York Times*, October 12, 1993: Eli Lilly announced a broad restructuring including eliminating 4,000 jobs—20% of its workforce. The cost of the restructuring had yet to be determined. Shares of the company rose 7% in "brisk trading."[22]

From the *Wall Street Journal*, December 9, 1993: Xerox announced job cuts of at least 10,000—10% of its workforce—in its third restructuring in three years. Although the size of the cuts "caught some analysts by surprise," shares of the company rose 7%.[23]

Why does the stock price go up when profit goes down?

The stock price goes up because Wall Street believes that the road to higher profits, higher stock prices, and higher returns on investment tomorrow is paved with lower costs today, particularly lower employee costs. Forget the mixed bag of actual experience. When a corporation announces that it will cut employees, Wall Street reflexively bids up the price of its stock on the assumption that fewer employees mean greater profits—not in the current year, perhaps, but in the next year (unless, like Xerox, the corporation announces cutbacks each year) and in the years following. What does Wall Street know?

But perhaps something else is going on. "The cuts began as a competitive drive," said Eric Greenberg, research director of the American Management Association, "but they seem to have become a way of life for many companies."[24] Downsizing can almost be counted on to raise the stock price (for no money down), and that pleases Wall Street, since a rising price stimulates trading, and also, of course, the shareholders. CEOs of public corporations know how important it is to keep both of these constituencies happy.

Do they feel the same concern for their workers? "We must start with the reality that corporations cannot guarantee anyone a lifetime job," said John Snow, chairman of CSX Corporation and the Business Roundtable, "any more than corporations have a guarantee of immortality. The challenge for corporate America is to maintain its competitiveness and in the process help employees prepare themselves for whatever changes lie ahead in this constantly changing world."[25] Donald Hastings, CEO of Lincoln Electric, expresses a somewhat different point of view. Everyone assumes that "layoffs are inevitable," he said, but "thinking ahead and having creative solutions for when there is a downturn is what management is all about."[26]

We will visit Lincoln Electric in the next chapter.

Chapter 23

Corporations Have to Lay Off Workers When Business Is Bad

Under a laissez-faire system, there may be great wastes due to unemployment and the business cycle [leading to] poverty that has no real cause but stems only from our intricate monetary system.
—Paul A. Samuelson, *Economics*[1]

What is good for the country is good for General Motors, and what is good for General Motors is good for the country.
—Charles E. Wilson, Secretary of Defense (and former CEO of General Motors)[2]

"Twice in the last year," wrote Paul Krugman in early 1997, "experts on America's economic statistics startled the public by declaring some well-known truths about our economy to be . . . inoperative."[3] At the beginning of 1996 the government decided that it had been overstating the real growth in productivity and the economy. At the end of 1996 a team of prominent economists appointed by Congress concluded that the government had been overstating the growth in inflation and therefore *under*stating the real growth in productivity and the economy—and also wages.

If we may now assume, as Krugman suggests, that the increase in wages has kept pace with the increase in productivity in recent years, as economists think it should (and did in the past), should we also assume that workers have shared *equally* in the increase in wages (as they did in the past)? No, Krugman says, the data on the growing disparity in income distribution weren't affected by the statistical revisions.

It is still true that families in the bottom fifth, who had 5.4 percent of total income in 1970, had only 4.2 percent in 1994; and that over the same period the share of the top 5 percent went from 15.6 percent [of total income] to 20.1 [percent].[4]

Nor is the increase in income inequality relieved by a corresponding increase in upward mobility. The percentage of poor people rising out of poverty decreased from the 35% measured over the period 1967–1979 to 30% in 1980–1991. The growing inequality, Krugman says, calls into question whether America should still think of itself as a middle-class society.

What's causing the growing inequality? Theories abound, but no one really knows. In an article entitled "Who Killed the Middle Class," John Cassidy reported that a straw poll taken at a conference at the New York Federal Reserve in November 1994 attributed 60% of the cause to the growth in technology, particularly computers, which increase the productivity (and pay) of computer-literate workers and replace many unskilled jobs, driving down the value of unskilled workers. Another 30% was attributed to such factors as the decline in union membership (and power) and the rise of immigration (and unskilled immigrant workers). The remaining 10% was attributed to global trade.[5]

According to a report in the *New York Times*, Kevin M. Murphy, 1997 winner of the Clark Medal awarded by the American Economic Association to an outstanding economist under age 40, "has clearly identified the growth in demand for skilled labor—as opposed to the rise in supply or decline in demand for unskilled labor—as the cause of the widening gap in wages between blue-and white-collar workers." And the cause of that growth in demand for skilled labor? "We've identified the suspects," Murphy said, which include both technology and global trade, "but don't have anyone in custody."[6]

Global trade supposedly raises the price of skilled labor in a developed country like the United States and depresses the value of unskilled labor because it exports products made by its skilled labor to developing countries and imports products made by their unskilled labor. Thus we are, in a sense, importing their unskilled labor by importing the products made by it, making unskilled labor in the United States more abundant (just as immigration does) and less in demand. At the same time, we are exporting our skilled labor and making it scarcer. So, in accordance with a theorem developed in the 1940s by Wolfgang Stolper and Paul Samuelson, the price of skilled labor in the United States should go up, and the price of unskilled labor should go down.[7] Except that, as we observed in discussing the myth that corporate management is strategic, the bulk of our trade is with developed countries paying wages at almost the same level as the wages we pay. So the theorem—and free trade—may not have that much impact.

"All these estimates are suspect," wrote John Cassidy in *The New Yorker*, "because some of the factors probably interacted and reinforced each other." So who killed the middle class? Nobody, concludes Cassidy, "it is just how capitalism has developed."[8] In other words, supply and demand applied to labor.

As Stephen Solomon wrote in a 1993 article about the U.S. airline industry, "A free market rewards the most efficient producers." Now that it's been deregulated, the airline market is very free indeed compared to what it used to be when fares and routes were controlled by the government. Now it not only rewards efficient airlines but also penalizes inefficient ones, which include most of the major airlines in the country.

Having inherited high labor costs and restrictive union contracts from the days of regulation, the major airlines made matters worse by buying other inefficient airlines to become bigger and building high-cost airport facilities called hubs. From 1990 to 1992, according to Solomon, the airlines collectively lost more than $10 billion. He concluded that "employees at the major carriers will either match the everyone-pitches-in efficiency of Southwest [Airlines] or face vast layoffs."

Corporations competing in a free market have to be cost-efficient to survive. Even if downsizing does not work well as a competitive strategy, corporations have to lay off workers when business is bad. Workers represent their single greatest expense. When they're losing money, corporations don't have the time to learn how to motivate their workers or increase their productivity or reengineer the way they perform the corporation's business—or increase sales.

Unlike the big national airlines, Southwest is a slow-growth, no-frills airline that flies you straight to where you want to go (if it goes there), not via some out-of-the-way hub. More to the point, it consistently makes money. Its office workers tag baggage and collect tickets, its flight attendants clean cabins, and its pilots fly half again as many hours as they do at, say, American Airlines to earn equivalent pay. While Southwest pays well, Solomon wrote, its operating costs are lower than those of other airlines, and "employees realize that their compensation and job security depend on productivity. . . . Southwest's people (almost all union members) are paid only for the time they fly."[9]

Martin Weitzman, whom we last met while discussing the myth of supply and demand, tells us that before *The General Theory of Employment, Interest and Money* by John Maynard Keynes was published in 1936, economists generally regarded the labor market as no different from, say, the potato market. Wages, like the cost of potatoes, rose and fell according to supply and demand. If potatoes were rotting in the fields, that's because their current price was higher than the equilibrium price. Similarly, if people were out of work, the price (wage) they were asking for their services was too high. Arthur Pigou, world-renowned economist and Keynes's teacher, said as much in 1933, at the depths of the Great Depression.

But Keynes pointed out that since three-quarters of our national income consists of what is paid to workers for working and only one-quarter for everything else that adds value to the economy (including growing potatoes and bringing them to market), the free market's solution for rotting potatoes (reduce prices) as applied to unemployed workers (reduce wages) reduces what the nation's consumers have to spend. If they spend significantly less, then corporations will produce significantly less—and hire fewer workers. Reducing wages in a recession (or depression) won't lead back to full employment for a long time.

The effect of Keynes's thesis was "profound," Weitzman wrote, as even Keynes's teacher conceded. In a stroke Keynes removed the wage issue from the table and substituted fiscal policy—government spending to influence total demand. But in the long run, Weitzman says, Keynes's accomplishment "must increasingly come to be viewed as something of a dazzling digression from the main route to economic prosperity [because] sooner or later the wage issue must be confronted head-on. How labor is paid remains the central issue."[10]

Fixed wages is the central issue.

In our capitalist economy, Alan Blinder has written, "[T]he profit motive is the wellspring of productivity and innovation. But large companies forget this simple lesson and pay their workers for hours spent on the job, not for output produced or profits generated."[11]

Southwest Airlines, which pays its crews only for the time they fly, hasn't forgotten Blinder's lesson, but a company that has traveled farther down the road of unfixed wages—indeed, said the *New York Times*, "farther than any other large manufacturer in matching compensation to each employee's productivity and to the profitability of the company"—is Lincoln Electric, the world's largest manufacturer of arc welding supplies and equipment. A private family-controlled corporation (employees own 30% of the stock), Lincoln is known for the high quality and low price of its products. That combination drove General Electric, Westinghouse, and many smaller competitors out of the market. But its employee policies, says the *Times*, are "brutally demanding, forcing workers into constant competition with each other to produce more with fewer mistakes." Why would anyone want to work there?

For one thing, no layoffs. Since 1934, Lincoln has guaranteed at least 30 hours of work a week to every worker who has been with the company three years.

For another thing, good pay. In 1993, workers averaged slightly over $50,000. In better years, some workers have been known to top $100,000. But workers are paid only for what they produce. They receive no base wage or payment for sick days or holidays. And they receive a very large part of their compensation as a bonus that is determined year by year—and allocated among individual workers—by management.

Although wages are directly tied to output produced, bonuses are not directly tied to profits generated. Lincoln, in fact, paid sizable bonuses in 1992 and 1993 after incurring the first losses in its 99-year history and omitting bonus dividends to its shareholders. (Management traces the losses to its decision to counter foreign competition by investing in overseas plants. Several of the investments turned out to be disasters. Concluded one director, "I doubt that Lincoln's [compensation] system is exportable.") But the bonuses were slimmer in those years—less than 65% of wages as compared to 70% or more in the late 1980s and an average of 105% in the 1950s, 1960s, and 1970s. So workers cannot be indifferent to company profit. One, a Lincoln welder for 17 years, told the *Times* reporter that he submitted nearly 50 cost-reduction suggestions during the spring and early summer of 1993, and about 30 were accepted. But, he said, "I don't work for Lincoln Electric; I work for myself. I'm an entrepreneur."

Harvard Business School uses Lincoln as a case study in how to motivate workers.[12]

In most corporations, profit sharing refers to employee ownership of shares of the corporation's stock. Under the typical profit-sharing plan, employees may not be able to sell their shares—and may not even receive dividends—until retirement. But even if they do receive dividends and can sell their shares, the amount that adds to their regular pay is much less than the 60 to 130% of wages that Lincoln employees receive each year as a bonus. Whether regarded as compensation for services rendered or an incentive to better performance, corporate profit sharing through stock ownership is remote and (compared to regular pay) insignificant.

Lincoln's profit sharing through large bonuses is current and significant. Having a significant part of current compensation related to profit is the trade-off Lincoln receives in return for guaranteeing no layoffs.

When a significant part of the employees' current compensation is *variable*—tied directly or indirectly to profit, as under Lincoln's bonus plan—a reduction in profit automatically reduces employee costs without layoffs. Since paying everyone 10% less (under profit sharing) reduces costs as much as paying 10% fewer people (after layoffs) the same amount, the benefit to the corporation is the same—and it hasn't lost any productive capacity. Having everyone's pay cut when business is bad is the trade-off workers concede in return for being guaranteed no layoffs.

If enough corporations and their workers agreed to a current and significant form of profit sharing, we would have what Martin Weitzman calls a *share system*, which he summarizes as follows:

To the working class, a share system promises permanent full employment at competitive remuneration, no inflation, and an improvement in working conditions and employer attitudes. It asks of the workers that they receive a substantial part of their pay as a negotiated share of company profits or revenues (per employee).[13]

A share system raises at least two problems. One is control over the conditions that govern the share system. The share of Lincoln profits paid to each employee isn't negotiated; management makes that decision each year on its own. But for six decades, at least, the Lincoln version of a share system worked well for Lincoln. It might not work so smoothly for corporations seeking to take advantage of variable compensation that don't have Lincoln's long experience with it.

At Monsanto, the committee that sets the performance objectives to which bonuses are tied includes worker representation. "We all have a say in setting goals,'' said one worker on the committee, ''but the people who make the final decision are not affected. They are in another pay structure with a different bonus plan, and that is frustrating.''[14]

The second problem is volatility in income—the profit-sharing part isn't an entitlement earned by working—and how that affects motivation. In 1995, 45% of the workers covered by major new labor agreements got (variable) bonuses instead of (fixed) raises, a significant union concession to the new business climate.[15] And in a survey the next year of 750 corporations by Towers Perrin, 27% said they intended over the next three years to replace traditional raises with bonuses and profit sharing. But when Allied Signal piloted a program to give bonuses tied to performance objectives to 5,000 workers averaging less than $30,000 and the objectives weren't met, the workers regarded it as a pay cut, not as the consequences of a performance shortfall.

These, surely, are solvable problems if management and workers have the will. It's a myth that in bad times corporations have to lay off employees when business is bad. **Meaningful profit sharing is a viable alternative to layoffs** and holds the promise of steadier employment and higher productivity, which in the long run is the key to the prosperity of everyone.

Chapter 24

Raising Productivity Benefits Workers by Raising What They Earn

So it makes sense to focus our attention on output per hour of work, that is, on the productivity of labor. It is slightly too simple, but only slightly, to say that standards of living advance in lockstep with labor productivity.
—Alan S. Blinder, *Growing Together*[1]

Nevertheless, the fact remains that all of the major shifts in the world's *military-power* balances have followed alterations in the *productive* balances.
—Paul Kennedy, *The Rise and Fall of the Great Powers*[2]

At the end of World War II, the United States, in a manner of speaking, held most of the world's chips. Then, when it encountered aggressive Soviet moves in Berlin, Eastern Europe, and elsewhere, it chose to spend some of those chips to revive, strengthen, and defend free economies around the world that might otherwise have been prey to Soviet or Soviet-sponsored subversion. Becoming a vast market for these revived and strengthened free economies, it spent other chips consuming the goods they exported to the United States.

Today, the United States no longer has a large reserve supply of chips—arguably less than it needs as the world's only superpower managing the world's principal reserve currency. It now owes more to other countries than it is owed, and the net foreign indebtedness continues to rise because the United States imports more than it exports. As previously noted, for the 10 years from 1985 to 1994 the annual deficit in the balance on current account in foreign trade averaged $110 billion a year. The $110 billion amounted to 2% of the average Gross Domestic Product for those years—what the country produced in goods and services. In 1994, the deficit exceeded $150 billion—2.3% of GDP.[3]

More is at stake than the $150 billion in U.S. assets transferred to foreign holders to finance the deficit. There's also the matter of jobs. Had Americans produced as much as they consumed in 1994, they would have increased their output of goods and services from facilities in the United States by $150 billion and employed otherwise unemployed (or underemployed) people to produce that output. Since the ratio of economic growth to reduction in unemployment is usually taken (under a "law" conceived by Arthur Okun, chairman of President Lyndon Johnson's Council of Economic Advisors) at 2:1, the increase in output could have reduced the unemployment rate by roughly a percentage point— from about 6% to 5%—and put a million or so people to work.[4]

How do we reverse the trade deficit?

One way might be to increase the productivity of Churchill's Horses at a faster rate. Productivity is the key to a nation's prosperity and power. It is also the key to the competitiveness of Churchill's Horses, lowering their costs and enabling them to sell more in their markets, domestic and export. Selling more in export markets reduces the trade deficit.

When workers, becoming more productive, produce more, they can be paid more. Although in recent years many have doubted that wage increases have kept pace with productivity increases, the statistical revisions of 1996 suggest, according to Paul Krugman, that these doubts may have been premised on a "statistical illusion."[5] That doesn't mean, as we have seen, that all workers share productivity gains equally. Still, for the workforce as a whole, it remains true that raising productivity benefits workers by raising what they earn.

When the United States had most of the chips (and factories not destroyed by the war), it led the world in productivity. But since that time, Japan and Germany and the other countries it trades with have made great progress in increasing their own productivity. Is the United States still in the lead?

As of 1990—yes, according to a study by McKinsey Global Institute and three economists that the *New York Times* called "the most authoritative comparison to date." In that year the average full-time American worker produced $49,600 worth of goods and services compared to $47,000 in equivalent purchasing power for a French worker, $44,200 for a German, $38,200 for a Japanese, and $37,100 for a Brit. Although the U.S. lead was greater in the manufacture of goods, it also led in the production of services, which by 1990 employed three out of four American workers. "We were all surprised," said Martin Baily, one of the participating economists, "at the extent of the U.S. lead in services. Most of us had concluded that the U.S. had been overtaken."[6]

Considering the relatively small amount of investment in productivity in the United States compared to either Japan or Germany (or even France?), one may marvel that the United States had *not* been overtaken, and not only in services but in manufactured goods as well. Starved by lack of investment, U.S. productivity between 1973 and 1990 grew at a substantially slower rate than between World War II and 1973. (The 1966 statistical revisions may have changed the numbers, but, Krugman says, the impression that "the first postwar generation experienced an immense improvement in living standards, while the second did not, is still correct.'')[7] How had the United States maintained any lead at all?

It had maintained its lead, according to the McKinsey study, because of less government regulation. Greater freedom to hire and fire workers, raise and lower prices, and open and close businesses allowed Corporate America to puts its smaller investment in productivity to more efficient use.

How about the future? Will the U.S. lead disappear because of continued low investment?

Not to worry, says Steven Rattner of the investment banking firm Lazard Frères. In an article written in 1993, he proclaimed the days of low-productivity growth to be over: ''After languishing for nearly two decades, American productivity is marching upward again, bringing the promise of higher incomes for more efficient workers and fewer jobs for everyone else.''

The upturn began in the 1980s in manufacturing, says Rattner, ''but was obscured by the bafflingly poor performance of service companies, which theoretically should have benefited most from new information technology.'' But service productivity turned around in 1992, leading overall productivity growth to ''the best result in several decades, according to Stephen Roach, chief economist at Morgan Stanley & Company.''[8]

But by 1996 Stephen Roach had changed his mind. Having maintained for years that the heavy investment by service businesses in computers had paid off in increased efficiency, he reversed himself because ''the improvements in operating performance and profits have been built on a steady stream of downsizings and cost cutting that is just not sustainable. If all you do is cut, then you will eventually be left with nothing, with no market share.'' In other words, the gains in service productivity have been temporary, not permanent.

And perhaps not even temporary for the economy as a whole. Banks, for example, having invested in automatic teller machines (ATMs), can process more customer transactions with fewer tellers, but if their customers don't transact more, the banking system hasn't grown and neither has the economy. The banks may be more productive because they process the same number of transactions with a smaller number of tellers, but the economy may not be unless the former tellers are engaged in producing goods and services somewhere else. And even the banks can't keep adding ATMs and laying off tellers indefinitely. ''The fatal flaw,'' said Roach, ''is that [corporate productivity gains in services] are built on the back of hollowing out labor.''[9]

Lazard's Rattner claimed that ''by all statistics, the companies that are most successful in improving productivity are often those companies that do the most to create jobs.'' But he admitted that it will take a long time for the new jobs that are created to make up for the old jobs that are eliminated. We have to understand, he wrote, that ''at the outset, the new jobs will not always pay as much as the old ones. That's because jobs are often lost when they cease to be economic.''[10]

How long will it be for new jobs to make up for the old jobs that are eliminated and to pay as much? In the case of the Industrial Revolution, it took upward of a *half century*. Industrialization substituted machines like the power loom of Luddite fame for work, reducing the demand for labor, and depressed wages for decades. In the nineteenth and twentieth centuries, mechanization and then automation of agriculture permanently reduced the number of farmers required to feed the world to a small fraction of what it used to be. Mechanical cotton-pickers, introduced in 1944, did the work of 50 sharecroppers—and by 1972 had replaced all of them! "In the short run—which may mean not years but decades," wrote Paul Krugman, "the social consequences of technological advances [that increase productivity] may be anything but benign. There is now a growing realization that we are living through one of those difficult periods." [11]

Writer Jeffrey Madrick called his book *The End of Affluence*. According to Madrick, the decline in the rate of U.S. economic growth from 1973 to 1993 compared to the century before that adds up to a loss of $12 trillion, which could have "paid off all of our government, mortgage and credit card debt, or replaced all of our nation's factories, including capital equipment, with new ones." What caused the decline? A major reason, said Madrick, is the decline of mass production, in which the United States excelled, in favor of flexible (lean) production, which is better suited to the array of international markets opened up by the lowering of global trade barriers. Productivity gains, he said, are more difficult to achieve under flexible production than under mass production. In a review of the book, the *Times'* Louis Uchitelle wrote that "this inevitable slowdown in productivity may one day become the most significant explanation for America's nearly stagnant wage growth and the reluctance of corporations to invest as heavily in expansion as they did in the past." [12]

Madrick's is a pessimistic view, not shared by everyone. After all, the Federal Reserve Board, the nation's inflation fighter, can influence the rate of growth in the economy by simply nudging interest rates down (or up). But the longtime chairman of the Fed, Alan Greenspan, believes that U.S. output is limited to its present, relatively slow rate of growth by limitations in machinery and manpower and how productively they are used. [13] Faster growth would push against the envelope of these limitations and, by creating shortages in critical skills, drive up the cost of labor and trigger an increase in inflation.

The trigger point is called the *Nairu* (for nonaccelerating inflation rate of unemployment), or the *natural rate of unemployment*, which economists usually put at 5.5 to 6%. [14] But there are those who believe that a lower unemployment rate (with the higher growth rate implied by Okun's Law) is possible without triggering inflation. Weak unions, the specter of corporate downsizings, and the millions of contingency and part-time workers (and dropouts) wanting permanent full-time jobs suggest that lower unemployment might not significantly increase the demand for higher wages. On the other side, a permissive business climate that allows corporations to offset wage increases with price increases and accordingly to agree more readily to demands for higher wages is increasingly rare, victim of the new era of intense competition at home and abroad.

Labor markets in the 1990s with only 5% unemployment, according to one authority, behave like labor markets in the 1980s with 6 to 6.5% unemployment.[15] Has the Nairu slipped while economists nodded?

And there are those like Robert Eisner, former president of the American Economic Association, who argue that unemployment *can't* be too low—the Fed should promote maximum employment (and economic growth) rather than minimum inflation.[16] But the Fed has its own hawks arguing that *inflation* can't be too low—the Fed should stomp *it* out and not worry about unemployment.

We've heard a pessimistic view from Madrick—fast growth is history; we've heard the views of hawks on both sides; and we've heard an optimistic view from Rattner—fast growth is the future. Let's take one last look at the optimistic view.

"The only way to improve living standards in any meaningful way over any period of time is via productivity growth," said Steven Rattner, quoting productivity expert Robert Litan.[17] And (by all statistics) the corporations that improve productivity the most will (often) create the most new jobs. On the other hand, it will take a long time for the new jobs that are created to make up for the old jobs that are eliminated. Also, the new jobs will not always pay as much as the old ones. In fact, Rattner made clear, productivity growth promises higher incomes *only for more efficient workers*. For everyone else, it promises *fewer jobs*.

It's a myth that raising corporate productivity benefits workers by raising what they earn. It doesn't benefit the millions whose jobs are eliminated, particularly if they have to wait a long time for a new job or take a job that doesn't pay as much as the old one. And it doesn't benefit the millions who are less efficient, promising this half (more or less) of the working population a future of lower incomes and fewer jobs. In fact, **corporate attempts to raise productivity harm millions of workers**.

Nor is it clear that in the crucial service sector—crucial because it employs three out of every four U.S. workers—corporate attempts to raise productivity largely by investing in computers and then downsizing actually raise productivity in any lasting or meaningful way that translates into economic growth. Computers (which still represent no more than 2% of business investment) may not make much difference in any event since they don't have that much impact on how we consumers live, certainly not when compared to the automobile—or the electric light bulb. "The hype about productivity has been much greater than the performance," said economist Robert Solow.

Maybe we have gotten so good at hype that the information revolution seems bigger to us than the electric motor seemed when it was invented. But the electric motor had a big impact on how many shirts you could sew in a day.[18]

People need shirts. "Computerized ticketing is a great thing," Krugman wrote, "but a cross-country flight still takes five hours; bar codes and laser scanners are nifty, but there's still time to read about celebrities and space aliens in the checkout line."[19] Corporations would do more to raise productivity if they invested in machinery and manpower development and products and services that people need—and long-term growth.

But one place where computers have undeniably had a big impact is Wall Street, changing not only *how* financiers of public corporations do what they do but even *what* they do. We turn now to discuss those changes.

Part VII

Capitalists

How the financiers of public corporations serve their corporate clients, their clients' shareholders, and the investing public; how they exert a beneficial influence on Churchill's Horses.

Chapter 25

Wall Street's Primary Function Is Raising Money for Public Corporations

During the 1980s, in a calculated move, every major [Wall Street firm] . . . changed from being solely or primarily agents to acting largely as principals.
                                        —Paul Gibson, *Bear Trap*[1]

The trend is that electronic trading in general is replacing advice as the major service the financial community sells.
                                        —Joel Kurtzman, *The Death of Money*[2]

Public corporations, as we observed in an earlier context, marry for money. When they go public to obtain money from public investors, they get hitched for life to Wall Street.

A public corporation provides goods and services to paying customers. That's its job. What does its spouse do?

Investment bankers on Wall Street provide access to capital by underwriting the sale of the corporation's stocks and bonds to public investors. That's always been Wall Street's primary function—raising money for corporate clients in what is referred to as the primary market. When investment bankers aren't actually raising money for their clients, they're providing them with high-priced advice on raising money, taking over other corporations, avoiding *being* taken over by other corporations, building shareholder value, and various other aspects of what may be thought of as corporate financial strategy.

Pretty much everyone else on Wall Street—everyone, that is, who isn't a trader or investor—services the secondary markets where traders and investors buy and sell the stocks and bonds that have been sold in the primary market. Their customers are the traders and investors rather than the corporate issuers, but what they do serves the interests of corporate issuers since a primary market with a strong secondary market attracts more buyers than one with a weak secondary market or (as in the case of a private offering) no secondary market at all.

That's how it has always been. Is it now?

In *Bear Trap*, Paul Gibson describes a few changes that have come to Wall Street. One occurred on Labor Day of 1974, when the Employee Retirement Income Security Act became law. ERISA requires pension fund managers to act prudently in their investments. "Initially this meant moving out of stocks and into safer bonds," said Gibson. "Later it meant indexing." But it also meant that "control over the single largest source of investable funds would shift from the sell side—Wall Street—to the buy side—the managers of the institutions with moneys to invest."

On May Day in 1975, deregulation brought supply and demand and a free market home to roost on Wall Street by unfixing fixed brokerage commissions. "Before the unfixing," said Gibson, "every second dollar of revenue on Wall Street came from commissions. Today [1993], fewer than one in five does."

In 1982 the Securities and Exchange Commission promulgated Rule 415 allowing so-called shelf registrations of securities that didn't have to be sold right away. Before Rule 415, said Gibson,

underwriting had been an orderly affair with the top bankers enjoying all the perks of an oligopoly. A compliant SEC had tilted the rules in their favor to such an extent that borrowers filing with the agency had to name the four or five underwriters they would use and stick with them. No shopping around for a better deal. An underwriting took months to pass through the Washington labyrinth, with the bankers' meters always ticking.

No more.

These changes forced Wall Street firms to reevaluate how they made money. Serving their traditional clients just wasn't as profitable as it used to be. So Wall Street took on a new client—itself. Now, writes Gibson, "the trading and investing of funds for their own accounts ranks far higher in importance [for Wall Street firms] than the making of markets for clients and the collecting of commissions and fees."[3]

In *Theory of Games and Economic Behavior*, John von Neumann and Oskar Morgenstern defined "games" in which the amounts paid by one or more "players" equal the amounts received by other "players" as *zero-sum games*. In these games "one can say that the players pay only to each other, and that no production or destruction of goods is involved." That is, zero-sum games don't add value to the economy. "All games which are actually played for entertainment are of this type. But the economically significant schemes are most essentially not such. There the sum of all payments, the total social product, will in general not be zero."[4]

"Trading," wrote Martin Mayer in *The Bankers: The Next Generation*, "is a zero-sum game: the bank [that is] trading financial instruments with its customer profits when the customer loses." Of course, when the bank is acting as an intermediary rather than a principal, its revenues "derive not from price movements that benefit the bank and harm the customer but from small dealer markups that can be taken when two customers have opposing needs and do their business through the bank." These aren't zero-sum games. But

> many of the instruments the banks have created for this trade are custom-designed for specific customers and are held by the bank as counterparty in the deal—and in constructing these instruments the bank has an enormous information advantage over its customer.[5]

Trading in financial instruments for house accounts whether as a principal or as an intermediary (customers often don't know which) is where the commercial banking that Martin was writing about and the investment banking that is Wall Street's stock in trade (as it were) come together. What instruments do all these banks trade? Well, stocks and bonds, of course, and the debt securities of all manner of governments, and dollars and foreign currencies, and options to buy or sell stocks and bonds and governments and currencies. Especially options, which are a form of *futures* securities collectively referred to as *derivatives* since their value depends on the value of other securities like stocks and bonds. Investors use options to insure against or hedge the risk that the price of the other securities they hold—or have agreed to buy or sell—will move in the wrong direction and lose them money.

A few chapters back we mentioned that trading in options took off beginning in 1973 when the Black-Scholes method of valuing options was published and the Chicago Board of Options Exchange opened for business. But the seeds of Black-Scholes were planted in the 1950s when finance economists and future Nobel laureates Harry Markowitz and William Sharpe were developing portfolio theory and the Capital Asset Pricing Model.[6]

Markowitz created a computer model to reduce the risk of an investment portfolio relative to its anticipated return through statistically planned diversification. Sharpe's Capital Asset Pricing Model measured the volatility of a given portfolio—its *beta*—relative to the market as a whole. A portfolio expected to decrease in value by 12% when the market goes down by 10% or increase 12% when the market goes up 10% would have a beta of 1.2—and to Wall Street's way of thinking would have to earn 1.2. times the overall market return to justify the extra downside risk. Similarly, a single stock with a beta of 1.2 would be expected to earn 12% more, relative to its price, than the stock market as a whole.

Not that the corporation issuing the stock would have to do anything itself. The market, being efficient—these models *made* it efficient—simply adjusts the price of the stock so that the earnings estimates for the corporation fulfill the market's return-on-investment expectations.

The Capital Asset Pricing Model, wrote Joel Kurtzman in *The Death of Money*,

is now [1993] used in investment houses around the world as the scaffold on which investment portfolios are built. It is so widely used that trillions of dollars have been traded based on how the equations turn out. It has nothing to do with quality or what companies make. It has nothing to do with how long or short term a manager thinks. It is simply mathematics.[7]

The mathematics became the scaffold on which Fisher Black and Myron Scholes built their models for valuing options and other derivatives so widely used in hedging. Both the investment and hedging strategies of the big players on Wall Street are now driven by mathematical computer models.

The basic hedging maneuver, covering in the futures market a position taken in the stock or bond market, is considered prudent and conservative. But taking the same action in the futures market when there is no position to hedge is the equivalent of speculating, which, being the equivalent of gambling, is considered neither prudent nor conservative—unless, of course, you happen to be a professional gambler.

"According to one source," wrote Jeff Madrick in a review of books about George Soros and other capitalists,

90 percent of all international financial transactions were once related to actual trade or long-term investment compared to only 10 percent in today's explosively growing markets, which are dominated by short-term investments in currencies, futures, "derivatives," and other investments.[8]

In other words, of all the money moving around the world financing *something*, only 10% finances the movement or production of real goods and services. The other 90% represents hedging or speculation in financial products. The financial economy is *nine* times the size of the real economy.

"The speculative markets now dwarf the 'real' markets," said Kurtzman.[9] He cited McKinsey economist Kenichi Ohmae to the effect that $20 to $25 billion changes hands each day to finance the world trade in real goods and services. But the total amount of money changing hands around the world each day is around $800 billion. That means that the financial economy is *30* times the size of the real economy, not 9 times. Another source cited by Kurtzman estimated that the financial economy is 30 to *50* times larger.[10]

The gambling capital of the world is no longer Monte Carlo or Las Vegas. The gambling capital of the world is Wall Street together with its counterpart streets all over the world—Global Wall Street.

Global Wall Street has far more money at its disposal than all the treasuries of all the countries in the world put together. One consequence is that governments have very little control over the value of their own national currencies. In 1992 a hedge fund (so-called) run by George Soros bet a reported $10 billion that the British government would not be able to prevent the devaluation of the British pound. When the smoke cleared, the Brits had folded, the pound had devalued, and the hedge fund (so-called) had pocketed a reported $1 billion in winnings.

Such a showdown would have been unheard of in the days when the pound and other currencies were linked to the dollar by fixed exchange rates and the dollar was supported by the commitment of the U.S. government to exchange dollars held by foreigners for gold at the rate of $35 an ounce. But the United States lived beyond its means for too many years. The performance of its obligations as the issuer of the world's reserve currency, as the only Western superpower in the Cold War, and as the principal market for goods produced by expanding economies abroad left a large amount of dollars in foreign hands. In the early 1970s the U.S. government unilaterally closed the gold window. The dollar quickly lost more than 17% of its value as measured by its rate of exchange with other major currencies, and over the course of the next year or so, all currencies, cut adrift from their anchor through the dollar to gold, started floating freely.

With gold and fixed exchange rates banished to history, what now determines the value of the dollar in international markets?

Public confidence and interest rates appear to be the main determinants.[11] Public confidence because money, having no intrinsic value, is worth what people think it's worth. And interest rates because, well, in the new financial economy driven by mathematical computer models, interest rates determine the value of just about everything!

In chapter 4 we noted that the stock market fell 3% on March 8, 1996, on the news of a major decline in the unemployment rate. Unemployment declines when business is good, we observed, but Wall Street worried that higher employment would lead to higher wages, higher inflation, and therefore higher interest rates. Not content just to worry, it took matters into its own efficient hands and raised interest rates by selling bonds (and lowering bond prices) and then lowered stock prices by selling stocks.

Now, the bond market has always worried about higher employment and higher wages because these conditions portend higher interest rates and, on the flip side, lower bond prices. According to labor economist Alan Krueger, who studied the correlation between interest yielded by the government's 30-year bond and employment data in the government's monthly employment report, 25,000 new jobs translate into one more basis point (1% of 1%) in the interest rate, and so does an additional $.02 in the hourly wage.[12]

But to the stock market, in the days when it was dominated by long-term investors, what was good for business was good for stock prices even if that meant higher interest rates (and higher costs) in the short term. In an earlier year the stock market would have gone *up* on March 6 as the bond market went down. But by 1996 the countermovement of stock and bond prices had largely disappeared. Why?

According to Martin Mayer, the stock market "is full of mutual and pension funds and bank trust departments that must buy stock in every company" in the Standard & Poor's index of the top 500 companies. And by buying and selling the market as a whole rather than individual stocks, they are turning the market into "just another commodity—as its recent volatility has shown." In a 1996 article entitled "Gaming on Wall Street," Mayer wrote that the big players in the market, being disciples of finance economics (which "is about making money, not about producing anything"), buy and sell stocks and index futures and options in combinations prescribed by their models to give them the safety of a Treasury bill but with a higher return. The stock market tends to move in the same direction as the bond market because "the mathematics used in trading today's index funds [and futures] emphasizes interest rate changes," just as it does in trading Treasury bills and bonds.[13] The stock and bond markets are in thrall to the same master.

Indeed, *all* financial markets are in thrall to the master of interest rates, including currency markets (as we just saw) that determine the value of the money invested. Stocks, bonds, indexes, index futures, options, and even currencies are just vehicles to arrive at the highest return on investment.[14] It makes little difference where the vehicle goes, or who drives it, or whether it even leaves the parking lot, so long as it ends up with more money than it started with—and more than other vehicles would have earned.

Picking the right vehicle has very rich rewards, and Wall Street puts its best players on the A team. Senior traders earn $1 to $2 million a year, according to a placement firm in 1996, but senior traders working on the firm's own proprietary accounts earn as much as $5 million a year.[15]

It's a myth that Wall Street's primary function is raising money for public corporations or financing the products and services they produce. As Joel Kurtzman said, "[M]athematical models . . . divorced the investor from [its] traditional role of bringing capital to a company in return for a share of the profits and a share of the company's net worth."[16] Today, **Wall Street's primary function is trading for its own account** in a financial market that is many times the size of the market for goods and services and that is all about making money, not producing anything.

But when its client *isn't* itself, Wall Street serves the interests of client and investor simultaneously—with great finesse.

Chapter 26

Investment Bankers Serve the Interests of Clients and Investors Simultaneously

Although compensated by and hence ostensibly serving those obtaining the capital, the investment banker must give equal consideration to the protection and interests of investors.
—Eric L. Kohler, *A Dictionary for Accountants*[1]

The mindset that increasingly regards companies as assets, casually to be bought and sold, is becoming more pervasive.
—Harvey H. Segal, *Corporate Makeover*[2]

For public corporations and for private corporations seeking to become public corporations, the heart of Wall Street is still investment banking. The investment banker acts "as a middleman for corporations needing original or additional financing and investors willing to risk their savings" and in so doing serves the interests of corporate client and public investors simultaneously.[3] It's a delicate balancing act, protecting the buyer while at the same time satisfying the seller, but that's why investment banking is so prestigious—and lucrative.

The prestige and reputation of Wall Street's bankers are well guarded by the financial press and media, but occasionally this great propaganda machine is caught nodding.

An article in the October 6, 1996, business section of the *New York Times* entitled "When Boards Say 'No Deal' to Holders" began this way: "Imagine that somebody knocks on your door and offers to buy your house for more than you thought it was worth." You're ready to sell, but your real estate broker prevents you. Of course, real estate brokers can't really prevent you from selling your house, but, according to the *Times*, "a board of directors can—and these days increasingly does—slam the door on an unsolicited bid for a company, even when shareholders favor the deal.''

The case in point was the rejection of an unsolicited offer to buy the stock of Wallace Computer Services by Moore Corporation, "a rival office-supply company." (That, incidentally, is the only description in the article of what either corporation did for a living.) The rejecters were the directors on Wallace's board, which was supported by the old-line investment banking firm of Goldman, Sachs, hired by Wallace as an independent expert, and ultimately by a federal district judge in Delaware, Wallace's state of incorporation. The rejectees were Wallace's shareholders, or rather the holders of the three-quarters of Wallace's stock that was tendered for purchase by Moore.

This was the cast of the drama as reviewed by the *Times*. Who in its view wore the white hats?

Well, certainly not Goldman. Investment bankers, despite their expertise, "may have a vested interest in keeping the management happy." (Goldman was paid $8 million for its advice to Wallace.) And not Wallace's board. Directors, despite their fiduciary duty to do right by the shareholders, "tend to circle the wagons whenever their salaries and perquisites are threatened." (The same, of course, may be said of management.) And not even the court. Judges, despite their legal training, are "but ill equipped to act as stock market analysts."

That leaves only the holders of Wallace's shares, even though an estimated 45%—three-fifths of the shares tendered to Moore—were held by equity arbitrageurs. Equity arbs are "professional investors . . . who jump into takeover frays in hopes of making a quick buck"—professional Wall Street gamblers speculating for their own account. But in the financial media, gamblers wear white hats when they costume themselves as shareholders.

One of the arbs, Guy Wyser-Pratte, claimed that Goldman's analysis of Wallace's worth was full of math errors. (Goldman's mathematical models full of math errors?) Other critics said that Goldman used multiples that were too high and discount rates that were too low—thus exaggerating the value of Wallace's equity and reducing by the same amount the value of Moore's takeover offer. Goldman had even used information provided by Wallace's management, despite management's natural proclivity toward optimism in matters pertaining to the corporation it is paid to manage.[4]

But why would anyone rely on the opinion of a hired gun when they can get an unbiased opinion from their own expert for free? The stock market divines all the earnings or cash flows that a company will ever generate (and the risk that it won't), computes their present value, and proclaims that value as the value of the company—efficiently, objectively, and in real time. In Wallace's case, it proclaimed that the company was worth less than the $30 a share Moore was offering. A year later it reached the same conclusion. How could Goldman maintain that the market *under*valued Wallace?

For that matter, why would Moore offer *more* than that value?

Moore's reason was control. Wallace shareholders were apartment dwellers, not house owners, and Moore wanted control of the whole building, not just their apartments. Control always sells for a premium since it allows you to do anything you want, including tearing down the building. But the premium attaches to a *collection* of shares (enough to control the corporation), not individual shares. Since the stock market values individual shares, it ignores the premium—until the arbs jump in and bid up the market in anticipation of a takeover at the premium price.

Goldman's task was to prove that Wallace's shares were worth more than their market value *plus* the control premium offered by Moore. Not so difficult a task, really, considering that all mathematical models, Goldman's included, are puppets supported by strings of assumptions like multiples and discount rates that have been input (and manipulated) by their master. The devil is in the inputs that the audience never sees. Thus, one banker's model can value a takeover target at more than an unsolicited bid for the company, another banker's model can value it at less, and a judge (if anyone sues) can reasonably conclude that reasonable directors can choose either value!

By choosing the higher value, the directors can just say no to the unsolicited bid and slam the door. But neither the directors nor the investment banker who came up with the higher value may be serving the best interests of the shareholders. In most cases, according to Joseph Grundfest, a former commissioner of the Securities and Exchange Commission, they are not: "Shareholders by a wide margin would make more money if target boards accepted the highest bid and then shareholders invested that money in the stock market. Over time, shareholders are worse off if premium bidders are rejected."[5]

How worse off, of course, varies with the size of the control premium, which in turn depends on the eye of the acquiring corporation or raider—the synergy that it sees the acquisition producing, or the financial leverage.

Although the two-plus-two-equals-five concept of synergy has acquired a bad reputation because (as previously observed) so many mergers fail, corporate mergers like the one that didn't happen between Moore and Wallace are all based on the synergistic assumption that the acquired corporation will be worth more to the acquiring corporation than the acquiring corporation is paying to the selling shareholders. Synergy makes these mergers *non-zero-sum games*. If the merger turns out badly for the acquiring corporation and the synergy is, in fact, negative, a destruction rather than a production of goods may occur. But in any event, the sum of all payments will in general not be zero, and neither will the total social product.

During the 1960s, investment bankers arranged many mergers and acquisitions in which the total social product was not zero. Thus were the great conglomerates like ITT created. In the 1970s, as the supply of eligible corporations willing to be bought—that is, whose managers (and directors) were willing to have them bought—got scarce, investment bankers promoted (and resisted) so-called hostile takeovers, which (as in the case of Wallace) created rifts between shareholders and their managers and directors. But hostile takeover battles generated great fees for the investment banks that lined up on both sides of the battlefield.

In the 1980s investment banks started arranging the breakup of large public corporations—many of them clients that the banks had built up in the 1960s and 1970s—in order (so they said) to make them more competitive. The favored tactic was to take the public corporations private (the reverse of going public) through leveraged buyouts, or LBOs. In an LBO, *leveraged* signifies that almost all the cash used to buy out the shareholders is debt borrowed from outsiders rather than equity contributed by the new owners. Inevitably, that debt becomes the corporation's debt. Now, since leverage can catapult a corporation into the poorhouse as readily as into the promised land, investment bankers once believed that too much of it—say, for a manufacturing company, a 50–50 debt/equity ratio, as much debt as equity—was worse than too little. LBOs, ended all that.

LBOs, being essentially one-corporation transactions, aren't premised on synergy. As such, they tend to be zero-sum gambles with little social benefit in which the acquiring party, with all or most of the money needed to make the acquisition borrowed from someone else, stands to profit immensely (if it doesn't fail). Take the buyout of Metromedia by John Kluge, its CEO. He became "America's first billionaire," wrote Michael Lewis, by turning "a $3 billion profit for himself in eliminating his shareholders."[6]

"What has to be recognized," said Harvey Segal in *Corporate Makeover*, "is that there is an inherent and irresolvable conflict of interest in any management-led buyout."[7] Investment bankers who finance management buyouts share that inherent and irresolvable conflict of interest.

But the prospect of making billions on an investment in which they had to put down no cash attracted a new breed of financiers specializing in leveraged buyouts for their own account. Many were individuals like Carl Icahn with little or no experience in the business acquired. But the champion was a firm named Kohlberg, Kravis and Roberts—KKR for short.

In May 1990 the *Wall Street Journal* published an account by Susan Faludi of the Safeway Stores LBO, the fourth largest of the 1980s. Safeway's CEO was 44-year-old Peter Magowan, the founder's son. Under his leadership, wrote Faludi, the corporation "produced earnings that more than doubled in the first four years of the 1980s, to a record [high] in 1985. The stock price tripled in three years, and dividends climbed four years in a row." But in July 1986, when the stock was trading at about $37 a share, corporate raiders Herbert and Robert Haft made an offer to buy the stock owned by Safeway's shareholders for upward of $64 a share. "Selling to the Hafts might have cost Chairman Magowan his job and, he felt, ultimately might have brought a breakup of the company." So Magowan called KKR.

Moving quickly, KKR formed a group of 70 institutional investors to lend a newly formed corporation $5,475 million to buy the stock of the old Safeway corporation at $67.50 a share and pay the costs of the buyout, including KKR's

$60 million advisory fee. KKR spent $2 million of its fee to purchase 20% of the shares of the new Safeway and pocketed $58 million. The institutional investors spent $173 million to buy the remaining 80% of the shares. After the LBO, Safeway's equity stood at $175 million, its debt at almost $5.5 *billion.*

In the third century B.C., Archimedes used this hyperbole to define leverage to the king of Syracuse: *Give me place to stand, and I will move the world.* On July 27, 1986, KKR used this debt/equity ratio to define leverage to the new private Safeway corporation: *97:3.*

"The Safeway LBO," said Faludi, who won the Pulitzer Prize for her article,

is often cited as one of the most successful in this regard. It brought shareholders a substantial premium at the outset, and since then the company has raised productivity and operating profits and produced riches for the new investors and top management.[8]

The shareholders of the old public Safeway corporation did indeed get a substantial premium for their shares, but they gave up ownership of a thriving, profitable, dividend-paying enterprise. Magowan and his top managers did indeed become rich, but they gave up control of Safeway. The leading investor, KKR, acquired control and 20% of what was then the largest supermarket chain in the world for *no investment whatsoever* in a transaction that netted it $58 million in advisory fees. Four years later, its 20% was valued by the market (in a Safeway public offering) at $160 million. Whose interests did this LBO primarily serve?

And how did the LBO raise productivity and operating profits so as to produce these riches?

LBO fans argue that the reason successful LBOs raise productivity and operating profits (and produce riches for their investors and managers) is precisely the leverage that the old breed of investment bankers would have deplored as too risky. When 97% of a corporation's financing involves fixed debt payments, all hands have to work diligently to avoid a default in those payments leading, potentially, to bankruptcy—or their being fired.

Listening to this argument, you might assume that Safeway got the money to pay down its $5.5 billion debt by selling groceries more diligently than it used to. In fact, most of the money came from selling grocery *stores*—almost half the stores Safeway owned before the buyout. More than a third of its employees—63,000 people—lost their jobs with Safeway. Most of those who continued working for the new owners of the stores or found other work had to take a cut in pay. Many could never find other work. One, a trucker and loyal Safeway booster for 30 years, marked the first anniversary of his being fired by shooting himself.

But Wall Street's models don't consider the return to workers or customers. All they consider is the return to the investors, among whom—first and foremost—was KKR. And KKR had a great return. Therefore, Wall Street pronounced the Safeway LBO to be a great success.

It's a myth that investment bankers serve the interests of clients and investors simultaneously. These days, **investment bankers put their own interests first**—and increasingly those interests conflict with the interests of the clients they are supposed to represent and the investors they are supposed to protect.

Nevertheless, Wall Street is still a level field when the game that's being played is one of its traditional functions—creating primary markets for corporate securities or maintaining secondary markets where the investing public can trade them.

Chapter 27

The Market Is a Level Trading Field for Public Investors

A market, then, is theoretically perfect only when all traders have perfect knowledge of the conditions of supply and demand, and the consequent rate of exchange.

—William Stanley Jevons[1]

Q. How many efficient-market economists does it take to change a light bulb? A. None—the market has already changed it for them.

—Economists' joke

One of the great assets of Wall Street is its propaganda machine. Its flagship publication the *Wall Street Journal* blends financial news with advocacy that, if Wall Street were a public corporation, would be thought of as public relations, government relations, and investor relations. But periodicals like *Forbes* or *Barron's* or even the Sunday business section of the *New York Times* focus mostly on just investor relations. And in the growing number of television and radio programs ostensibly devoted to business, business seems to mean investing—period.

The very language of business is changing to accommodate this narrowing focus. The word *money*, as in *Money* magazine, no longer refers to dollar bills and change in your pocket or what you've got in the bank. Now it refers to the return you earn from the financial products you invest in—money as in *money management.*

"In Real Life," as the *Times* titled a 1996 chart showing how much (in millions) Wall Street traders made, "Wall Street's a Hit."[2] Employment is increasing and pay is skyrocketing. The obsession with Wall Street led writer

Colleen Boyle into taking a job in investment banking rather than in her first love, publishing. In "Surviving a Detour to Business School," Boyle wrote that in her detour years (at Columbia Business School), she was trained for little else and socialized by peers and professors alike to value no career more." But at the investment bank she encountered "the personalities of those to whom I reported. Initial cockiness was surpassed by conceit only to be exceeded by insolence." And the absence of "goals of building a better consumer good or creating a manufacturing concern" troubled her. Looking back, she asks: "Is this why business schools exist, as expensive training grounds for the trading floor?"[3]

The new financiers that emerged in the 1980s—individuals and firms acting for their own account and specializing in hostile tender offers and leveraged buyouts—are indeed traders, but what they trade are whole companies rather than stocks or bonds or derivatives or commodities. Some use coercive tactics that have earned them the title of *raider*. One such tactic is the two-tiered tender offer where the raider offers to pay a control premium for the shares required to gain control and a lesser amount for shares tendered after that time. (At Harvard Law School, I recall learning that what was offered for any shares had to be offered for all—but often what we learned was what the law *should* be, not what it *was*.) Another tactic is greenmail, buying enough stock in a corporation to threaten management with loss of control, then demanding that the corporation buy back the stock at a hefty premium above the market price and a hefty profit to the raider—and a corresponding charge to shareholders' equity.

If old-line investment bankers sometimes subordinate the interests of shareholders to the interests of managers (their clients), the new breed of investment bankers often subordinates the interests of shareholders and managers to its own interests.

The arena where companies are fought over is largely unpoliced, a modern-day Dodge City (with the nearest marshal in Wilmington, Delaware) compared to the regulated markets on Wall Street where registered securities are bought and sold. Since members of the public trade in these markets, rules are enforced and guns are checked at the door. ("Markets," says Martin Mayer, "are entirely the creatures of a legal order."[4] Particularly *free* markets.) According to the Stock Market Course materials prepared by the publisher of *Forbes* magazine, we all should feel grateful:

For the purpose of realizing capital gains, the stock market is ideal in many respects. It is continuously in operation—one can always locate a buyer or a seller for a major stock. Unlike real estate, there is never any question of the prevailing price for a specific listed stock. Rather, prices are determined by millions of buyers and sellers, and are out in the open for all to see.[5]

The message is clear, isn't it? Each of us may use the stock market to increase our personal wealth, confident in the knowledge that all transactions are above-board where we can see them. Each public corporation can trust the stock market to value its stock correctly and treat its shareholders and the investors who are potential shareholders honestly. The market is a level trading field.

Let's go take a look at how some of the players on this field trade.

Underwriters price shares of stock in an initial public offering at "roughly 10% below their perceived fair market value," according to the *Wall Street Journal*. Many of these discounted shares are sold to institutional investors that *invest* no longer than it takes to resell the shares to the public at market value. According to a survey by Salomon Brothers, a quarter to a half of all IPO shares are flipped in this manner on the first day of the offering. So who cares? The "companies whose shares are flipped and the legions of small investors who are barred from the party," says the *Journal*—the companies because the discounts reduce their proceeds from the offering without benefiting their future shareholders.[6] Does anyone besides the flippers benefit? Well, yes: the issuing companies' underwriters who minimize their underwriting risk by pricing the issue at such a large discount; and the brokers who curry the favor of big customers by feeding them shares to flip. Level trading field?

Dealers in the Nasdaq "try to get in on virtually every trade," wrote Floyd Norris in the *New York Times*, preventing direct customer-to-customer transactions that would benefit the customers but reduce the dealers' income.[7] Stock exchanges, on the other hand, facilitate direct trading between customers and bar dealers (called *specialists*) from competing with them when they place an order to buy or sell shares. Nasdaq dealers make even more money if the customer is an individual by not sharing or even revealing the better prices quoted in a private market—Reuters' Instinet—to which only institutional investors are invited. (In the bond market, brokers and dealers don't reveal *any* prices other than what the customer pays or receives since "information on mark-ups and mark-downs is irrelevant to most investors"—according to the Public Securities Association.)[8] "A fundamental change of philosophy is needed," says Norris, "in which market markers [dealers] get involved only when they are needed, not whenever they scent a way to make money off a customer." [9] Some such change may be coming, if only because both the Justice Department and the Securities and Exchange Commission concluded in 1996 that Nasdaq firms had illegally conspired among themselves to keep prices high.

Brokers are commonly accused of churning their customers' accounts—trading them more than necessary. "Like sharks who must keep moving or suffocate," says Robert Nylen, "brokers must transact . . . or else" because they earn a commission only when a customer buys or sells. Mutual fund managers, on the other hand, earn a fee each year based on the value of the assets being managed; if the fund's value increases, so does the manager's fee—and vice versa. Nylen, editor in chief of *Media and the Law*, believes that a broker should be compensated by asset-based fees, the way mutual fund managers are compensated, rather than by transaction-based commissions that encourage brokers to act like sharks.[10]

Analysts who work for an investment bank are expected to say nice things about the stock of the bank's clients, according to the *Wall Street Journal*, and they're also "expected through their recommendations to drum up interest in stocks, producing a flow of trading commissions." And that's not all that's expected of them. Wayne Whipple, executive director of the New York Society of Security Analysts, says that their bonus, which typically represents more than half their income, "depends heavily on the amount of investment banking business they bring in."[11] (A study out of Columbia Business School that quantified analysts' ratings of companies involved in investment banking transactions such as an offering of securities found that ratings of banking clients averaged 8% higher than nonclients and, in mergers and acquisitions, 12.5% higher.)[12] The more time analysts spend on investment banking, of course, the less time they can devote to researching the companies they report on—perhaps as little as one day out of five.[13]

Money managers, says Andrew Cox, a mutual fund trustee, "can all say, 'I do it at home after my kids are in bed,' but, well, give me a break." He was referring to trading for their own account. Security analysts, writes Susan Antilla in the *New York Times*, are "making money at their day jobs of picking stocks for customers, and trading their personal portfolios on the side. So why not mutual fund portfolio managers?"[14] What's really a conflict of interest for money managers (and brokers) is *front-running*—executing personal trades *before* executing client trades in the same security. "It's all a big no-no and against the rules," wrote Paul Gibson in *Bear Trap*. "It's also widely practiced."[15]

Corporate executives may sell or sometimes buy stock of their corporation on the basis of inside information—information that's not (yet) been made available to the public or (presumably) the other party to the transaction. One apparent instance of such trading was described by Kurt Eichenwald in the *New York Times*. Optical Data Systems, a computer networking corporation, announced in September 1993 that it expected quarterly earnings to be 30% below the prior quarter's earnings because of weak sales. The next day the price of its shares dropped by a third. But in the weeks before the announcement and the price drop, three senior executives sold a large percentage of their stock holdings.[16] Level trading field?

Since 1989 the *Wall Street Journal* has staged a contest between investment pros and a dartboard in what it calls "a lighthearted test of the 'efficient-market theory.'" The theory, which is "hated on Wall Street [it could put thousands of people out of business] but accepted by many academics," according to *Journal* reporter John Dorfman,

states that stock-picking success is basically a "random walk," or a matter of luck. The notion is that, since all publicly known information is instantaneously factored into stock prices, an uninformed person—or a chimp throwing darts—can do as well as a knowledgeable professional.

But even efficient-market believers concede that "people who possess non-public 'inside information' can beat the market."[17] That's why trading with inside information is against the law. The typical case involves a conflict of interest between a corporate manager buying or selling shares of the corporation's stock while possessing inside information that was acquired during the course of employment, and that, as a consequence (so say the lawyers), belongs to the corporation, and a present or future shareholder selling or buying those shares without the benefit of that information. The conflict of interest subverts the stock market by distorting the price that the market—any market—is supposed to set.

But so do all the conflicts of interest described earlier—between underwriters and the corporate issuers they represent (and the issuers' shareholders), between Nasdaq dealers and their customers, between commission brokers and their clients, between stock analysts and the investors who rely on their reports, between money managers and the institutions whose money they manage. All these conflicts distort the prices the market is supposed to set, making it less perfect, less efficient.

It's a myth that Wall Street is a level trading field. **On Wall Street, insiders are always looking down on outsiders**.

Among the newer insiders on Wall Street are some commercial banks whose basic business, making loans to corporations, had declined as corporations found it less costly to borrow money by issuing securities. One heavy hitter among the newcomers is Bankers Trust Company, which specialized in complex derivative products. In 1994, derivatives brought it notoriety.

Multinational corporations use derivatives to hedge against fluctuations in foreign currencies and interest rates so that they can plan the profit from future operations abroad with greater certainty. Originally, they used publicly traded options and futures, but as the number of foreign markets grew, so did the complexity and hazards of hedging. Corporations increasingly turned to specialists like Bankers Trust that sold customized products. Customized products aren't traded in public markets. Both parties to the contract have to live with them until maturity. Customized products are zero-sum games. One party wins what the other party loses.

What Bankers Trust excelled at were exotic products such as leveraged interest rate swaps that its clients sometimes used not just to lock in favorable long-term interest rates but to bet on them. When rates were low, the clients made money on those bets. When rates jumped up in 1994, some of them claimed that they had been gulled—and sued. One of the suers was Procter & Gamble.

P&G's swap involved giving up a fixed interest rate and agreeing to pay a floating interest rate instead. The formula as described by the *Times*' Floyd Norris is as follows (it won't be on the quiz):

Six months after the deal was signed, multiply the yield on 5-year Treasuries by 17.0415 and then subtract the price of the outstanding 30-year Treasury, which had a coupon of 6.25 percent. That figure, less 0.75 percentage points, was the margin above commercial paper that would be paid, in most cases.[18]

According to Norris, P&G might have had to pay interest of more than 30% a year—and it did have to pay about 20% a year for four years. "Derivatives are truly remarkable things," says finance professor Andre Perold, but they're not for the uninitiated. On the other hand, "You can't say, 'We never speculate, we only hedge.' That's impossible and if it weren't it would probably be too costly. A little bit of speculation is probably good, if you are any good at it."[19]

Bankers Trust was good at it—better, apparently, than many of its customers. "What is clear from interviews with former Bankers Trust executives" and others, concluded the *Wall Street Journal*, "is that Bankers Trust has been unusually aggressive in selling the products as well as in using them to its own advantage, even if this turned out to be at the expense of its clients."[20]

Level trading field? That's the kind of issue that's ultimately decided in a court of law. But even if insiders on Wall Street take advantage of outsiders, overall, we can say, Wall Street's influence on the economy (and public corporations in particular) is beneficial.

Chapter 28

Wall Street's Influence on Public Corporations Is Beneficial

What's good for the United States is good for the New York Stock Exchange. But what's good for the New York Stock Exchange might not be good for the United States.
—William McChesney Martin, chairman of the Federal Reserve Board[1]

It is a well-understood point that the returns to society from an investment may be either much less or much more than their payoff to the private investor.
—Paul Krugman, *Peddling Prosperity*[2]

Public corporations are married to Wall Street, and their spouse, scion not only of the world's richest financial empire but also of the world's loudest publishing network, influences (not to say dominates) everything the corporations do. Some corporations like Safeway get a divorce by going private—the divorce, typically, being financed by investment bankers—but then, like Safeway, they usually get married again because the bankers want the kind of return on their investment that only public markets can finance. Once more, everything they do is influenced (not to say dominated) by Wall Street.

Fortunately, Wall Street's influence on public corporations is beneficial. Their performance is continuously measured against what they said they were going to do, what they did previously, and what other comparable companies are doing currently. Any discrepancies are denounced by stock analysts and punished by docking the share price. If the discrepancies are persistent or egregious, those institutional investors who have remained loyal may offer constructive criticisms, and directors representing the public may even suggest changes in management.

Attention to duty is encouraged along with frugality. Take each day as it comes and let the market take care of the future. Stick to your knitting and leave diversification to portfolio managers. Satisfy customers, but don't spoil them. Don't spend money on anything that isn't sure to pay you back in the near future with interest exceeding what that money cost you. Don't hire too many people; don't pay them more than necessary; don't keep them longer than needed. Outsource whenever possible so that costs can be monitored and controlled. If competitors can do the job at lower cost, let them—even if they're foreigners. If you can't be first or second in your market, get out of it, downsize, if necessary liquidate, and pay back the people who invested in you.

Never forget that the people who invested in you entrusted you with their hard-earned savings. They could have invested in risk-free Treasury bills or bonds instead.

Wall Street loves public corporations, but it's tough love.

The government also adds its own tough love, the kind provided by regulators, the cops on the Street who make sure that you don't keep bad company, don't hang out with price-fixers or swindlers or unlicensed gamblers. And then there's the tough love provided by the government's own banker, the austere federal agency that regulates the business cycle in order to control inflation and perhaps (if it's feeling kindly) moderate unemployment. Since its weapon of choice is the rate of interest, which (we have seen) controls the value of just about everything that Wall Street trades, the head of this agency, the Federal Reserve Board, is considered on the Street to be the second most powerful person in the country, if not the world.

Some on Wall Street think that the Fed's role is misconceived. "There will always be cycles in markets and economies," wrote James Grant, editor of *Grant's Interest Rate Observer* newsletter. Booms "are the financial expression of innovation and derring-do. In the natural course of things, promoters will err on the side of excess." If the Fed (feeling kindly) seeks to subsidize an up cycle by holding interest rates down, the boom will be exaggerated because "in the heat of the up cycle, error is so financeable." But eventually the "robust American capacity to fail" comes into play.

If the Fed (feeling kindly) seeks to moderate that capacity to fail, again by holding rates down, growth in the next up phase may be stunted. Grant believes that governmental intervention in the natural cycle of markets may account for the slow growth in the economy since the 1960s, and governmental intervention in Western Europe and Japan for even slower growth in those economies. "Any economic system can cope with success," he says. "But capitalism excels at failure: recognizing it, cutting it short and, through the process of bankruptcy, forgiving it."[3]

Perhaps. But in a study by three economists of the "Economic Freedom of the World: 1975–1995," one of the tests of economic freedom is this: "Does government protect money as a store of value and allow it to be used as a medium of exchange?" This test, according to the *Economist*, "includes the volatility of inflation [and] monetary growth relative to the potential growth capacity of [the] economy''—exactly the focus of the U.S. Federal Reserve Board.

Other measures of economic freedom include how much the government taxes its citizens, whether they can hold foreign currencies and engage in international trade, the size of the trade deficit, and the amount of government spending relative to the size of the economy. The study's conclusion, said the *Economist*, "could scarcely be more emphatic: the more economic freedom a country had in that period, the more economic growth it achieved and the richer its citizens became." The least-free countries had the lowest standard of living (measured by gross domestic product per person) and a negative growth rate—the low standard of living was getting lower. The more freedom, the higher the standard of living and the higher the growth rate.[4]

The study ranked the U.S. fourth in economic freedom in the period 1993–1995 behind the city-states Hong Kong (not yet part of China) and Singapore and directly behind New Zealand. (A separate index rated New Zealand as the least corrupt country in the world in 1995, the United States only fifteenth.)[5] Japan was tenth in economic freedom, Germany twentieth. But why (corruption aside) wasn't the U.S. number one?

Taxation has something to do with why the United States is not ahead of Singapore—and why it's ahead of almost every other country it trades with. The U.S. has earned enough national income to pay its annual taxes (federal, state, and local) by April 11, but Singapore pays its taxes by March 4. The tax-free date for Japan is April 12, but the major European countries have to wait until sometime in May or June.[6] So compared to almost everyone else in the economically developed world where Churchill's Horses compete, Americans are not heavily taxed.

But the U.S. government also spends a lot more than the Singapore government relative to the size of its gross domestic product (although less on health care), and it has a larger public debt compared to GDP than New Zealand. The bulk of the U.S. debt that was outstanding in 1993–1995 was incurred to finance the large budget deficits in the 1980s and early 1990s. In borrowing so much, the government drove up the cost of money. Interest rates on short-term business borrowings in the 1980s averaged 4.25% above the rate of inflation. In the 1960s and 1970s, those rates averaged less than 2% above the rate of inflation.[7] Thus, the deficits raised real interest rates by almost 2.5%.

High interest rates deter investment. In the 1980s net investment in new plant and equipment as a percentage of national income declined by almost 1%. At the end of 1992, business investment in plant and equipment came to $63,000 per worker. But for the decline in the 1980s, the amount would have been $76,000—20% more.[8]

Lower investment rates impede the growth in productivity and therefore the growth in the economy and in national wealth and prosperity. Interest rates are the boss of all of us. In this case the rise in interest rates was caused in part—

probably in large part—by government spending and tax policies, not by the Fed—or Wall Street.

But less investment in productivity and growth means more money available for investment in Wall Street's products and markets. "In fact," wrote Floyd Norris, "the overall stock market seems to do best when economic growth is far from robust." The same was true in the Roaring Twenties, after economic growth had slowed down but before the Great Crash—people figuring why "build a new plant when you could get rich a lot faster by simply speculating in stocks."[9]

When a corporation uses the cash it earned to buy back its own shares from its investors—to *decapitalize*—rather than invest in its own products and services and productivity and growth, Wall Street applauds. Without in any way affecting total profit, decapitalization increases earnings per share (shares now being fewer in number) and return on equity investment (now reduced) and boosts the stock market price. Decapitalization takes money from the real economy and diverts it to the financial economy.

"There is competition for capital between the real economy and the financial economy," said equity strategist David Shulman. Wall Street, of course, is the home of the financial economy, the place where business is reduced to finance, and trading is increasingly for the trading firm's own account. As far as the real economy is concerned, Norris said, "slow growth, with the expectation of faster growth someday, seems to be just what Wall Street wants."[10]

The real world to Wall Street is trading securities, and the real markets are the securities markets. The trading is short term, of course (that's what distinguishes *trading* from *investing*), increasingly so, galvanized by the mindless speed of computers and the information—any information—they disgorge.

Like a stray dog scrounging the neighborhood garbage for scraps of food, Wall Street devours information as if all scraps were equally nourishing, significant, reliable, and true. Hip-shooting before aiming (or reflecting) makes trading whimsical and markets volatile. The actively managed mutual funds (those not indexed) appear to be the worst offenders. A recent increase in the volatility of both stocks and bonds, said the *New York Times* in February 1996, reflected the seeming "desire of mutual fund managers to leap in and out of the market at a moment's notice."[11] As Paul Gibson wrote, mutual funds, unlike pension funds, "don't ride out storms. When money flows in or out from investors, they react immediately."[12]

Financial markets, said economist Lawrence Summers, "often react to events far more than the fundamentals suggest they should."[13]

Market volatility increases the risk and therefore the cost of corporate investment, especially long-term investment. We saw the mechanics a few chapters back in the Capital Asset Pricing Model, which defines the rate at which all future earnings of a corporation are discounted back to their present value, that value representing one calculation of the current worth of the corporation. In defining the discount rate, CAP-M factors in the volatility of the corporation's stock based on its past market performance. The more volatile the stock, the greater the risk, which to risk-averse Wall Street is always bad, although risky stocks may have higher as well as lower returns. (Indeed, some efficient-market true-believers hold that picking volatile stocks is the only way to beat the efficient market.)[14] The greater the risk, the higher the discount rate and the lower the corporation's current value. And since the discount rate also represents the corporation's cost of equity capital, the more volatile the stock, the higher the corporation's cost of capital and therefore the higher the hurdle rate for its investments.

According to Michael Porter, the hurdle rates that corporations use to evaluate their investment projects appear to be higher than the calculated cost of capital.[15]

Discounting the future reduces the future to the present. And the present is where Wall Street's head is. When a few chapters back we cited Alan Krueger's correlation of higher employment and higher wages with interest rates yielded by government bonds, we were talking about the Treasury's *long bonds*, the ones that mature in 30 years, not short-term bills or notes. In reality, all financial markets are immediate. All react to news and rumors of current events that may affect current interest rates, even the market in long-term government bonds. Wall Street trades; it doesn't buy bonds to hold until maturity, and it doesn't buy stocks for the long haul. Its computer models comparing corporate operating and market performances rarely look more than a year into the future, if that.

"Long-term growth has declined as an influence on U.S. stock prices," concluded Michael Porter.[16]

Dealing in large portfolios of stocks, Wall Street does not have the patience to master the fundamentals of the different business it trades in. So it reduces all worth to simple numbers—productivity to profit, profit to profitability ratios, profitability ratios to share price—and relegates the future to CAP-M and growth to the back burner.

If the return from an investment can't be measured in numerical terms, Wall Street can't assign any value to it in its mathematical models. That makes it harder to justify research and development projects. In the 1990s, wrote Louis Uchitelle in the *New York Times*, corporate R&D became "a victim of downsizing, stiffer competition and the growing corporate view that the return from most research and development spending should come in three years or less." The biggest loser was basic research into new technologies that in the past "created new industries [and] helped to expand the national economy at a rapid pace." According to Uchitelle, "[M]any experts worry that in 20 years or so a shortfall of new technology could shackle the economy, even though the stock market does not show much concern."[17]

"We are eating our seed corn," said economist Paul Romer.[18] But *the stock market does not show much concern*.

It's a myth that Wall Street's influence on public corporations is beneficial. By reducing business to finance, the real world to its own trading world, the future to the present, and all worth to simple numbers—and then, adding insult, presuming to be the arbiter of all things corporate—**Wall Street has corrupted the basic purpose of public corporations**, producing goods and services for paying customers and thereby adding wealth and purchasing power to the economy. In so doing, it has inhibited corporate investment in innovation and productivity and growth.

We are all of us, consumers and workers, even investors, the poorer for it.

Afterword: We Are All Consumers, We Are All Workers

Americans, perhaps more than any other people in the world, define themselves in relationship to their work. . . . Employment is far more than a measure of income: for many it is the essential measure of self-worth.
—Jeremy Rifkin, *The End of Work*[1]

The key to long-term success—even survival—in business is what it has always been: to invest, to innovate, to lead, to create value where none existed before. Such determination, such striving to excel, requires leaders— not just controllers, market analysts and portfolio managers.
—Robert H. Hayes and William J. Abernathy,
"Managing Our Way to Economic Decline"[2]

You really can observe a lot by just watching—and listening. We have, for example, observed that the shareholders of Churchill's Horses, those great public corporations powering the American economy, don't control the corporation they own—and don't even own it in any meaningful sense of the word. Nor do they (except in rare instances) elect its directors, although they go through the motions every year. And even if they did elect its directors, they still wouldn't control the corporation since the directors (except in rare moments) don't control it either.

We may be thankful that Churchill's Horses are *not* controlled by either shareholders or directors who represent shareholders. Democracies and republics are not exactly known for their efficiency. Nations, of course, have interests more vital than efficiency to serve, so we accept democracies and republics (in Churchill's words) as "the worst form of government except all those other forms that have been tried from time to time."[3] But in our competitive economy, efficiency is the essence of business corporations, which survive by producing economic results with the economic resources entrusted to them.

We refer to that efficiency as profitability because we account for the economic results as profit.

But both profit and profitability (or profit ratioed against some other value like sales, assets, equity, market price, or profit from a prior period) are built up by what customers pay in and used up by what the corporation pays out. Two implications fairly leap off the page. First, customers have everything to do with the day-to-day, month-to-month, and year-to-year profit that keeps a corporation in business—but shareholders almost nothing. Second, cutting costs as a way to increase the profitability that measures efficiency is a piece of cake compared to expanding revenue since costs are inside the corporate fence where management can get its hands on them—but customers are not.

But that piece of cake, which usually comes from slicing jobs and people, goes only so far. Downsizing may increase profitability (after the downsizing costs have been accounted for), but the increase is apt to be short-lived. In the not-very-long-run increasing profitability means building markets and customers and revenue and profit itself by developing innovative new products and services and processes and techniques and increasing productivity—some or all of the above. In other words, growing better. Corporations that stand still ultimately lose their competitive edge and become soft and dull and less profitable.

It all takes investment that takes time to bear fruit, but Churchill's Horses don't invest as much of their profits as they used to. We ask the question we've asked before: Why not?

Well, we may believe that shareholders have almost nothing to do with a corporation's profit, but Wall Street holds to the faith that corporations have everything to do with shareholders—and trumpets that faith daily through its financial press and media. Lest corporate managers not heed the trumpet, its special advocacy group, the corporate governance movement, advocates that corporate executives and particularly CEOs and even directors (why leave them out?) first qualify as corporate shareholders and then be compensated according to how the corporation's *stock* performs—how much its value in the stock market increases. The device preferred by all parties to confer this form of compensation is, as we know, the stock option, which the corporation can issue without charge either to its own P&L or to the optionee.

Although stock-optioned managers don't necessarily remain shareholders of the corporation any longer than they have to, they've become true believers nonetheless. Managing the corporation *financially* for short-term market performance that favors shareholders seeking a quick profit (including the trader mentalities that dominate Wall Street) can make them a lot wealthier a lot faster than managing the corporation *strategically* for long-term profit performance. Thus, Churchill's Horses often seem to spend more money buying back their shares to boost the value of the outstanding stock (and stock options) than they do investing in the research and development of products and services for paying customers.

Does it matter? At the end of 1996, upward of one-quarter of all U.S. households owned shares of mutual funds that invest in corporate stocks, and the more than $200 billion these households invested during the year was the main force behind the bull market.[4] As employers transfer more of the cost of pension plans to employees and make more of them corporate shareholders under profit-sharing plans, the stock market is slowly but steadily becoming us. Someday corporate actions designed to benefit shareholders (and managers) may benefit more of us than not.

Someday. But even then investment income will never equal the wages and salaries we earn as workers or offset the loss of our paycheck when we're laid off—anymore than the lower prices we receive as consumers from foreign trade can ever offset the loss of our job to foreign competition.

Our economy, like all economies, really comes down to one essential: *jobs*. Work may define us, but at a more basic level—the level every economy comes down to—work provides us with the money to subsist and to consume. We are all workers (or have been or will be), we are all consumers—but relatively few of us are capitalists earning our living by investing. Eliminate jobs and you eliminate consumers. Eliminate enough jobs and enough consumers and then you eliminate capitalists and eventually gut the whole economy. More than one out of four workers was unemployed in the Great Depression, and more than one out of four banks failed.[5]

But America is hardly facing another great depression. (Although I can still hear Pearson Hunt cautioning his financial management class at Harvard Business School that not having experienced the Great Depression shouldn't lead us to believe that it couldn't happen again.) With jobs increasing, inflation under wraps, interest rates low, and the stock market bulling, the economy is looking good. And with profits increasing, especially in the large corporations, Churchill's Horses must be doing something right. Yet despite the favorable economic indicators, workers are insecure and consumption less than robust. The disparity between income at the top and bottom levels of the economy is widening. Productivity does not seem to be improving much in the service sector, where most of us work and computers abound. Corporations continue to underinvest in R&D even as the trade deficit hovers around $100 billion a year, meaning that we are producing less than we are consuming at a cost of something like a million jobs. Almost overnight, it seems, stores have become stocked with goods *made in China*.

Churchill's Horses are doing a lot of things right—and better than most foreign corporations—but increasingly they're being co-opted by the myth of shareholder supremacy and taking their eyes off the ball. They're focusing on the stock market instead of their own market. They're devoting too much time and attention and money placating current shareholders and not enough securing future customers—and their own survival. And they still haven't figured out how to motivate their employees or make them more productive or compensate them in such a way that the employees don't have to walk the plank every time corporate profits are threatened.

Churchill's Horses are doing a lot of things right—but they're still underachieving.

They have to invest more, innovate more, lead more, and create more value where none existed before. And take care of the people who do the corporation's work.

Table of Anti-Myths

PART I. CONTROL

How Churchill's Horses—our great public corporations—
became so powerful; who owns them, who controls them,
and in whose interests are they governed.

PART II. SHAREHOLDERS

How the value of the investment of the shareholders of
public corporations is maximized, measured, and distributed;
why public corporations exist.

7. Only Profit That the Corporation Distributes in Dividends Is Owned by the Shareholders

8. The Function of a Public Corporation Is to Satisfy the Needs of Paying Customers

PART III. CUSTOMERS

How the needs of the customers of public corporations are satisfied through marketing, brand enhancement, low pricing (as required by the law of supply and demand), and innovation.

9. Corporations Engage in Marketing to Satisfy Their Own Needs— Selling

10. Corporations Invest in Brands to Increase the Value of the Brand to Themselves

11. Corporations Mark Up Their Prices and Limit Demand to Maximize Profit

12. Public Corporations *Under*invest in Innovation

PART IV. MANAGERS

How the managers of public corporations are entrepreneurial, strategic, and capable of running any business; how their competence is enhanced through team management.

13. Public Corporations Are Too Bureaucratic for Management to Be Entrepreneurial

14. Public Corporation Planning Is Too Short Term for Strategic Management

15. Professional Management Requires On-the-Job Experience and In-depth Knowledge

16. Corporate Management Is CEO Management, and Corporate Power Is CEO Power

PART V. CEOS

How the chief executives of public corporations are controlled by outside directors; how they are fairly compensated; how their compensation is linked to performance; how they perform.

PART VI. WORKERS

How workers are motivated by public corporations, although downsizing and layoffs are required by global competition and the business cycle; how they benefit from increased productivity.

PART VII. CAPITALISTS

How the financiers of public corporations serve their corporate clients, their clients' shareholders, and the investing public; how they exert a beneficial influence on Churchill's Horses.

Notes on Sources

Introduction: Our Underachieving Corporations

1. Quoted in Louis E. Boone, *Quotable Business* (New York: Random House, 1992), 226–227.

2. Commencement address, Yale University, 1962.

3. "Sixty Years of American Business: Great Businessmen," *Forbes*, September 15, 1977, P30.

4. See Robert J. Schoenberg, *Geneen* (New York: W. W. Norton, 1958), chaps. 18, 19.

5. Harvey H. Segal, *Corporate Makeover: The Reshaping of the American Economy* (New York: Viking, 1989), vii–viii, 2.

6. "The Pain of Layoffs for Ex-Senior I.B.M. Workers," *New York Times*, December 23, 1993.

7. Nicholas von Hoffman, *Capitalist Fools: Tales of American Business, from Carnegie to Forbes to the Milken Gang* (New York: Doubleday, 1992), 99, referring to "these organizations, these companies, these corporations and protected partnerships."

8. Joel Kurtzman, *The Death of Money: How the Electronic Economy Has Destabilized the World's Markets and Created Financial Chaos* (New York: Simon & Schuster, 1963; Boston: Little, Brown, 1993), 58 (page citation is to the Little, Brown edition).

9. *The American Heritage Dictionary of the English Language* (New York: Dell, 1977), 467.

10. Quoted in Boone, *Quotable Business*.

PART I. CONTROL

1. Corporations Are Nothing More or Less Than Their People

1. Quoted in *The International Thesaurus of Quotations* (New York: Crowell, 1970), 102.

2. Thurman Arnold, *The Folklore of Capitalism* (New Haven: Yale University Press, 1937), 185.

3. *Dartmouth College* v. *Woodward*, 17 U.S. 518 (1819).

4. Data derived from *The American Almanac, 1995–1996: Statistical Abstract of the United States* (Austin, TX: Reference Press, 1995), tables 666, 708, 848, 854, 883.

5. See Jeremy Rifkin, *The End of Work: The Decline of the Global Labor Force and the Dawn of the Post-Market Era* (New York: G. P. Putnam's Sons, 1995), 9–10.

6. "The Forbes 500's Annual Directory," *Forbes*, April 25, 1994, 264.

7. *Dartmouth College* v. *Woodward*.

8. *Liggett Co.* v. *Lee*, 288 U.S. 564 (1933).

9. Anthony Sampson, *Company Man: The Rise and Fall of Corporate Life* (New York: Times Books, 1995), 223–229.

10. " '60 Minutes' Case Illustrates a Trend Born of Corporate Pressure, Some Analysts Say," *New York Times*, November 17, 1995; "Cigarette Defector Says CEO Lied to Congress about View of Nicotine," *Wall Street Journal*, January 26, 1996.

11. Quoted in Sampson, *Company Man*, 17.

12. Jethro K. Lieberman, *The Evolving Constitution: How the Supreme Court Has Ruled on Issues from Abortion to Zoning* (New York: Random House, 1992), 138.

13. "Justices Split on Just What a 'Person' Is," *New York Times*, January 13, 1993.

14. "Move in Senate Aims at Cutting Corporate Aid," *New York Times*, March 6, 1996.

15. Paul Krugman, *Peddling Prosperity: Economic Sense and Nonsense in the Age of Diminished Expectations* (New York: W. W. Norton, 1994), 240.

16. "Top Contributors of 'Soft Money,' " *New York Times*, September 8, 1996.

17. Lieberman, *The Evolving Constitution*, 138.

18. Arnold, *The Folklore of Capitalism*, 190.

2. Public Corporations Are Just Private Corporations with Many Owners

1. Quoted in Nicholas von Hoffman, *Capitalist Fools: Tales of American Business, from Carnegie to Forbes to the Milken Gang* (New York: Doubleday, 1992), 196.

2. Quoted in [Adam Smith], *The Money Game* (New York: Random House, 1969; New York: Dell, 1969), 183 (page citation is to the Dell edition).

3. "Wall Street Plans to Crack Down on IPO 'Flippers,' " *Wall Street Journal*, December 29, 1993.

4. Harvey H. Segal, *Corporate Makeover: The Reshaping of the American Economy* (New York: Viking, 1989), 109.

5. Robert C. Pozen, "Institutional Investors: The Reluctant Activists," *Harvard Business Review*, January–February 1994, 142–143.

6. "Sears, Returning to Its Roots, Is Giving Up Allstate," *New York Times*, November 11, 1994.

7. "Do Your Duty, Retirement Managers," *New York Times*, January 30, 1994.

8. "Fixing Corporate America's Short-Term Mind-Set," *New York Times*, September 2, 1992.

9. William G. Bowen, *Inside the Boardroom: Governance by Directors and Trustees* (New York: John Wiley, 1994), 85n.

10. "A Bond Market That Could Use a Psychiatrist," *New York Times*, May 22, 1994.

11. Pozen, "Institutional Investors: The Reluctant Activists," 141.

12. "Ode to the Money Masters," *Wall Street Journal*, October 19, 1993.

13. [Smith], *The Money Game*, 187.

14. "Invoking a Must to Explain Markets," *New York Times*, March 13, 1994.

15. "Fixing Corporate America's Short-Term Mind-Set."

16. John Maynard Keynes, *The General Theory of Employment, Interest and Money* (1936; reprint, London: Macmillan, 1973), 131.

3. The Owners of a Public Corporation Control It by Electing Its Directors

1. New York Stock Exchange, *You and the Investment World* ([New York]: Author, 1972), 4.

2. "Debate on Outside Directors," *New York Times*, October 29, 1972.

3. William G. Bowen, *Inside the Boardroom: Governance by Directors and Trustees* (New York: John Wiley, 1994), 46.

4. Edward S. Herman, *Corporate Control, Corporate Power: A Twentieth Century Fund Study* (New York: Cambridge University Press, 1981), 31.

5. Bowen, *Inside the Boardroom*, 48, 59.

6. Bowen, *Inside the Boardroom*, 61.

7. Herman, *Corporate Control, Corporate Power*, 48.

8. "Stop Us Before We Meet Again," *New York Times*, March 18, 1994.

9. "Stop Us Before We Meet Again."

10. *The American Heritage Dictionary of the English Language* (New York: Dell, 1977), 229, 634, 777, 556.

11. Harvey H. Segal, *Corporate Makeover: The Reshaping of the American Economy* (New York: Viking, 1989), 170.

4. The First Concern of Public Corporation Management Is Shareholder Value

1. Quoted in *The Macmillan Book of Business & Economic Quotations* (New York: Macmillan, 1984), 127.

2. Alfred D. Chandler, Jr., *The Visible Hand* (Cambridge, MA: Harvard University Press, 1977), 10.

3. Adolf A. Berle, Jr., and Gardner C. Means, *The Modern Corporation and Private Property* (New York: Commerce Clearing House, 1932).

4. Gordon Donaldson, *Managing Corporate Wealth: The Operation of a Comprehensive Financial Goals System* (New York, Praeger, 1984), 21–23.

5. G. Bennett Stewart III, *Stern Stewart Corporate Finance Handbook* ([New York]: Stern Stewart Management Services, 1986), 6.

6. Quoted in Rand V. Araskog, *The ITT Wars* (New York: Henry Holt, 1989), 227.

7. "Amos Tversky, Expert on Decision Making, Is Dead at 59," *New York Times*, June 6, 1996.

8. Joel Kurtzman, *The Death of Money: How the Electronic Economy Has Destabilized the World's Markets and Created Financial Chaos* (New York: Simon & Schuster, 1963; Boston: Little, Brown, 1993), 195 (page citation is to the Little, Brown edition).

9. Kurtzman, *The Death of Money*, 200.

10. Araskog, *The ITT Wars*, 105.

PART II. SHAREHOLDERS

5. Corporations Maximize Shareholder Value by Maximizing Current Profit

1. Quoted in *The Macmillan Book of Business & Economic Quotations* (New York: Macmillan, 1984), 46.

2. Pearson Hunt, Charles M. Williams, and Gordon Donaldson, *Basic Business Finance: Text and Cases* (Homewood, IL: Richard D. Irwin, 1958), 14.

3. Michael Porter, "Capital Disadvantage: America's Failing Capital Investment System," *Harvard Business Review*, September–October 1992, 71.

4. Porter, "Capital Disadvantage," 73.

5. Porter, "Capital Disadvantage," 67

6. "How H-P Used Tactics of the Japanese to Beat Them at Their Game," *Wall Street Journal*, September 8, 1994.

7. "David Packard, 83, Pioneer of Silicon Valley, Is Dead," *New York Times*, March 16, 1996.

8. "How H-P Used Tactics of the Japanese."

9. Porter, "Capital Disadvantage," 74.

10. "Suiting Up for America's High-Tech Future," *New York Times*, December 3, 1995.

11. "Dow Jones Will Overhaul Telerate Unit," *New York Times*, January 21, 1997.

12. "Fixing Corporate America's Short-Term Mind-Set," *New York Times*, September 2, 1992.

13. "Creating Gain without Pain," *New York Times*, July 23, 1995.

14. "Fair Stock Markets: The Hidden Cost," *New York Times*, January 22, 1995.

6. Corporate Profit Is the Best Measure of Real Shareholder Value

1. Eric L. Kohler, *A Dictionary for Accountants* (Englewood Cliffs, NJ: Prentice-Hall, 1957), 389.

2. John N. Myer, *Accounting for Non-Accountants* (Rye, NY: American Research Council, 1967), 173.

3. Alfred P. Sloan, Jr., *Adventures of a White Collar Man* (New York: Doubleday, 1940); quoted in Nicholas von Hoffman, *Capitalist Fools: Tales of American Business, from Carnegie to Forbes to the Milken Gang* (New York: Doubleday, 1992), at 199.

4. "A Changing Vision for a Giant: Once Scorned, a Breakup Strategy Is Now Being Embraced," *New York Times*, June 14, 1995.

5. "Singer's Success Requires Reading between the Bottom Lines," *New York Times*, May 14, 1995.

6. Myer, *Accounting for Non-Accountants*, 173.

7. Myer, *Accounting for Non-Accountants*, 129.

8. "Company News: McDonnell Douglas Altering Pension and Health Plan," *New York Times*, October 9, 1992.

9. Kohler, *A Dictionary for Accountants*, 206.

10. "Leslie Fay Restates Three Years' Profits, Trims Duties of CEO," *Wall Street Journal*, September 30, 1993.

11. "Cooking Books: How Hurricane Losses Vanished," *New York Times*, September 5, 1993.

12. "The Winners and (Many) Losers of '92," *New York Times*, December 27, 1992.

13. "Singer's Success Requires Reading between the Bottom Lines."

7. Corporate Profit Is Owned by the Shareholders Who Own the Corporation

1. Eric L. Kohler, *A Dictionary for Accountants* (Englewood Cliffs, NJ: Prentice-Hall, 1957), 389.

2. Pearson Hunt, Charles M. Williams, and Gordon Donaldson, *Basic Business Finance: Text and Cases* (Homewood, IL: Richard D. Irwin, 1958), 648–649.

3. "Bad Times for Mesa, But Not for Pickens," *New York Times*, November 22, 1992.

8. Corporations Exist to Maximize Shareholder Value

1. Paul A. Samuelson, *Economics: An Introductory Analysis*, 2d ed. (New York: McGraw-Hill, 1951), 646.

2. Quoted in Louis E. Boone, *Quotable Business* (New York: Random House, 1992), 143.

3. "Reward Genuine Capital Investment," *New York Times*, November 19, 1995.

4. "And in the Long Run We Should Win," *New York Times*, May 19, 1996.

5. "Why Must Chrysler Be Driven Off a Cliff?" *New York Times*, May 2, 1995.

6. "Chrysler Stock Rise Was Aim of Kerkorian," *New York Times*, February 14, 1996.

7. "And in the Long Run We Should Win."

8. Richard N. Goodwin, *The American Condition* (New York: Doubleday, 1974), 220.

9. "Baxter International, Dragged Down by Woes, Begins to Draw the Interest of Bottom Feeders," *Wall Street Journal*, September 29, 1993.

10. "Why Must Chrysler Be Driven Off a Cliff?"

11. Peter F. Drucker, *Management: Tasks, Responsibilities, Practices* (New York: Harper & Row, 1974), 42.

12. Drucker, *Management*, 40

13. Drucker, *Management*, 40.

PART III. CUSTOMERS

9. Corporations Engage in Marketing to Satisfy Their Customers' Needs

1. Peter F. Drucker, *Management: Tasks, Responsibilities, Practices* (New York: Harper & Row, 1974), 61.

2. Theodore Levitt, "Marketing Myopia," *Harvard Business Review*, September–October 1960, 41, 46.

3. Quoted in *The Macmillan Book of Business & Economic Quotations* (New York: Macmillan, 1984), 131.

4. *Triumph of the Nerds: The Rise of Accidental Empires in Silicon Valley* (program broadcast on Public Television, 1995).

5. "Xerox's New Strategy Will Not Copy the Past," *New York Times*, December 18, 1994.

6. Levitt, "Marketing Myopia," 50.

7. "Consumer Product Companies Seek Better Methods to Gauge the Effect of Marketing on Their Sales," *New York Times*, October 19, 1993.

8. "50 Cents Off! 2 for 1. But Get Them While You Can," *New York Times*, March 17, 1996.

9. Drucker, *Management*, 64.

10. "The Five Deadly Business Sins," *New York Times*, October 21, 1993.

11. "The Five Deadly Business Sins."

12. "Xerox's New Strategy Will Not Copy the Past."

13. "Marketers, Stop Your Tinkering," *New York Times*, June 19, 1994.

14. Levitt, "Marketing Myopia," 52.

10. Corporations Invest in Brands to Increase Consumer Value

1. Quoted in Louis E. Boone, *Quotable Business* (New York: Random House, 1992), 151–152.

2. "Grand Met's New CEO Emphasizes Premium Brands," *Wall Street Journal*, October 7, 1993.

3. Martin L. Weitzman, *The Share Economy: Conquering Stagflation* (Cambridge: Harvard University Press, 1984), 35.

4. "Coping with the Private-Label Threat," *The Food Industry Newsletter*, 1993, 1.

5. "Consistency Is Not a Hobgoblin for the Minds behind Tide's Miracle," *New York Times*, February 6, 1996.

6. "Who Says Brands Are Dead?" *Financial World*, September 1, 1993, 3.

7. "A New Survey Finds That Responsibility for Brand Management Sits on Some Surprising Shoulders," *New York Times*, June 21, 1995.

8. "Ah, Loyalty. Always a Warm Concept, But the Industry Hears Just How Vital It Is for Brands," *New York Times*, October 20, 1993.

9. "A New Survey Finds That Responsibility for Brand Management Sits on Some Surprising Shoulders."

10. "Consumers Wake Up to Increase in Cereal Prices," *New York Times*, August 10, 1993.

11. "Consumers Wake Up to Increase in Cereal Prices."

12. "Who Says Brands Are Dead?"

11. Corporations Are Required by Supply and Demand to Charge Their Lowest Prices

1. *The Columbia Encyclopedia*, 3d ed. (New York: Columbia University Press, 1963), 2070.

2. Martin L. Weitzman, *The Share Economy: Conquering Stagflation* (Cambridge: Harvard University Press, 1984), 19.

3. See Weitzman, *The Share Economy*, 16.

4. Weitzman, *The Share Economy*, 37.

5. Weitzman, *The Share Economy*, 35.

12. Corporations Innovate to Satisfy Their Customers' Needs

1. Peter F. Drucker, *Management: Tasks, Responsibilities, Practices* (New York: Harper & Row, 1974), 65.

2. Paul Krugman, *Peddling Prosperity: Economic Sense and Nonsense in the Age of Diminished Expectations* (New York: W. W. Norton, 1994), 99.

3. Theodore Levitt, "Marketing Myopia," *Harvard Business Review*, September–October 1960, 46.

4. "The Five Deadly Business Sins," *New York Times*, October 21, 1993.

5. Henry Ford, *My Life and Work* (New York: Doubleday, 1923), 147.

6. Alfred P. Sloan, Jr., *My Years with General Motors* (New York: Doubleday, 1964), 163.

7. Krugman, *Peddling Prosperity*, 59.

8. "Big Steelmakers Shape Up," *New York Times*, April 16, 1996.

9. "Big Steelmakers Shape Up."

10. Simon Head, "The New, Ruthless Economy," *New York Review*, February 29, 1996, 47.

11. "Big 3 and Japan," *New York Times*, June 28, 1995.

12. "Ford Presents the Importance of Being Taurus, Act III," *New York Times*, September 3, 1995.

13. "With a Rare Opportunity, Ford Blew It," *New York Times*, October 24, 1993.

14. "With a Rare Opportunity, Ford Blew It."

15. *The American Almanac, 1995–1996: Statistical Abstract of the United States* (Austin, TX: Reference Press, 1995), table 1319.

16. "Radically New, Easily Familiar," *New York Times*, September 3, 1995.

PART IV. MANAGERS

13. Corporate Management Is Entrepreneurial

1. Quoted in *The International Thesaurus of Quotations* (New York: Crowell, 1970), 263.

2. Received by author.

3. *The American Heritage Dictionary of the English Language* (New York: Dell, 1977), 241.

4. A. David Silver, *Venture Capital: The Complete Guide for Investors* (New York: John Wiley, 1985), 163.

5. Silver, *Venture Capital*, 164.

6. Silver, *Venture Capital*, 108–109.

7. *Tort Cost Trends: An International Perspective* (Tillinghast-Towers Perrin, 1995).

8. "On Wall Street, Masters of Innovation," *New York Times*, October 24, 1993.

14. Corporate Management Is Strategic

1. Quoted in Louis E. Boone, *Quotable Business* (New York: Random House, 1992), 33.

2. Quoted in Boone, *Quotable Business*, 31.

3. *The Random House Dictionary of the English Language*, unabr. ed. (New York: Random House, 1966), 1404.

4. Gary Hamel and C. K. Prahalad, "Strategic Intent," *Harvard Business Review*, May–June 1989, 63, 64.

5. Michael E. Porter, *Competitive Strategy: Techniques for Analyzing Industries and Competitors* (New York: Free Press, 1980), 4.

6. Porter, *Competitive Strategy*, 361.

7. Hamel and Prahalad, "Strategic Intent," 73.

8. Hamel and Prahalad, "Strategic Intent," 73.

9. "Fantasy Economics," *New York Times*, September 26, 1994.

10. Paul Krugman, *Peddling Prosperity: Economic Sense and Nonsense in the Age of Diminished Expectations* (New York: W. W. Norton, 1994), 147–148.

11. "Fixing Corporate America's Short-Term Mind-Set," *New York Times*, September 2, 1992.

12. Hamel and Prahalad, "Strategic Intent," 75.

13. Krugman, *Peddling Prosperity*, 235.

15. Professional Managers Can Run Any Corporate Business

1. Rand V. Araskog, *The ITT Wars* (New York: Henry Holt, 1989), 23.

2. Harvey H. Segal, *Corporate Makeover: The Reshaping of the American Economy* (New York: Viking, 1989), 187.

3. "The Greed and the Glory of Being Boss," *Economist*, June 17, 1989, 79.

4. J. Sterling Livingston, "Myth of the Well-Educated Manager," *Harvard Business Review*, January–February 1971, 79.

5. Livingston, "Myth of the Well-Educated Manager," 82.

6. Livingston, "Myth of the Well-Educated Manager," 84.

7. Gary Hamel and C. K. Prahalad, "Strategic Intent," *Harvard Business Review*, May–June 1989, 63, 74.

8. Hamel and Prahalad, "Strategic Intent," 74–75.

9. Robert J. Schoenberg, *Geneen* (New York: W. W. Norton, 1958), 334.

10. "An Idea Whose Time Never Came," *New York Times*, November 21, 1993.

11. Susan Cartwright and Cary L. Cooper, "If Cultures Don't Fit, Mergers May Fail," *New York Times*, August 29, 1993.

12. Thurman Arnold, *The Folklore of Capitalism* (New Haven: Yale University Press, 1937), 351.

13. "NCR Stock Is Trading High, and Some Analysts Wonder Why," *New York Times*, December 31, 1996.

14. "Merger Made in Heaven? For Now," *New York Times*, September 4, 1994.

15. "Marketer's Dream, Engineer's Nightmare," *New York Times*, December 12, 1993.

16. "Hiring a New Boss? Look No Further," *New York Times*, August 22, 1993.

16. Corporate Management Is Strong Because It's Team Management

1. Quoted in Louis E. Boone, *Quotable Business* (New York: Random House, 1992), 90.

2. "The Cult of the Coach," *Economist*, January 13, 1996, 81, 82.

3. Peter F. Drucker, *Management: Tasks, Responsibilities, Practices* (New York: Harper & Row, 1974), 618.

4. "Job Hunting Isn't Always Goodbye," *New York Times*, December 5, 1993.

5. *The Random House Dictionary of the English Language*, unabr. ed. (New York: Random House, 1966), 1113.

6. J. Sterling Livingston, "Myth of the Well-Educated Manager," *Harvard Business Review*, January–February 1971, 79, 87.

7. "Unisys Advances a Trend, Eliminating President's Job," *New York Times*, August 10, 1993.

8. James Drury, "Tomorrow's Leaders Sidelined," *New York Times*, May 14, 1995.

9. "Jobs Die So Companies May Live," *New York Times*, January 7, 1996.

10. Robert Cole, "Learning from Learning Theory: Implications for Quality Improvement of Turnover, Use of Contingent Workers, and Job Rotation Policies," *Quality Management Journal*, October 1993, 9, 11, 15.

11. Drury, "Tomorrow's Leaders Sidelined."

12. Paul Krugman, "Would You Buy a New Car from This Man?" *New York Times Book Review*, July 23, 1995, 7 (reviewing *Behind the Wheel at Chrysler: The Iacocca Legacy* by Doron P. Levin).

13. "Paranoia in the Ranks? No, Realism," *New York Times*, August 23, 1992.

PART V. CEOs

17. In Public Corporations the CEO Is Controlled by Independent Directors

1. Quoted in Louis E. Boone, *Quotable Business* (New York: Random House, 1992), 38.

2. *American Bar Association Model Business Corporation Act* (1984), section 8.04(b); reprinted in *Martindale-Hubbell Law Digest* (New Providence, NJ: Martindale-Hubbell, 1995), UMA-8. The model act was approved by the ABA's Committee on Corporate Laws but never, apparently, acted upon by the association itself.

3. Edward S. Herman, *Corporate Control, Corporate Power: A Twentieth Century Fund Study* (New York: Cambridge University Press, 1981), 39–40, table 2.5.

4. Herman, *Corporate Control, Corporate Power*, 45.

5. "When a CEO's Pain Is a Gain," *New York Times*, November 1, 1992.

6. See William G. Bowen, *Inside the Boardroom: Governance by Directors and Trustees* (New York: John Wiley, 1994), app. B.

7. "If the Boss Walks Out the Door, Investors May Rush In," *New York Times*, January 7, 1996.

8. Bowen, *Inside the Boardroom*, 84.

200 Notes on Sources

9. Graef S. Crystal, *In Search of Excess: The Overcompensation of American Executives* (New York: W. W. Norton, 1991), 214.

10. Crystal, *In Search of Excess*, 214.

11. Herman, *Corporate Control, Corporate Power*, 48.

12. "Moves by Campbell Soup Send Shares Surging to Reach a High," *New York Times*, September 6, 1996.

18. CEOs Are Paid What They're Worth

1. Quoted in Louis E. Boone, *Quotable Business* (New York: Random House, 1992), 104.

2. Quoted in *The Macmillan Book of Business & Economic Quotations* (New York: Macmillan, 1984), 158.

3. *The American Almanac, 1995–1996: Statistical Abstract of the United States* (Austin, TX: Reference Press, 1995), table 571.

4. "Vestiges of Success: Laid-Off Workers Complain That IBM, in Distress, Is Still Spending Big on Perks," *Wall Street Journal*, October 27, 1993; "10 Years Later, I.B.M. Sets a New High in a Changed Market," *New York Times*, May 14, 1997.

5. "IBM's Short List in Search for a Chief Dwindles Once Again," *Wall Street Journal*, March 16, 1993.

6. Graef S. Crystal, *In Search of Excess: The Overcompensation of American Executives* (New York: W. W. Norton, 1991), 27.

7. *Business Week*, May 6, 1991, 96.

8. Paul Krugman, *Peddling Prosperity: Economic Sense and Nonsense in the Age of Diminished Expectations* (New York: W. W. Norton, 1994), 58.

9. "Corporate Greed, Meet the Maximum Wage," *New York Times*, June 16, 1996.

10. Crystal, *In Search of Excess*, 222.

11. "1995 Was Good for Companies, and Better for a Lot of CEOs," *New York Times*, March 29, 1996.

12. See *Internal Revenue Code of 1985*, sec. 162.

13. "Business Diary: Executive Pay, Unlimited," *New York Times*, February 19, 1995.

14. "Tax Law Expected to Bring Little Shift in Executive Pay," *New York Times*, August 24, 1993.

15. "1995 Was Good for Companies, and Better for a Lot of CEOs."

19. CEO Compensation Is Linked to Corporate Performance

1. Quoted in Louis E. Boone, *Quotable Business* (New York: Random House, 1992), 104.

2. Ben R. Rich and Leo Janos, *Skunk Works: A Personal Memoir of My Years at Lockheed* (New York: Little, Brown, 1994), 317–318.

3. William G. Bowen, *Inside the Boardroom: Governance by Directors and Trustees* (New York: John Wiley, 1994), 100.

4. "And in the Long Run We Should Win," *New York Times*, May 19, 1996.

5. *Business Week*, April 26, 1993, 59.

6. "Fired Tambrands CEO Was Unusually Close to a Consulting Firm," *Wall Street Journal*, August 23, 1993.

7. "Put More Incentive in Incentive Pay," *New York Times*, January 16, 1994.

8. "The Boss's Stock: To Short or Not," *New York Times*, December 10, 1995.

9. "The Boss's Stock: To Short or Not."

10. "Who Pays Capital Gains Taxes?" *New York Times*, December 3, 1995.

11. "And in the Long Run We Should Win."

12. Joel Kurtzman, *The Death of Money: How the Electronic Economy Has Destabilized the World's Markets and Created Financial Chaos* (New York: Simon & Schuster, 1963; Boston: Little Brown, 1993), 142 (page citation is to the Little, Brown edition).

13. "Top Executives See Method in Stock Option Madness," *New York Times*, March 26, 1993.

14. "Accounting Board Yields on Stock Options," *New York Times*, December 15, 1994.

15. "In Accounting, Truth Can Be Very Scary," *New York Times*, April 11, 1993.

16. "1995 Was Good for Companies, and Better for a Lot of CEOs," *New York Times*, March 29, 1996.

20. CEOs Devote Full Time to Managing Their Corporation

1. Alan Farnham, "The Trust Gap," *Fortune*, December 4, 1989, 56, 60.

2. "Fran Lebowitz Knows Why You Never Have Enough Time. Got a Minute?" *Mirabella*, July 1993.

3. "Casings Firm Is Tough Meat for Deal Whiz," *Wall Street Journal*, November 23, 1993.

4. "Acquire, Merge or Get Out of the Way," *New York Times*, September 24, 1995.

5. "Acquire, Merge or Get Out of the Way."

6. "Can a Firm Be Active in the Takeover Market and Still Stay Innovative? Only with Difficulty," *Economist*, December 14, 1996, 63.

7. "AT&T Chief, Who Cut Jobs, Defends Pay," *New York Times*, February 28, 1996.

8. "An Argument That Big Ego Is Behind a Lot of Mergers," *New York Times*, September 28, 1995.

9. "Follow the Leader," *New York Times*, October 13, 1995.

10. "Medco Chief Began Early in Mergers," *New York Times*, July 30, 1993.

11. "Storm after Storm," *New York Times*, July 19, 1996.

12. Dennis C. Carey and Ralph S. Saul, "Have Spinoffs Spun Out of Control," *New York Times*, July 14, 1996.

13. "ITT Will Split into 3 Units to Be Spun Off to Investors," *New York Times*, June 14, 1995.

14. "Birthdays, Not Assets, Tip Off Bank Mergers," *Wall Street Journal*, November 16, 1993.

15. Nicholas von Hoffman, *Capitalist Fools: Tales of American Business, from Carnegie to Forbes to the Milken Gang* (New York: Doubleday, 1992), 24.

PART VI. WORKERS

21. Public Corporations Are Proficient at Motivating Their Workers

1. Quoted in Ben R. Rich and Leo Janos, *Skunk Works: A Personal Memoir of My Years at Lockheed* (New York: Little, Brown, 1994), 295.

2. Quoted in Louis E. Boone, *Quotable Business* (New York: Random House, 1992), 52.

3. "The Bottom Line on 'People' Issues," *New York Times*, February 19, 1995.

4. "A Job Coach's Sobering Pep Talk," *New York Times*, October 2, 1994.

5. "Do People and Profits Go Hand in Hand?" *New York Times*, May 9, 1996.

6. "Getting on the Merit-Go-Round," *New York Times*, January 30, 1994.

7. Frederick Herzberg, "One More Time: How Do You Motivate Employees?" *Harvard Business Review*, January–February 1968, 53, 56.

8. Abraham H. Maslow, *Motivation and Personality* (New York: Harper, 1954), 83.

9. Herzberg, "One More Time: How Do You Motivate Employees?" 53.

10. Herzberg, "One More Time: How Do You Motivate Employees?" 59–61.

11. Robert C. Ford and Cherrill P. Heaton, *Principles of Management: A Decision-Making Approach* (Reston, VA: Reston Publishing Company, 1980), 166–167.

12. "LTV's Weld of Worker and Manager," *New York Times*, August 2, 1994.

13. Alan S. Blinder, *Growing Together: An Alternative Economic Strategy for the 1990s* ([Knoxville, TN]: Whittle Direct Books, 1991), 55–56.

14. "LTV's Weld of Worker and Manager."

15. "What, Us Worry? Big Unions' Leaders Overlook Bad News, Opt for Status Quo," *Wall Street Journal*, October 5, 1993.

16. Harvey H. Segal, *Corporate Makeover: The Reshaping of the American Economy* (New York: Viking, 1989), 142.

17. Quoted in *The Macmillan Book of Business & Economic Quotations* (New York: Macmillan, 1984), 121.

22. Corporations Stay Competitive in a Global Economy by Downsizing

1. Lance Morrow, "The Temping of America," *Time*, March 29, 1993, 40, 41.

2. Quoted in *The International Thesaurus of Quotations* (New York: Crowell, 1970), 665.

3. "Though Upbeat on the Economy, People Still Fear for Their Jobs," *New York Times*, December 29, 1996.

4. "Despite Drop, Rate of Layoffs Remains High," *New York Times*, August 23, 1996.

5. "The Year Downsizing Grew Up," *Economist*, December 21, 1996, 97.

6. "Though Upbeat on the Economy, People Still Fear for Their Jobs."

7. "Despite Drop, Rate of Layoffs Remains High."

8. "The Year Downsizing Grew Up."

9. "Survey Finds 6 Million, Fewer Than Thought, in Impermanent Jobs," *New York Times*, August 19, 1995.

10. "The Labor Picture in July" (chart), *New York Times*, August 3, 1996.

11. "What's Wrong with the Fed's Picture?" *New York Times*, September 4, 1994.

12. "When Surviving Just Isn't Enough,"*New York Times*, June 25, 1995.

13. "The Year Downsizing Grew Up."

14. "U.S. Earnings Depend on Dollar and Foreign Economies," *New York Times*, December 24, 1996.

15. "The Year Downsizing Grew Up."

16. "Big Companies Cloud Recovery by Cutting Jobs," *New York Times*, December 17, 1992.

17. "Why Shake-ups Work for Some, Not for Others," *Wall Street Journal*, October 1, 1993.

18. "Why Shake-ups Work for Some, Not for Others."

19. "We're Leaner, Meaner and Going Nowhere Faster," *New York Times*, May 12, 1996.

20. "The Year Downsizing Grew Up."

21. "Big Companies Cloud Recovery by Cutting Jobs."

22. "Lilly to Cut 4,000 in Wide Revamping," *New York Times*, October 12, 1993.

23. "Xerox to Cut 10,000 Jobs, Shut Facilities," *Wall Street Journal*, December 9, 1993.

24. "Big Companies Cloud Recovery by Cutting Jobs."

25. "Lots of Bobbing and Weaving on Issue of Company Layoffs," *New York Times*, May 18, 1996.

26. "Lots of Bobbing and Weaving on Issue of Company Layoffs."

23. Corporations Have to Lay Off Workers When Business Is Bad

1. Paul A. Samuelson, *Economics: An Introductory Analysis*, 2d ed. (New York: McGraw-Hill, 1951), 744.

2. Quoted in Louis E. Boone, *Quotable Business* (New York: Random House, 1992), 196.

3. Paul Krugman, "New Math, Same Story," *New York Times Magazine*, January 5, 1997, 32.

4. Krugman, "New Math, Same Story," 32.

5. John Cassidy, "Who Killed the Middle Class?" *The New Yorker*, October 16, 1995, 113, 122–124.

6. "Economist Wins Top Medal for Pay Study," *New York Times*, March 14, 1997.

7. "Trade and Wages," *Economist*, December 7, 1996, 74.

8. Cassidy, "Who Killed the Middle Class?"

9. "A Sharp Increase in Cabin Pressure," *New York Times*, November 28, 1993.

10. Martin L. Weitzman, *The Share Economy: Conquering Stagflation* (Cambridge: Harvard University Press, 1984), 54.

11. Alan S. Blinder, *Growing Together: An Alternative Economic Strategy for the 1990s* ([Knoxville, TN]: Whittle Direct Books, 1991), 52.

12. "Recasting Model Incentive Strategy," *New York Times*, September 5, 1994.

13. Weitzman, *The Share Economy*, 138.

14. "A New Era of Ups and Downs: Volatility of Wages Is Growing," *New York Times*, August 18, 1996.

15. "A New Era of Ups and Downs: Volatility of Wages Is Growing."

24. Raising Productivity Benefits Workers by Raising What They Earn

1. Alan S. Blinder, *Growing Together: An Alternative Economic Strategy for the 1990s* ([Knoxville, TN]: Whittle Direct Books, 1991), 4.

2. Paul Kennedy, *The Rise and Fall of the Great Powers: Economic Change and Military Conflict from 1500 to 2000* (New York: Random House, 1987), 439.

3. *The American Almanac, 1995–1996: Statistical Abstract of the United States* (Austin, TX: Reference Press, 1995), table 1319. GDP from table 699.

4. Paul Krugman, *Peddling Prosperity: Economic Sense and Nonsense in the Age of Diminished Expectations* (New York: W. W. Norton, 1994), 114.

5. Paul Krugman, "New Math, Same Story," *New York Times Magazine*, January 5, 1997, 32.

6. "U.S. Output per Worker Called Best," *New York Times*, October 13, 1992.

7. Krugman, "New Math, Same Story."

8. Steven Rattner, "If Productivity's Rising, Why Are Jobs Paying Less?" *New York Times Magazine*, September 19, 1993, 54.

9. "A Top Economist Switches His View on Productivity," *New York Times*, May 8, 1996.

10. Rattner, "If Productivity's Rising, Why Are Jobs Paying Less?"

11. "Long-Term Riches, Short-Term Pain," *New York Times*, September 25, 1994.

12. Louis Uchitelle, "Beyond Our Means," *New York Times Book Review*, October 1, 1995, 15, reviewing *The End of Affluence* by Jeffrey Madrick.

13. "It's a Slow-Growth Economy, Stupid,"*New York Times*, March 17, 1996.

14. Krugman, *Peddling Prosperity*, 46.

15. "Letting the Good Times Roll: The Case against a Rate Rise," *New York Times*, September 12, 1996.

16. "Who's Afraid of Jobs and Growth?" *New York Times*, March 31, 1996.

17. Rattner, "If Productivity's Rising, Why Are Jobs Paying Less?"

18. "We're Leaner, Meaner and Going Nowhere Faster," *New York Times*, May 12, 1996.

19. Paul Krugman, "Stay on Their Backs," *New York Times Magazine*, February 4, 1996, 36, 37.

PART VII. CAPITALISTS

25. Wall Street's Primary Function Is Raising Money for Public Corporations

1. Paul Gibson, *Bear Trap: Why Wall Street Doesn't Work* (New York: Atlantic Monthly, 1993), 5.

2. Joel Kurtzman, *The Death of Money: How the Electronic Economy Has Destabilized the World's Markets and Created Financial Chaos* (Boston: Little, Brown, 1993), 24.

3. Gibson, *Bear Trap*, 5, 16, 19–20, 22–23.

4. John von Neumann and Oskar Morgenstern, *Theory of Games and Economic Behavior* (1944: Princeton, NJ: Princeton University Press, 1953), 46–47.

5. Martin Mayer, *The Bankers: The Next Generation* (New York: Truman Talley Books/Dutton, 1997), 285–286.

6. "3 U.S. Economists Win Nobel," *New York Times*, October 17, 1990; also see related articles in the *New York Times* of that date.

7. Kurtzman, *The Death of Money*, 134.

8. Jeff Madrick, "How to Succeed in Business," *New York Review*, April 18, 1996, 22.

9. Kurtzman, *The Death of Money*, 64.

10. Kurtzman, *The Death of Money*, 39–40.

11. See Kurtzman, *The Death of Money*, 93.

12. "Putting a Number to the Monthly Gyration in Bonds," *New York Times*, August 3, 1996.

13. "Gaming on Wall Street," *New York Times*, March 12, 1996.

14. Kurtzman, *The Death of Money*, 163.

15. "In Real Life, Wall Street's a Hit" (chart), *New York Times*, September 1, 1996.

16. Kurtzman, *The Death of Money*, 135.

26. Investment Bankers Serve the Interests of Clients and Investors Simultaneously

1. Eric L. Kohler, *A Dictionary for Accountants* (Englewood Cliffs, NJ: Prentice-Hall, 1957), 276.

2. Harvey H. Segal, *Corporate Makeover: The Reshaping of the American Economy* (New York: Viking, 1989), 80.

3. Kohler, *A Dictionary for Accountants*, 276.

4. "When Boards Say 'No Deal' to Holders," *New York Times*, October 6, 1996.

5. "After Spurned Bids, It's Often the Shareholders Who Pay," *New York Times*, February 11, 1996.

6. Michael Lewis, *The Money Culture* (New York: W. W. Norton, 1991; New York: Penguin, 1992), 65 (page citation is to the Penguin edition).

7. Segal: *Corporate Makeover*, 96.

8. "Safeway LBO Yields Vast Profits But Exacts a Heavy Human Toll," *Wall Street Journal*, May 16, 1990.

27. The Market Is a Level Trading Field for Public Investors

1. Quoted in *The Macmillan Book of Social Science Quotations* (New York: Macmillan, 1991), 108.

2. "In Real Life" (chart), *New York Times*, September 1, 1996.

3. "Surviving a Detour to Business School," *New York Times*, September 10, 1995.

4. Martin Mayer, *The Bankers: The Next Generation* (New York: Truman Talley Books/Dutton, 1997), 331.

5. *Forbes Stock Market Course* ([New York]: Forbes, Inc., 1977), 2.

6. "Wall Street Plans to Crack Down on IPO 'Flippers,' " *Wall Street Journal*, December 29, 1993.

7. "A Timely Call for Reform in Nasdaq Trading," *New York Times*, January 30, 1994.

8. "Keeping Mum about Bond Prices," *New York Times*, September 11, 1994.

9. "A Timely Call for Reform in Nasdaq Trading."

10. "Curbing Wall Street's Seamier Side," *New York Times*, November 21, 1993.

11. "Some Question If Analysts Are Worth Their Pay," *Wall Street Journal*, September 15, 1993.

12. "Do Analysts Favor Firms' Customers?" *New York Times*, August 18, 1996.

13. "A Guide to the Goofs of Wall Street's Wizards," *New York Times*, December 1, 1996.

14. "Fund Managers Testing the Rules," *New York Times*, January 23, 1994.

15. Paul Gibson, *Bear Trap: Why Wall Street Doesn't Work* (New York: Atlantic Monthly, 1993), 99.

16. "Insiders' Trades Point the Way for Optical Data Systems' Stock," *New York Times*, September 10, 1993.

17. "Luck or Logic? Debate Rages on Over 'Efficient-Market' Theory," *Wall Street Journal*, November 4, 1993.

18. "Procter's Tale: Gambling in Ignorance," *New York Times*, October 30, 1994.

19. "Derivatives as the Fall Guy: Excuses, Excuses," *New York Times*, October 2, 1994.

20. "Bankers Trust Thrives Pitching Derivatives, But Climate Is Shifting," *Wall Street Journal*, April 22, 1994.

28. Wall Street's Influence on Public Corporations Is Beneficial

1. Quoted in Louis E. Boone, *Quotable Business* (New York: Random House, 1992), 169.

2. Paul Krugman, *Peddling Prosperity: Economic Sense and Nonsense in the Age of Diminished Expectations* (New York: W. W. Norton, 1994), 125–126.

3. "The Downside of an Upturn," *New York Times*, October 9, 1996.

4. "Of Liberty, and Prosperity," *Economist*, January 13, 1996, 21.

5. "A Global Gauge of Greased Palms," *New York Times*, August 20, 1995.

6. "Assessing the Inevitable," *Economist*, September 21, 1996.

7. Benjamin M. Friedman, "There They Go Again," *New York Review*, October 31, 1996, 27, 30–31.

8. Friedman, "There They Go Again."

9. "You're Fired! (But Your Stock Is Way Up)," *New York Times*, September 3, 1995.

10. "You're Fired! (But Your Stock Is Way Up)."

11. "Those Wild Swings, Examined," *New York Times*, February 20, 1996.

12. Paul Gibson, *Bear Trap: Why Wall Street Doesn't Work* (New York: Atlantic Monthly, 1993), 175.

13. See Joel Kurtzman, *The Death of Money: How the Electronic Economy Has Destabilized the World's Markets and Created Financial Chaos* (New York: Simon &

Schuster, 1963; Boston: Little, Brown, 1993), 198 (page citation is to the Little, Brown edition).

14. "Luck or Logic? Debate Rages on over 'Efficient-Market' Theory," *Wall Street Journal*, November 4, 1993.

15. Michael Porter, "Capital Disadvantage: America's Failing Capital Investment System," *Harvard Business Review*, September–October 1992, 67.

16. Porter, "Capital Disadvantage: America's Failing Capital Investment System," 68.

17. "Basic Research Is Losing Out as Companies Stress Results," *New York Times*, October 8, 1996.

18. "Basic Research Is Losing Out as Companies Stress Results."

Afterword: We Are All Consumers, We Are All Workers

1. Jeremy Rifkin, *The End of Work: The Decline of the Global Labor Force and the Dawn of the Post-Market Era* (New York: G. P. Putnam's Sons, 1995), 195.

2. Robert H. Hayes and William J. Abernathy, "Managing Our Way to Economic Decline," *Harvard Business Review*, July–August 1980, 67, 77.

3. *The Macmillan Book of Social Science Quotations* (New York: Macmillan, 1991), 38.

4. "Some Worries about the Rush into Mutual Funds," *New York Times*, December 27, 1996; "1996 Changed the Way Americans Think About Stock Funds," *New York Times*, January 14, 1997.

5. See William Manchester, *The Glory and the Dream: A Narrative History of America, 1932–1972* (Boston: Little, Brown, 1974; reprint, Toronto: Bantam, 1975), 72–73 (page citation is to the Bantam edition).

Selected Bibliography

Araskog, Rand V. *The ITT Wars*. New York: Henry Holt, 1989.

Arnold, Thurman. *The Folklore of Capitalism*. New Haven: Yale University Press, 1937.

Blinder, Alan S. *Growing Together: An Alternative Economic Strategy for the 1990s*. [Knoxville, TN]: Whittle Direct Books, 1991.

Bowen, William G. *Inside the Boardroom: Governance by Directors and Trustees*. New York: John Wiley, 1994.

Crystal, Graef S. *In Search of Excess: The Overcompensation of American Executives*. New York: W. W. Norton, 1991.

Drucker, Peter F. *Management: Tasks, Responsibilities, Practices*. New York: Harper & Row, 1974.

Ford, Robert C., and Cherrill P. Heaton. *Principles of Management: A Decision-Making Approach*. Reston, VA: Reston Publishing Company, 1980.

Gibson, Paul. *Bear Trap: Why Wall Street Doesn't Work*. New York: Atlantic Monthly, 1993.

Herman, Edward S. *Corporate Control, Corporate Power: A Twentieth Century Fund Study*. New York: Cambridge University Press, 1981.

Krugman, Paul. *Peddling Prosperity: Economic Sense and Nonsense in the Age of Diminished Expectations*. New York: W. W. Norton, 1994.

Kurtzman, Joel. *The Death of Money: How the Electronic Economy Has Destabilized the World's Markets and Created Financial Chaos*. New York: Simon & Schuster, 1963; Boston: Little, Brown, 1993.

Lewis, Michael. *The Money Culture*. New York: W. W. Norton, 1991; New York: Penguin, 1992.

Lieberman, Jethro K. *The Evolving Constitution: How the Supreme Court Has Ruled on Issues from Abortion to Zoning*. New York: Random House, 1992.

Mayer, Martin. *The Bankers: The Next Generation*. New York: Truman Talley Books/ Dutton, 1997.

Porter, Michael E. *Competitive Strategy: Techniques for Analyzing Industries and Competitors*. New York: Free Press, 1980.

Rich, Ben R., and Leo Janos. *Skunk Works: A Personal Memoir of My Years at Lockheed*. New York: Little, Brown, 1994.

Rifkin, Jeremy. *The End of Work: The Decline of the Global Labor Force and the Dawn of the Post-Market Era*. New York: G. P. Putnam's Sons, 1995.

Sampson, Anthony. *Company Man: The Rise and Fall of Corporate Life*. New York: Times Books, 1995.

Schoenberg, Robert J. *Geneen*. New York: W. W. Norton, 1958.

Segal, Harvey H. *Corporate Makeover: The Reshaping of the American Economy*. New York: Viking, 1989.

Silver, A. David. *Venture Capital: The Complete Guide for Investors*. New York: John Wiley, 1985.

[Smith, Adam]. *The Money Game*. New York: Random House, 1969; New York: Dell, 1969.

Von Hoffman, Nicholas. *Capitalist Fools: Tales of American Business, from Carnegie to Forbes to the Milken Gang*. New York: Doubleday, 1992.

Weitzman, Martin L. *The Share Economy: Conquering Stagflation*. Cambridge: Harvard University Press, 1984.

Index